THE HORSE SOLDIER

1776–1943

The United States Cavalryman: His Uniforms, Arms,
Accoutrements, and Equipments

VOLUME I

The Revolution, the War of 1812,
the Early Frontier
1776–1850

VOLUME II

The Frontier, the Mexican War,
the Civil War, the Indian Wars
1851–1880

VOLUME III

The Last of the Indian Wars,
the Spanish-American War,
the Brink of the Great War
1881–1916

VOLUME IV

World War I, the Peacetime Army,
World War II
1917–1943

THE HORSE SOLDIER

1776–1943

VOLUME I

The Revolution, the War of 1812, the Early Frontier

1776–1850

The Horse Soldier
1776-1943

The United States Cavalryman: His Uniforms, Arms, Accoutrements, and Equipments

Sergeant, the Regiment of Dragoons (ca. 1837), in fatigue dress and with the 1833 horse equipments packed for service in the field. (See Figure 84.)

Volume I

*The Revolution,
the War of 1812,
the Early Frontier*

1776-1850

by Randy Steffen

illustrations by Randy Steffen

UNIVERSITY OF OKLAHOMA PRESS
NORMAN AND LONDON

By Randy Steffen

Horseman's Scrapbook, 3 vols. (Colorado Springs, 1959–65)
Horsemen Through Civilization, All (Colorado Springs, 1967)
United States Military Saddles (Norman, 1973)
The Horse Soldier, 1776–1943: The United States Cavalryman, His Uniforms, Arms, Accoutrements, and Equipments; Volume I, *The Revolution, the War of 1812, the Early Frontier, 1776–1850*; Volume II, *The Frontier, the Mexican War, the Civil War, the Indian Wars, 1851–1880*; Volume III, *The Last of the Indian Wars, the Spanish-American War, the Brink of the Great War, 1881–1916*; Volume IV, *World War I, the Peacetime Army, World War II, 1917–1943* (Norman, 1977–79)

The Company of Military Historians takes pride in sponsoring *The Horse Soldier, 1776–1943: The United States Cavalryman: His Uniforms, Arms, Accoutrements, and Equipments* as a standard reference work in military history.

George S. Pappas
President

Library of Congress Cataloging-in-Publication Data

Steffen, Randy, 1917–1977
    The horse soldier, 1776–1943.

    Includes index.
    CONTENTS: v. 1. The Revolution, the War of 1812, the early frontier, 1776–1850.
    1. United States. Army. Cavalry—Equipment—History. 2. United States. Army. Cavalry—History.
I. Title.
UE443.S83   357'.1'0973   75–26946
ISBN: 0–8061–1283–2

To Harold A. Geer, who, in accordance with the finest traditions of the United States Cavalry, came charging to the rescue when succor was sorely needed. Without his unselfish material help and constant encouragement this work might never have been completed.

PREFACE

IF I HAD A NICKEL for every time I have wished that someone had published a work like this a hundred years ago—and another about 1920—I would be able to add a few fine Paterson, Walker, and dragoon Colts to my collection! Believe me, such books would have saved me a rough self-imposed more-than-ten-year sentence at hard labor.

This work had its real beginning in the early 1950's. I had been involved with horses and horse equipment almost all my life, and when my articles and drawings had started appearing in magazines a few years earlier, naturally, most of them were about horses and horsemen—many about old-time cavalry.

Central Texas, where my home and studio were located, is far from the centers where primary sources of information on cavalry are preserved. After a great deal of fruitless searching, I realized that most of the information and detail I needed was hundreds of miles away—Washington, West Point, Fort Riley, Richmond, Fort Lee, Leavenworth, Fort Laramie, and many other places that would require years to search out.

It did not take long for me to realize how few and far between were existing works on the subject of cavalry. I do not mean to imply that many books have not been written on the subject; their titles run into the hundreds. But none revealed more than smatterings of the details I needed to know about. What uniform clothed the dragoon in 1837? What was the exact pattern of his saddle and bridle, and what color was his saddle blanket? What kind of a buckle did he wear on his saber belt, and what, exactly, did his spurs look like? These and literally thousands of other details I needed to know were rarely mentioned in the hundreds of books I poured through. I was always hopeful that the next page would include at least a description of some article of dress, or mention of a specific type of bit, or at least a sketchy word picture of

something that would help my illustrations be accurate and authentic.

My formal education had been dominated by the engineering courses crammed into me at the Naval Academy, and I suppose the dominance of accuracy and preciseness, always a requisite in engineering drawing, had a great deal to do with both my style of drawing and my own perpetual demands for authenticity.

At any rate, I have never allowed myself the short cuts that *faking* a detail here and there affords an illustrator. I am the first to admit that many of my early drawings, used as illustrations for my own articles on cavalry and some to illustrate pieces by others, had errors in them. But they were honest errors, made because of inadequate or careless research, and not by attempts to fake something I had no complete knowledge of.

I am fortunate that this did not happen too often, but when it did I was the most embarrassed human on the face of the earth!

About 1956 a whole new world of information opened up for me when the late Colonel Harry Larter, living in San Antonio, invited me to become a member of The Company of Military Collectors & Historians (later renamed The Company of Military Historians). The Company journal was filled with a treasure trove of information on military subjects I had been able to find nowhere else, and this began an association that I value more highly than any other I have ever had.

But even the *Military Collector & Historian*, as the quarterly journal is called, came up with far too few cavalry details. The uniform plates published by the Company were done by the best military artists in the world and have been a source of information and inspiration since I laid eyes on the first one.

I had thought some about writing a work on early

cavalry in the mid-1950's, but with all the research I was doing constantly for my bread-and-butter work, there just wasn't time in a 24-hour day to more than daydream about it while I was at the easel or drawing board struggling to meet deadlines.

Open-heart surgery the summer of 1957 slowed me down to a crawl, and it was months after my session with the surgeons in Dallas before I could hold a pen or brush steadily enough to do any kind of a drawing or painting. I had a lot of time to think, and that is when I made up my mind that some day I would *take* enough time to write a work on the uniforms, arms, and equipments of the horse soldier!

The next year I moved to northern California, about as far from West Point, the National Archives, the Smithsonian, and the Library of Congress as you can go and still be in the United States. But I managed to make an extended trip to the East about every other year to spend weeks poring through age-yellowed records and thousands of photographs in the facilities maintained by the national government for the preservation and display of this type of information and artifacts of the past.

It was hard for me to tear myself away from those great sources of information, but pure economic necessity always saw to that. Slowly my files became stuffed with notes, photocopies of uniform regulations, and 8x10 prints of negatives I had made by the thousands of articles of cavalry uniforms and equipment.

In 1960 I acquired a small ranch in the foothills of the Sierras and started building a log studio, which took better than two years to complete. What a studio that was! A friend who had been one of the construction superintendents during the building of Disneyland pitched in with a few more friends to help construct that big two-story log building.

Everything was done in the way it would have been built a hundred years before. The rafters and floor joists were heavy peeled pine poles tied together with rawhide. The stairs to the second floor were hewn from logs, and the atmosphere of the whole structure was a real inspiration for someone occupied with the kind of work I was doing.

While the studio was being built, I made the decision to write my work on the cavalry. I had already done a series of illustrated articles for the *Western Horseman* magazine on the Civil War cavalryman, and I suppose that the reception it got from horsemen and military buffs was the deciding factor in making

up my mind to go ahead with the book I had wanted to do for so long.

Another series for the *Western Horseman* on the Indian-fighting cavalryman that I planned to include in my work was shipped off to their editorial offices in the fall of 1962, shortly after the new studio was completed. I had been able to devote more than a year to the project by that time, and, except for the index, it was about ready to be delivered to the publisher.

There were 150 pages of black-and-white illustrations on the big table in the downstairs library, and 350 pages of text, including those pages not yet returned by the magazine in Colorado Springs.

Three 4-drawer filing cabinets full of the research material accumulated for the work stood against the wall at the end of the shelves holding a few more than 3,500 reference books that made up the library I had been able to accumulate over a period of a good many years. One wall across from the library shelves was filled with carbines, pistols, and sabers—the models I had used to make the illustrations for the work.

Upstairs the walls were lined with uniforms, cartridge boxes and belts, saddles, bridles, bits, and the thousand and one items that had served as models for the drawings and 24 paintings of cavalrymen and their gear that were stacked downstairs.

Near the end of January, 1963, the drawings and text came back from the magazine, and, except for a little more work on the index, the manuscript would have been ready to ship within a week at the latest.

To make a long story short, I spent nearly all the afternoon and early evening of January 25 thirty miles away in Sacramento. When my car headlights illuminated the end of the driveway as I turned in to the ranch shortly after dark, I saw nothing but a still-smoldering pile of ruins. Everything in the studio had been completely destroyed when the building burned to the ground that afternoon.

I won't try to tell you how I felt. A lifetime accumulation of uniforms, arms, horse equipment, and Early West articles was gone, including the completed work and every scrap of research material that had made it possible.

So, you see, this is the second version of *The Horse Soldier*. It has taken a lot longer to put it together this time, for I had to start all over from scratch and, besides, work like the devil to recoup the monetary loss the fire caused.

There was one advantage, I kept telling myself—

this time I will know where *not* to go when I start gathering the material for the next go at the project. I do not remember ever having a doubt in my mind about writing this work the second time. In spite of the fact that I had been way underinsured and had suffered a terrific financial loss, it seemed to have been a foregone conclusion to me that *The Horse Soldier* had to be put together again.

That old saying about everything happening for the best is hard to swallow sometimes, but in this case I must admit that the present work, as you will see it when you finish wading through these first few pages, is much more nearly complete and, I believe, a much more valuable source of reference.

There are a few facts you should know about this work before you turn to the first chapter.

Perhaps the most important fact is that this is *not* a history of the United States Cavalry. There are many fine books (and some a fraction less than fine) that tell the stories of the regiments, their officers and men, and their charges and battles during the life span of our horse cavalry. This work deals with the way the dragoon, the mounted rifleman, and the cavalryman looked; the weapons they fought with; and the saddles, bridles, and other horse gear they draped on their horses.

But *The Horse Soldier* will prove to be a source of reference for more than just cavalry buffs! Each change of uniform and improvement in arms and equipment was, almost without exception, reflected in similar changes for all branches of the Army. True, for many years the length of both dress and field coats or blouses was shorter for the mounted man than for the foot troops—but the cut was generally the same or very similar. Colors of facings and insignia were different for each branch of the service, but with a basic knowledge of facing colors a student of military history can pinpoint important changes in uniforms, insignia, and, in a good many cases, weapons from the pages of these volumes. By using the dates of changes in regulations and specifications contained herein, a researcher can readily refer to the complete regulations as published by the War Department to pinpoint changes for any branch of the Army.

Throughout the years spent gathering material on which to base both illustrations and text, I have avoided pictorial representation by artists, except for the meticulously researched plates by a few artists in the Company of Military Historians' series "Military

Uniforms in America." Before the days of reproducing photographs by the photoengraving process, illustrations in nineteenth-century publications were from steel engravings, woodcuts, or lithographs on stone, executed by artists who worked from sketches and drawings done in the field by other artists. Mistakes and misinterpretations by the field artist were compounded by the engraver, so that published illustrations were seldom if ever accurate enough to rely on.

Whenever possible—and this has been the case with most of the illustrations in this work—drawings were made from actual specimens of the uniforms, arms, accoutrements, and horse equipment. My present collection includes a large percentage of these items, but many details were drawn from sketches I made and photographs I took of articles in many private collections, as well as those in municipal, state, and national museums throughout the United States.

When it was necessary to make a drawing from an *official description* of an article of equipment, I have indicated that such was the case, either in the text or in the caption for that particular illustration.

In the cases of articles of uniform or equipment that I have been unable to document, I have been careful to announce that fact.

I have tried to make the information, both that shown by the drawings and paintings and that described in the text, as factual as I know how. Undoubtedly there are details I may have missed, and perhaps an error or two may show up. If such is the case, I claim full responsibility for them!

This work has been made possible by the unselfish interest and help of many people in many walks of life. A list of every individual who contributed information and assistance throughout the years it has taken to complete *The Horse Soldier* would require many pages. But there are some who deserve more than mere acknowledgment for their part in making this work possible.

Harold Geer, a former horse soldier in an Ohio National Guard regiment, did more to encourage me, both materially and with his enthusiasm for the project, than any other person in the country. I want my appreciation for this man's help to be especially understood, and recorded here.

My friend the late Gerald C. Stowe, curator and historian at the West Point Museum, made it possible for me to spend countless hours in the museum and in the study collection where so much of the detailed information found in these pages came from. His help, encouragement, and hospitality were largely responsible for the accuracy of much of the contents of this work.

I am also greatly indebted to the rest of the staff at the West Point Museum—Robert Fisch and Phil Cavanaugh, both curators who devoted many hours posing for sketches and photographs in uniforms and equipment of many periods of history; Mrs. Leona Patton in the museum office who graciously helped with accession-card verification of hundreds of items in the museum and anything else she was asked to help with; Frederick P. Todd, former Director of the West Point Museum, and Richard E. Kuehne, the present Director.

Egon Weiss, Librarian at the West Point Library, made it possible for me to photocopy dozens of uniform regulations and excerpts from other vitally important records and volumes necessary for the documentation of a major portion of this book. Further assistance came from J. Thomas Russell, Rare Book Section; Joseph M. O'Donnel, Archives Section; and William Kerr, Assistant Librarian. All helped make the facilities of the huge library at the military academy available to me.

Colonel Richard Johnson, then stationed at West Point, made the hundreds of items of military accoutrements in his valuable personal collection available for photographing, and spent hours of his time identifying the articles which appear so frequently in the text and illustrations.

Edgar M. Howell, Director of the Military History Section of the Smithsonian Institution, as well as Don Kloster and Craddock Goins of his staff, provided invaluable assistance and advice, making the vast national collection of military uniforms and equipment available for study and photographing. Throughout the years required for compiling the information found in this book the information they furnished in frequent correspondence helped unravel some of the many mysteries surrounding the clothing, arms, and equipment described and pictured.

Horace Mann, Director of the Quartermaster Museum at Fort Lee, and Jesse H. Travis, Historian, made the large collection housed there available to me for unlimited study.

Mrs. Sarah Jackson and Harry D. Ryan of the Military Records Division at the National Archives spent hours helping me track down thousands of military orders, correspondence, and records deposited there—on so many occasions.

Hirst D. Milhollen, specialist in photography at the Library of Congress, made the huge files of photographic prints available to me, and spent much of his time finding suitable photographs of horse equipment for my use.

Mrs. Mary W. Stubbs and Detmar H. Finke, at the Office of the Chief of Military History in Washington, provided me with much valuable information and material.

I am especially indebted to Phil Kelleher, Gaithersburg, Maryland, for the hundreds of pages of copies of uniform regulations he obtained so willingly from the National Archives, the Smithsonian, and the Library of Congress, and without which this book could not have been completed without additional months of laborious work and many more visits to Washington.

In addition to many others, the following contributed much in allowing me to pour over their personal collections, and in providing and arranging for information that would have been unobtainable without their assistance: Gordon Chappell, Sacramento, California; Lieutenant Colonel Roy T. Huntington, Charlottesville, Virginia; Lieutenant Colonel William N. Todd, Gatewood, Illinois; Norman Wilson and Jack L. Dyson, Sacramento, California; Major General John F. Ruggles, Washington, D.C.; Frank E. Morse, Mount Vernon, Virginia; Donald A. Heckaman, Cleveland, Ohio; Colonel Glenn I. Epperson, Del Mar, California; the late John M. Lee, Cypress, California; Chester J. Yatcak, Westminster, California; Gillett Griswold, Fort Sill, Oklahoma; Olaf Wieghorst, El Cajon, California; H. Charles McBarron, Jr., Chicago, Illinois; Stanley J. Olsen, Tallahassee, Florida; John Carraci and Frank Carraci, Fort Pierce, Florida; Carl Pugliese, Yonkers, New York; Carter Rila, Washington, D.C.; John Rossi, Denver, Colorado; Lyle Thoburn, Gates Mills, Ohio; Arthur Sherman, Sacramento, California; Miss Eleanor Murray, Fort Ticonderoga, New York; Miss Mildred C. Cox, Fort Leavenworth, Kansas . . .

and to my wife, Dorothy, without whose help, inspiration, and constant encouragement this book might never have been completed.

Walking S Ranch
Dublin, Texas

TECHNICAL NOTES

FORMAT

REFERENCE NOTATIONS throughout this work are found adjacent to that part of the text requiring documentation, either as a part of the text, or in parentheses in or after the sentence to which the reference pertains.

I have used this method, rather than footnotes, for several reasons. Perhaps the most important is the fact that so much of the documentation is direct reference to paragraphs from uniform regulations or specifications, or from published general orders, bulletins, circulars, and reports. The use of footnotes, therefore, would have been more confusing than helpful, and highly repetitious.

In cases where quotations from non-War Department publications or material originating from such publications have been used, complete credit and details have been given in the text.

SPELLING AND TERMINOLOGY

Throughout this work I have used the spelling for articles described and illustrated that was common throughout the era covered by each chapter. Thus *saber* is spelled for the twentieth century as it is shown at the beginning of this sentence, and as *sabre* for before 1900, which was the way it was spelled in every military document and communication. The same is true with other military terms used throughout the work.

SOURCES

You will find no bibliography at the end of this work. With few exceptions the text is documented by constant reference to particular paragraphs of official uniform regulations, uniform specifications, general orders, circulars, ordnance memoranda, government documents, annual reports by the Secretary of War, and other War Department publications. All these are available at libraries, the Library of Congress, and the National Archives.

Wherever possible, and certainly wherever necessary to provide adequate descriptions of cavalry articles important to the serious student of the U.S. Cavalry, regulations, specifications, and entire sections of reports, orders, and published pamphlets are reproduced verbatum.

The few commercially published works from which quotations or specific information have been used are noted in the text.

During the more than 10 years it has taken to write and illustrate this work, I have read literally thousands of books written about or containing information on the U.S. Cavalry. Unfortunately, the amount of *documented* material that could be used as reference was almost nonexistent. Pages and pages of bibliography, therefore, would in this case be superfluous. Those books containing information of real value to this subject are listed in appropriate places throughout the text.

ILLUSTRATIONS

The drawings and paintings used as illustrations have been executed with great care. In every case possible I have used models wearing authentic uniforms and posing with the weapons and equipment shown with them. For those cavalrymen portrayed in uniforms impossible to obtain, I used coats cut in the same style and changed details to conform to the correct specifications.

The same was true with the illustrations of arms, accoutrements, and horse equipment. In cases where no specimens exist, or could not be located, descriptions found in regulations and specifications were used to *reconstruct* this equipment on paper. But in each case where these conditions existed, I have made specific mention of this fact in the text or in the caption for the illustration. This was necessary in only one or two instances, however.

Thousands of photographs and sketches of uniforms, arms, and equipment, all made from specimens in private collections and municipal, state, and national museums, were used to supplement the articles in my own collection and specimens borrowed from others.

All black-and-white drawings were done with Number 2 Robert Simmons Series-80 pure red sable water-color brushes and Pelikan India ink.

The color plates have been done with tempera, opaque water colors, on medium-weight cold-press illustration board. The same illustration board was used for the black-and-white brush and ink drawings.

CONTENTS

ILLUSTRATIONS

THE HORSE SOLDIER

1776–1943

VOLUME I

The Revolution, the War of 1812, the Early Frontier

1776–1850

INTRODUCTION

THE MASSIVENESS of the material included in *The Horse Soldier* has made publication of the work as a single volume impractical. Much thought and many conferences between the author and the editorial and production departments of the University of Oklahoma Press were necessary before the decision was made to publish in four volumes.

Of primary consideration was reader convenience. A single volume of this format with more than a thousand pages would be extremely difficult to handle for constant reference; its weight alone would discourage carrying it from library shelf to working area, and it would be most unhandy.

Perhaps the biggest drawback to such an oversize and overweight book would be the difficulty in seeing easily those parts of the illustrations near the inner margins of the pages, especially near the middle of the book.

Since each individual chapter with its accompanying illustrations covers specific eras in which major changes were made in uniform and equipment specifications and regulations, it was relatively easy to divide *The Horse Soldier* into four separate volumes. The periods covered by each volume are listed below:

Volume I	1776–1850
Volume II	1851–1880
Volume III	1881–1916
Volume IV	1917–1943

Volume I covers the Revolutionary War and the Continental Light Dragoons, the first horse soldiers authorized by the Continental Congress and the first mounted troops employed by the brand new nation that was soon to become the United States of America.

It also covers that indecisive but critical period between 1783 and 1797 when mere token forces of mounted men were shuffled in and out of existence by a government that was sick of war and overly conscious of economy.

Included are the years preceding the War of 1812 and this second conflict with Great Britain in which the mounted arm of the American forces played a very minor role.

Special emphasis is placed on the first permanent mounted troops of our infant nation, beginning with the United States Mounted Ranger Battalion organized in 1832, and the first Regiment of United States Dragoons authorized and recruited in 1833. Their colorful and unique uniforms, arms, and equipment are covered in great detail through the years of the Seminole Wars in Florida and their campaigns in Mexico.

Volume I concentrates heavily on the dragoon and the mounted rifleman up to the year 1851, when a major change in uniforms and considerable changes in equipment dictated a practical stopping place for the book.

CHAPTER ONE

The Continental Light Dragoons

1776–83

CONSIDERING THE SCARCITY of material, either written or pictorial, in our national depositories concerning the Continental soldier, his uniform, arms, and accoutrements, several other writers—Harold Peterson, Warren Moore, George Neumann—have done remarkable jobs in presenting what evidence is available to the serious military buff. And a number of equally talented illustrators working with these writers have contributed much to the available knowledge of the cavalrymen of this period.

Since the Continental Army actually preceded the United States Army, which this work attempts to cover, I shall make no bones about having drawn extensively from the existing reliable works on the Continental Dragoons. And I shall not attempt to portray the Continental Dragoons as thoroughly as I have every one of the United States mounted soldiers—for several reasons.

First, the reference material concerning every part of the Continental Dragoons' dress, arms, and equipment just does not exist in enough detail to illustrate or describe accurately every part of the uniform or equipment; and, second, the above-mentioned writers and illustrators have covered this subject so thoroughly, considering the source material available, that I feel the following list of publications will enable anyone to avail himself of the most accurate descriptions of the Continental Dragoon that exist:

The Book of the Continental Soldier, by Harold Peterson (Harrisburg, Stackpole Books, 1968).
The History of Weapons of the American Revolution, by George C. Neumann (New York, Harper & Row, 1967).
Weapons of the American Revolution, by Warren Moore (New York, Funk & Wagnalls, 1967).
Sketch Book 76, by Robert L. Klinger and Richard A. Wilder (published by the authors, 1967).
Picture Book of the Continental Soldier, by C. Keith Wilbur (Harrisburg, Stackpole Books, 1968).

It must be remembered that the Continental Army was one raised from scratch—and that, in spite of published regulations concerning uniforms, insignia of rank, and equipment, soldiers and officers alike wore what they could get, and used whatever arms and equipment they were lucky enough to put their hands on.

So it was with all arms of the Continental Army—they read the published orders on what their dress should be, on how to distinguish ranks, on the proper equipment for the mounted forces—and went right ahead using what they had.

As with the remainder of this work, this era of military significance will be covered under separate headings: "Uniforms," "Arms," "Accoutrements," and "Horse Equipments."

UNIFORMS

Dress of the Continental Dragoons, according to published orders and regulations, are well covered in Harold Peterson's *The Book of the Continental Soldier*, pages 235–38. Much of his material was drawn from Leffert's *Uniforms of . . . the War of the American Revolution, 1775–1783*, known to contain a number of errors, but for the most part accurate and reliable.

Officers were required to furnish their own horses, saddles, and other horse equipment as well as their arms and accoutrements. But each trooper of the *First Regiment of Continental Light Dragoons*, raised in June, 1776, was to be furnished with a coat, cap, a pair of leather breeches, and a pair of boots and spurs—at public expense. When first formed, this regiment was to have blue coats with gilt buttons, but there was no supply of helmets, caps, or hats in public stocks. As a consequence they undoubtedly wore their citizen's tricorn hats as they were, or decorated them with whatever cockade or plume they could lay their hands on.

In 1777 and 1778 regimental orders for the First Regiment prescribed short brown coats with green lapels, cuffs, and collars; green waistcoats; leather breeches; gilt or yellow buttons of regimental pattern(?); black leather caps with perpendicular fronts and green turbans with yellow tassels. As was the custom with European armies, trumpeters, farriers, and saddlers had reverse uniforms of green trimmed with brown.

In 1780 clothing was provided from stores in Virginia, and from then until the end of the war the uniform of the First appears to have been short blue or black coats with green lapels, cuffs, and turnbacks and blue lining; black stocks; and blue overalls. Some wore leather breeches. Helmets were black leather with black cockades on the left side. Both stable jackets and linen shirts were furnished.

But helmets were in short supply and records show most of the regiment had to wear hats until the regiment was mustered out in 1782.

Not much documentary evidence exists regarding the uniform of the *Second Regiment of Light Dragoons*, perhaps because the Second was the only cavalry regiment active to the end of the war. John Trumball included figures of both officers and enlisted men in several of his most important paintings. According to these paintings the uniform of the Second, from 1780 through 1783, was a blue coat with buff lapels, cuffs, and turnbacks; buff waistcoat and breeches; white belts, metal(?) helmets with light blue turbans and yellow tassels. (*See Uniform Color Plate I, Figure A.*) When dismounted the Second wore brown or dark-colored overalls. Apparently the uniform for the period between 1776 and 1780 has never been pinned down.

And this was also the case of the *Third Regiment of Continental Light Dragoons*—uniforms for the first two years of its existence, 1776–78, are unknown. Records of cloth received by the Virginia Public Stores at Williamsburg and delivered to the regiment in May, 1779, indicate, along with a portrait of an officer of the Third, that uniforms were white coats, faced, lapelled and lined with blue. Again, in 1780, records indicate the uniforms had white coats but with green facings, and leather breeches, white stockings, white shirts, and stable jackets were issued. A contemporary German drawing shows the uniform to be substantially the same, but with a black leather billed jockey cap with red turban and drooping foxtail. The *Fourth Regiment of Continental Light Dragoons*, as impractical as it may seem, wore scarlet coats during the early years of the war. Because the officers of the regiment had gone to considerable personal expense to outfit themselves with scarlet uniforms, the commander in chief gave the clothier general permission to issue 240 captured coats of red faced with blue to the regiment. But for the remainder of the period from 1777 to 1779 hunting shirts, leather breeches, stockings, shoes, and some kind of helmets were worn by most of the Fourth.

Deserter descriptions list the uniform of this regiment for the years 1780–82 as green coats faced with red, red waistcoats, leather breeches, green overalls, helmets trimmed with bearskin, and green cloaks with red capes.

Since the invention of the photographic process came many decades later, we have only contemporary paintings, drawings, and illustrations on which to rely for the details of these uniforms. With the exception of a few dragoon-type caps and helmets that are found in the collections of the National Museum, Fort Ticonderoga, and undoubtedly a few private collections, few, if any, items of Continental Light Dragoon uniforms exist.

Contemporary drawings and paintings are risky, at best, for complete reliability. With few exceptions, most painters and artists, even to this day, are prone to "fake" a detail with which they are not completely familiar. This is especially evident in paintings portraying horse equipment—details are *almost* correct, but most have flaws that are quickly evident to any experienced horseman. The same must be taken for granted in military uniform and equipment portrayal. The *documentary* illustrator does not dare use such material for irrefutable reference without offering reservations in his captions or descriptions. This is why I chose to treat this chapter on the Continental Dragoons as less than documentary in its descriptions and illustrations. I have used the material available to me as evidence that *points toward* the *conclusions* I have drawn as to what the uniforms, arms, and equipment *looked like*, and as to *how* they were used.

INSIGNIA OF RANK

At the beginninng of the war there were no prescribed badges of insignia or rank, so it was difficult to distinguish officers from enlisted men. In the summer of the first year, sashes across the shoulder were chosen to designate general officers, while other commissioned officers wore cockades on their hats. Noncommissioned officers wore worsted epaulettes or strips of cloth on the shoulders of their coats.

The cockade insignia that officers wore on their hats or helmets distinguished ranks by their colors. Field officers wore red or pink, captains yellow, and subalterns green. Captains' cockades were changed from yellow to white or buff in 1776.

Noncommissioned officers in the grade of sergeant wore red strips of cloth or red epaulettes on each shoulder, while corporals were authorized to wear similar badges of green.

In June, 1780, new regulations for the insignia of rank for all grades were adopted and generally remained unchanged until the end of the war.

Special uniforms were worn by general officers, and their rank was further indicated by the number of silver stars on their epaulettes and by the plumes on their hats. Two stars and a black and white plume marked a major general, while a single silver star on the epaulette and a white plume indicated the rank of brigadier general.

Field grade officers, colonels, lieutenant colonels, and majors were authorized to wear an epaulette on each shoulder; captains and lieutenants, one epaulette each—captains on the right shoulder and subalterns on the left. Epaulettes for dragoons (and infantry) were to be of silver; gold was specified for artillery.

In March, 1779, both Congress and General Washington agreed on epaulette insignia to be prescribed for noncommissioned officers—dragoon sergeants, corporals, farriers, and saddlers were to wear epaulettes of blue. Equivalent grades of other arms were to wear different colors. The sergeants were directed to wear epaulettes on both shoulders, corporals, just one on the right shoulder, but no written record of what the farriers and saddlers were to wear seems to exist.

SPECIAL MILITARY DECORATIONS

In mid-1872 the first "honorary mark of distinction," actually a service stripe, was established in one brigade of the Continental Army. It was a single stripe of white tape worn on the left sleeve of the regimental coat, running from seam to seam and located 3 inches below and parallel with the shoulder seam so that the tape formed a herringbone figure. If a soldier served

8 years, he was authorized to place a second tape one inch below and parallel with the first.

Later that same year Washington issued orders for honorary badges of distinction for noncommissioned officers and privates in all branches of the Army who had served for 3 or more years "with bravery, fidelity and good conduct." This badge was a "narrow piece of white cloth, of angular form" to be placed on the left arm of the uniform coat. For those serving more than 6 years of the same type of unsullied service, another piece of cloth of similar shape was set parallel with the first. No doubt these were the first chevrons in the American service. Shortly after this order was published, it was changed to allow the stripes of cloth to be made the same color as the facings of the uniform.

At about the same time, Washington also created a badge called "the badge of military merit" for unusual gallantry and extraordinary fidelity. Award of this badge was limited to those acts certified to Washington by the individual's regimental or brigade commander. This was the famous purple heart, which was revived in 1932 for award to men wounded in battle. The award itself was the figure of a heart in purple cloth mounted on narrow lace, and was worn on the facings over the left breast of the uniform coat. The word "Merit" with floral decorations on each side was embroidered in silver thread on the purple heart. Only 3 men are known to have received this award, one being a Sergeant Elijah Churchill of the Second Continental Light Dragoons. After the war this decoration was discontinued completely for almost 150 years.

THE UNIFORMS IN DETAIL

The uniform as prescribed by regulations is illustrated in Figure 1, with the standard military coat of the period, leather breeches, waistcoat, stock, linen shirt, and leather dragoon cap, or helmet, with horsehair plume, turban, and knot in the back with its protective tassels.

The two figures at the left show front and back views of the clothing regulation for enlisted men of the various regiments of Continental Light Dragoons. Each regiment was distinguished from the others by the colors of the coats and the colors of the facings.

Coats were made of wool or broadcloth, and facings referred to were collars, lapels, cuffs, and the turnbacks

FIGURE 1. Left: Front and rear views of the typical Continental Light Dragoons' uniform for privates. The various regiments, according to regulations, were distinguished by the colors of their coats and facings and by the color of turbans and tassels on their helmets. Right: Commissioned officers. Coats and facings are same colors as those of the men, but cloth and workmanship are finer. Helmets were also better quality and more ornate.

of the skirts. Normally lapels were worn turned back and buttoned, with the upper edges of the lapels fastening with hooks and eyes. While descriptions of coats for the Light Dragoons called for short coats in many cases, the skirts were much longer than later styles of cavalry coats, reaching well below the buttocks, and were styled exactly the same as the coats for infantry and artillery.

At the right of Figure 1 are front and rear views of commissioned officers, and it will be seen that the pattern of their coats is identical to those of their men. It seems that there must have been much tolerance for variation in the ways lapels were buttoned to collars, for some reference works show that buttons were on the collars, as worn by the officer facing forward in this drawing; others show the top of the lapel

under the collar, so that the button must have been fastened to the lapel instead of the collar, as on the enlisted man at the left.

The officer facing forward is of field grade, for he wears an epaulette on each shoulder; the officer with his back turned is a lieutenant, since he wears a single epaulette on his left shoulder. Both officers wear heavy leather helmets with metal crests, most likely made of sheet brass, since it was easy to work and would not rust. Plumes are white horsehair, allowed to droop for parade and duty in the field, but plaited in strands for ordinary duty to keep it from becoming tangled and snarled. Chin straps are made of brass scales on leather.

The enlisted man with his back turned carries a white buff-leather carbine sling with a chain and toggle that suspends the carbine from its carrying ring.

FIGURE 2. Left: Dragoon on dismounted duty wearing the linen overalls adopted for wear by most regiments after 1778. Right: Private dragoon wearing stable jacket and fatigue cap.

Buff leather has a roughened finish and is made from cowhide—not *buffalo* hide, as some writers have erroneously stated. This man's sabre belt is the shoulder type, and is also made of white buff leather with brass buckle and billet cap.

The sabre belt on the field officer is the waist type with slings to support the sabre. The subaltern wears a shoulder-type sabre belt of the same pattern as the enlisted man, but with better buff leather and better finish to the metal parts, which might be gilt.

Boots on both officers and enlisted men are black with light tan or buff-leather tops, as was the style of that period both for civilian boots and for military boots.

FIGURE 3. Private of one of the regiments of light dragoons dressed and equipped for duty in the field. He wears the linen hunting shirt instead of the fancy and ungainly (for a mounted man) coat prescribed by regulations. But Washington considered it an ideal military garment, and sooner or later the hunting shirt was adopted by almost every unit in the Continental Army for wear on some occasions.

The dragoons shown in Figure 2 are wearing slightly different clothes prescribed for nonmounted and stable duty. The figure on the left wears the full-leg-length garment called overalls. The commander in chief considered overalls a most practical military garb, and after 1778 most regiments of all branches of the Army adopted them. Overalls made of wool were much sought after for winter wear, while those made of linen were preferred for summer.

H. Charles McBarron, one of the outstanding military illustrators of all times, depicted the stable jacket and cap as on the figure at the right in a drawing that appeared in the *Military Collector & Historian*, the journal of The Company of Military Historians, a few years ago. This was an illustration accompanying a comprehensive article by McBarron and Detmar H. Finke, both distinguished historians and Fellows of The Company of Military Historians. ("Continental Army Uniform and Specifications, 1779–1781," *Military Collector & Historian*, Vol. XIV, No. 2, 35–41.) Lefferts states that stable jackets were green, and this may have been true for all regiments.

The stable cap, or fatigue cap, is certainly European in its origin. I have not been able to find a source that reveals the color of this cap or the material from which it was made.

Figure 3 shows an enlisted light dragoon dressed and equipped for campaign against the British. He wears one style of linen hunting shirt with open front and fringed decorations on shoulder yokes and sleeves that were typical of most styles. Washington considered the hunting shirt an ideal military garment and sooner or later it was adopted by almost every unit in the Continental Army for wear on some occasions.

Under the hunting shirt is the usual waistcoat, over which is buckled a waist belt with the style of cartridge box most often used by the light dragoons. His captured British flintlock carbine is suspended from the chain and toggle on the carbine sling slide, and his American-made horseman's sabre in its leather scabbard is slung from a shoulder-type sabre belt.

His breeches are the usual yellowish buff-leather ones worn by most horsemen, when they could get them, and his boots are black with tan tops. His leather jockey-style cap is made of stiffened heavy leather. A cloth turban with a small cockade on the left side encircles the cap and ties at the back with a bulky knot, whose tasseled ends hang down over the back of his neck as a sort of protection against sabre blows. A leather chin strap keeps the cap-helmet in place. White horsehair fastened to the leather crest in clumps form a plume that droops over the cap and helps distinguish the light dragoon from soldiers of other arms.

His horse is equipped with a civilian-type saddle that has had rings and staples added to it for fastening holsters, blanket, saddlebags, and breast harness. The bridle and halter are semimilitary types in wide use during this period. Four thicknesses of folded blanket pad the horse from the saddle's bars and skirts. A crupper aids the breast harness in keeping the saddle in place on the horse's back, no matter how rough the going.

Helmets for the light dragoon regiments were considered vital for protection against sabre blows, but it seems there was a shortage of them all through the war. Most were made of heavy leather that had been stiffened by one means or another. Some were fitted with strap-iron bands riveted around the bottom with two or more pieces crossing over the rounded top as additional protection. Almost all of them had a crest made of either leather or metal that served to hold the small hanks of horsehair making up the drooping plume.

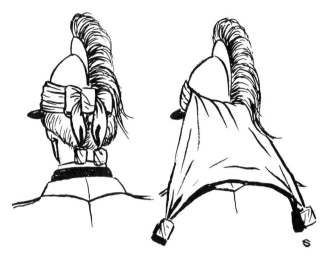

FIGURE 4. Rear views of a common type of helmet worn by some of the dragoon regiments. At left, the turban and neck protection are shown tied up, as normally worn for protection against sabre blows. At right, the knot is untied, and the cloth covers the neck to protect ears and neck from the sun and the weather.

Figure 4 shows the manner in which the bulky knot with its hanging tasseled ends was normally arranged at the rear of the helmet and fastened to the cloth turban. The right view shows how the knot, untied, allowed the cloth with its tassels to form a sort of scarf, or havelock, as this arrangement later became known, to drape over the back of the neck, affording protection from the sun, wind, snow, or rain.

The light dragoon carried cartridges for his musket or carbine on his person—if and when he was armed with a musket or carbine, for long arms for the mounted service were in extremely short supply. In his valuable small book, *Some Notes on the Continental Army*, available through the reconstructed cantonment near Newburgh, New York, Colonel John W. Wright states that almost no long arms except carbines captured from the British and Jaeger rifles from the Hessian dragoons were available to the light dragoons, so most were armed with pistols and sabres.

Undoubtedly there were a number of dragoons equipped with captured carbines, and others with all manners of long arms, from the French Charleville musket to the British Brown Bess to the Pennsylvania rifles made right there in the Colonies.

Ammunition for the military-type weapons was carried in a cartridge box attached to a leather waist

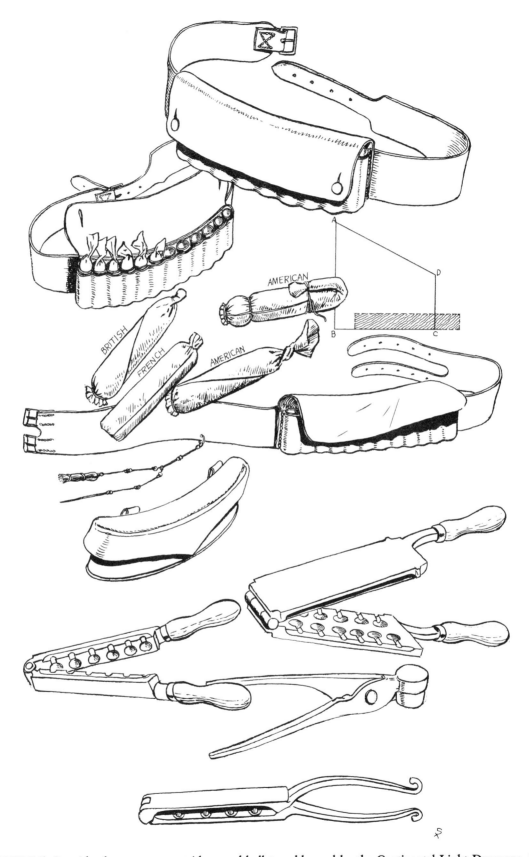

FIGURE 5. Cartridge boxes, paper cartridges, and bullet molds used by the Continental Light Dragoons, 1776–83.

belt and worn in the center of the body in front. Figure 5 shows three different styles of this type of cartridge box, each made to hold about a dozen paper cartridges in the tin-tube-lined leather loops protected by the overhanging leather flap. Most such cartridge-box and belt outfits were equipped with a vent pick and brush on a small wire chain fastened to the belt. These implements were used to keep the vent and pan of the flintlock clean and free of sludge from the burned powder to insure proper ignition each time the flint struck the frizzen.

At the bottom of Figure 5 are several types of gang- and single-cavity bullet molds used to cast bullets for the pistols and long arms used by the Continental soldier.

Below the top two cartridge boxes are shown several different types of paper cartridges that were used with the pistols, carbines, and muskets with which the Continental soldier was armed. A man by the name of Timothy Pickering described the process of making such cartridges at the beginning of the war, using the diagram shown on the illustration next to the cartridges:

> ... the best method of making paper cartridges seems to be that used in the [British] army. It is this ... take the soft brown paper called whitish brown, or wrapping paper, and cut it into pieces ... of these dimensions; the side AB measures about six inches, BC about five inches and a half, and CD about two inches. A piece of wood about six inches long is to be made round so as to fit exactly the size of the ball; this is called a former: make one end of it hollow to receive a part of the ball: lay the former upon the straight edge BC (as represented by the dotted lines) with its hollow end about an inch from the side AB: roll the paper around the former; then with the ball press in the corner of the paper so as to cover the hollow end of the former, and keeping fast the ball, roll on until the paper is all wrapped round the former; having before taken a piece of twine and fastened its two ends to something that will not easily be moved, and so far apart as to leave it slack, you are now to take with the twine a single turn around the paper, below the ball; then running in the end of your fore finger till it touches the ball, pull upon the string that it may girt the paper, and by turning round the former with one hand you will presently form a neck below the ball; which being afterwards tied with a piece of coarse thread will secure the ball from slipping out: then withdrawing the former, the cartridge is ready to be charged with powder; in doing which you must put in the more because part of it is to be taken for priming: having properly filled the cartridge, twist the top and the work is done. The size of the paper above described will serve for an ounce ball: if your ball be less, the paper may be somewhat smaller. One thing should be remembered, that if the cartridge exactly fits your firelock when the barrel is perfectly clean, it will be too large and difficult to be rammed down, when it becomes foul by firing; and 'tis dangerous firing when the ball is not rammed well home: for this therefore you are to make allowance.

French-style cartridges also became popular after the French entered the war. They were made much the same way, but the cartridge was pasted shut below the ball and along the side seam instead of being tied with string. The other two cartridges shown are both American and are made in much the same manner as the British method described above.

The use of paper cartridges greatly speeded the loading of smoothbore muskets and pistols, but there are some facts that seem to indicate paper cartridges were also used to speed the loading of some of the rifles used in the war.

The equipment illustrated in Figure 6 is typical of that used by the Continental Light Dragoons. Saddlebags at top left are the two-strap type approved by Congress. As shown on Figure 3, the straps are designed to allow the saddlebags to hang just behind the cantle of the saddle, supported across the seat by one strap and behind the cantle by the other. The bags shown in Figure 3 are made slightly different than those shown in this drawing, but the principle is the same. A leather string at the forward bottom corner of each bag is used to tie the bag down to a ring in the rear edge of the saddle skirt to prevent its flopping around when the horse is in motion.

To the right of the saddlebags is the standard buff-leather carbine sling that was used by both the British and American cavalry. Buckle, loop, and billet end were usually made of brass. Chain and toggle fastened to the sliding metal loop at the bottom of the sling are shown attached to the sliding ring of the carbine. This sling, kept glistening white by applications of chalk or clay, was worn over the soldier's left shoulder with the carbine suspended at his right side.

Below the carbine sling are shown three different types of haversacks carried by mounted men during this period. The one with the three straps is a captured British dragoon haversack made of white linen. Directly above it, with the flap fastened by three pewter buttons, is another popular version patterned after a British type. The bulky one to the right is a combination haversack-knapsack with compartments in each half. This one could be carried with the strap over the shoulder and the bags hanging at the side, as with regular knapsacks, or the compartmented bags

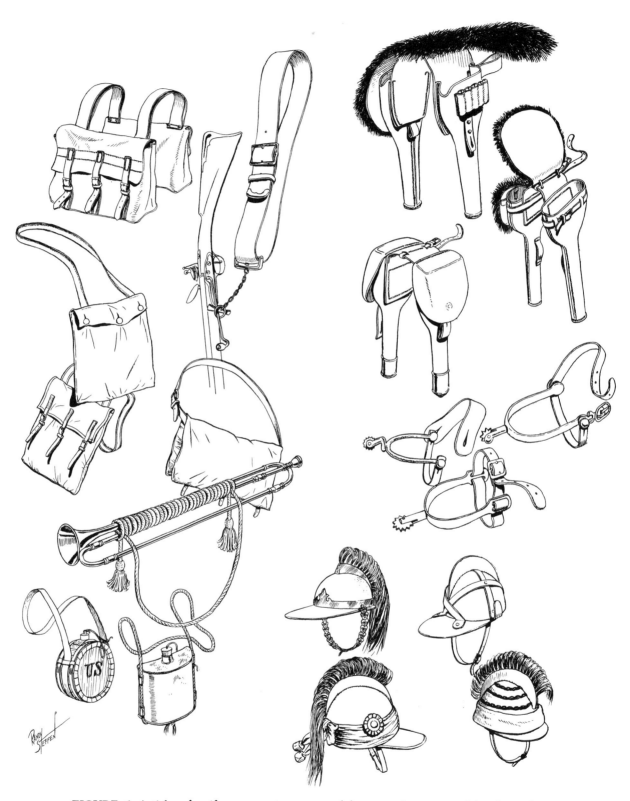

FIGURE 6. Articles of uniform, accoutrements, and horse equipments used by the regiments of Continental Light Dragoons.

could be slung across the back, with the supporting strap across one shoulder and under the other arm. This bag had more room for the soldier's gear than did the other two types.

The elongated trumpet below the haversacks is the type used by trumpeters of the Continental Light Dragoons during the war. There was a separate mouthpiece, and the brass tubing made just one loop between the mouthpiece and the bell. The trumpet cord is shown wrapped and secured, with a loop for supporting the trumpet over one shoulder and across the back when it was being carried on horseback.

The two canteens shown are the types most frequently used by the Continental soldier. The ends of the round one were solid wood about 6 to 9 inches in diameter. The sides were made of wood staves about 4 inches long, held in place by tinned-iron or brass hoops on some canteens, but most utilized hoops of willow or hickory with a buttonhole-and-eyelet joint. Three flat metal loops held the linen sling strap in place. The metal canteen shown is a British type, and many captured ones were used by the American soldiers. There is evidence that these were also made in this country.

At top right of Figure 6 are shown three different types of saddle holsters for holding the big flintlock pistols with which all light dragoons were armed. The holster at the top was drawn from a specimen in the writer's collection and is made of leather obviously formed wet over a wood pattern, then sewn as shown with linen thread. On the outside of each holster are leather pockets containing tin tubes for the paper cartridges. A wide leather piece joins the two holsters; it has a leather string attached to a hole near its center for securing the holsters to a ring at the head, or pommel, of the saddle. A broad, flat loop at the rear of each holster allows the surcingle, passing across the seat of the saddle, to be threaded through to help hold the holsters securely in place. The other two types shown are made in the same manner, but have slightly different methods of attachment to the saddle. The holster cover on the specimen shown at the top, and the one below to the right, are made of bearskin with the hair on it—most effective in shedding rain and snow. The cover on the lower set is made of leather formed wet over a pattern block.

Spurs shown below the holster are three types used by civilians and soldiers alike during the latter part of the eighteenth century, and are from the writer's collection. The spur at the left is made of wrought iron with an iron rowel. To its right is a forged-steel spur made in two pieces, with the shank riveted to the heel band. The rowel of this one is offset, so the bottom half is concealed by the shank. A small buckle is attached to the outside of the spur by a cast-brass jointed arrangement, as shown on the drawing. The bottom spur is unusual in that its rowel is set horizontally in the shank, which is riveted to the flat brass forming the slotted heel band.

At the bottom of the drawing are four different types of leather jockey-cap-style dragoon helmets known to have been worn by troopers of the different regiments of Continental Light Dragoons. The two at the left rely on their heavy leather construction for protection, while the two at the right are reinforced—the top one with iron straps and the bottom one with lengths of light chain attached to each side above the turban.

ARMS

The sabre was by far the most important weapon employed by the Continental Light Dragoons. Military men of this period of history, both on this continent and in Europe, contended that a charge by cavalry in line swinging sabres against opposing cavalry in line awaiting the charge with pistols ready to fire would, in every case, run over the horsemen with pistols. This may or may not have been an indisputable fact, but it was greatly believed in by American cavalry commanders, and the sabre was indeed the "weapon supreme," as far as they were concerned.

The Continental Light Dragoons were armed with a surprisingly large assortment of sabres; there was no pretense at any one or two patterns. The primary reason for the big variety was, of course, the short supply. But there were some exceptions. A sword maker at Rappahannock Forge supplied 1,000 sabres patterned after the British light cavalry sabre to the American forces. And several hundred German broadswords captured from the Brunswick Dragoons at the Battle of Bennington were issued to the Second Continental Light Dragoons on orders from General Washington in January, 1778. But for the most part the rule was great variety, even among the individual troops.

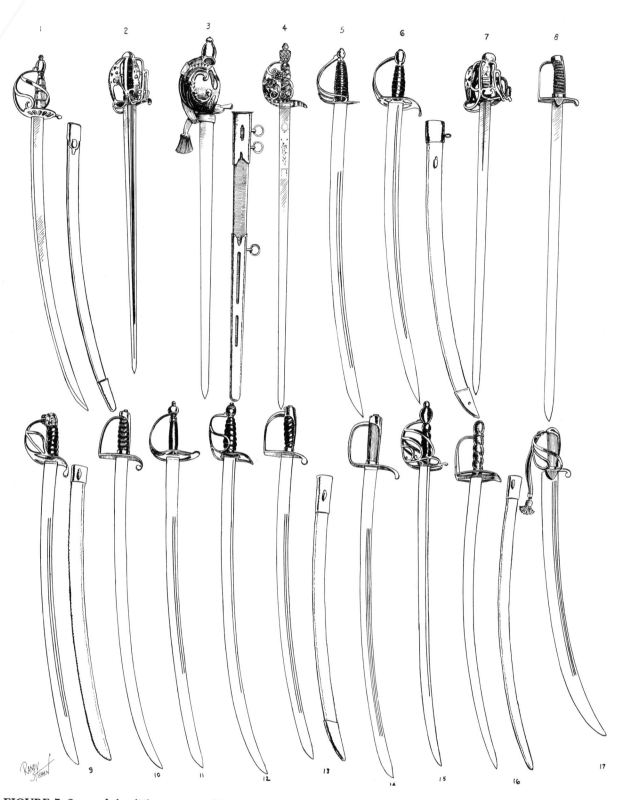

FIGURE 7. Some of the different types of horsemen's sabres used by officers and men of the 4 regiments of Continental Light Dragoons in the war against the British, 1776–83.

Figure 7 shows 17 different types of both light and heavy sabres known to have been used by American light dragoons during the war.

1. British dragoon sabre, with steel hilt and leather scabbard brass-mounted. For use with shoulder belt.
2. British cavalry backsword with steel hilt and 34-inch blade.
3. German brass-hilted broadsword captured from the Brunswick Dragoons and issued to the Second Continental Light Dragoons. Blade length, 36¾ inches.
4. British dragoon officer's steel-hilted sabre with 36-inch blade. Used by American dragoon officer.
5. American dragoon officer's brass-hilted sabre with 32½-inch blade and walnut grip.
6. American brass-hilted sabre with cherry grip and brass-mounted black leather scabbard. Blade length, 34 inches.
7. British dragoon trooper's broadsword with Scottish basket hilt and double-edged 34-inch blade.
8. British brass-hilted light dragoon sabre of the 1773–88 pattern with 36-inch blade.
9. American brass-hilted sabre with lion-head pommel and cherry grip. Its blade is 32 inches long and the scabbard is black leather with an iron throat.
10. American sabre with brass stirrup hilt and cherry grip. The blade is 34 inches long.
11. American brass-hilted sabre with maple grip. Blade length is 33 inches.
12. American brass-hilted sabre with cherry grip and 34½-inch blade.
13. American sabre with steel stirrup hilt, brown leather grip bound with wire, and brown leather scabbard with stud for suspending from shoulder-type belt. Blade length is 33 inches.
14. American sabre with steel stirrup hilt and black leather scabbard with brass mountings. Blade length is 33 inches.
15. Steel-hilted dragoon-pattern sabre with black leather grip and 32-inch blade.
16. American sabre with steel hilt and black leather grip. The scabbard is black leather with an iron throat and stud for shoulder-belt frog. The blade is 36 inches long.
17. French sabre. The hilt is steel, and the wide three-fuller blade is 32 inches long. Drawn from a specimen in the author's collection.

The sabre belts shown in Figure 8 are the types used by the light dragoons. At left is a white buff shoulder belt, probably the most common device by which sabres were carried by rank and file, although many officers carried their sabres with this type of belt, and enlisted men are known to have used waist belts with slings, as shown by the other two drawings on this page. The top waist belt is leather and the kind most likely used by most; the lower drawing shows a cloth waist sabre belt probably used by officers. Both brass and iron fittings were used.

Next to the sabre the big flintlock pistol was the most important light dragoon weapon, and each dragoon was certain to have a pair of these single-shot muzzle-loaders in his saddle holsters. If he was lucky enough to be armed with a carbine, or musket, or rifle in addition to his sabre and pistols, these long arms could be used only when his horse was standing or when he was fighting afoot. But the pistols could be fired—even though accuracy was replaced by pure luck most of the time—when the horse was at a trot or even full gallop. The theory then was to fire the pistol only at pointblank range, so the weapons *were* practical when used up close.

Figure 9 shows some of the many different types of pistols used by officers and men of the Continental Light Dragoons. Some were issued from Army arsenals, stored there originally by the British or colonial governments. A great many were captured from the British; pistols in conservative numbers were manufactured by American gunsmiths during the war. After France began to supply men and material, French pistols were used by some troopers.

British heavy dragoon-type pistols were used almost universally by both sides during the early years of the war. Of slightly *smaller* caliber than the light dragoon-type pistols used later, which fired a .69-caliber ball, the heavy dragoon pistols used by the American horsemen were either captured or were British arsenal pieces issued by the colonies before the war.

The pistols manufactured by American gunsmiths to alleviate the shortage as the war progressed were patterned after the light dragoon pistols of the British, although many American-made "Kentucky" pistols spit lead and fire at the British before the war ended.

In the light dragoon regiments both officers and enlisted men very often carried the same type and quality pistols, since the supply of these weapons made finicky selection impossible. But some officers did

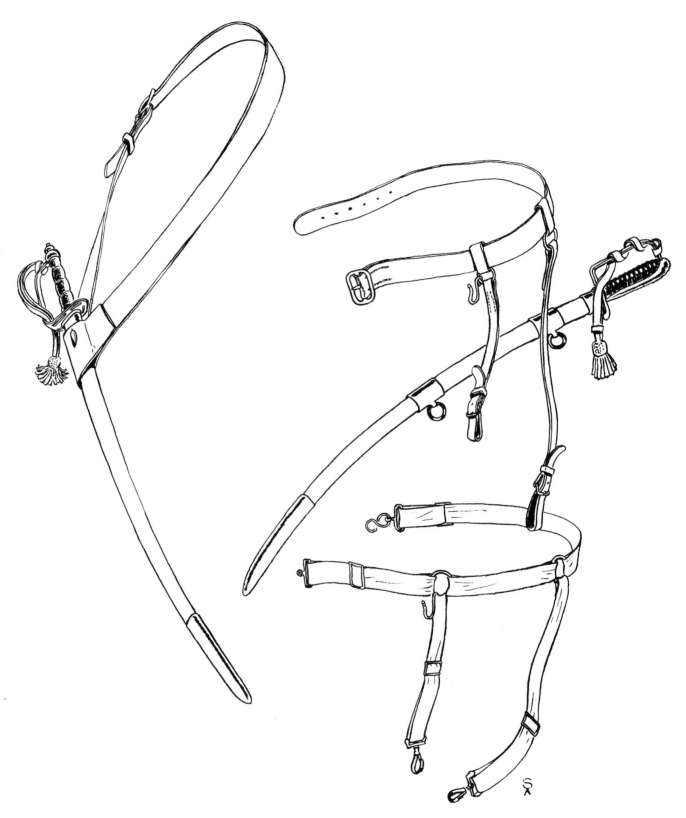

FIGURE 8. Sabre belts used by the Continental Light Dragoons. Left: Shoulder belt, most common method of carrying the sabre. Right: Two types of waist sabre belts with slings, much used by officers and by some enlisted men.

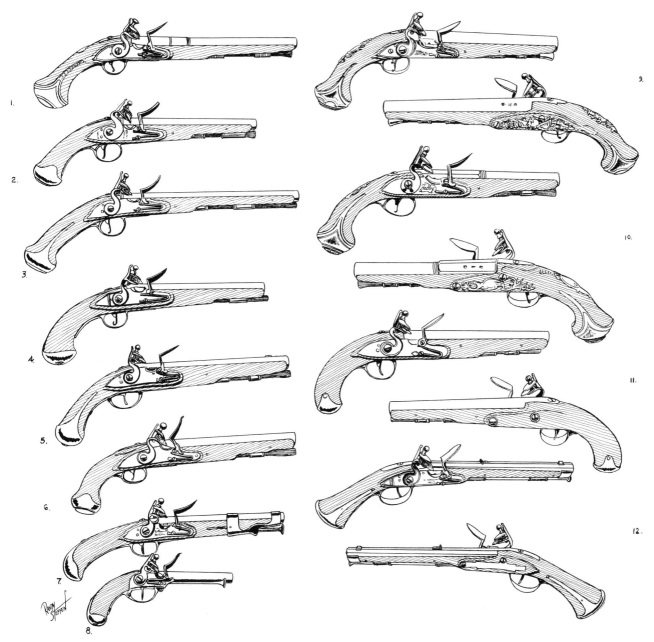

FIGURE 9. Some of the different types of pistols carried in saddle holsters and used by the Continental Light Dragoons.

manage to equip themselves with pairs of ornate pistols, specimens of which are shown in this illustration.

Reference for the pistols illustrated here were the excellent photographs found in Warren Moore's *Weapons of the American Revolution* and Harold Peterson's *Book of the Continental Soldier*.

1. A British heavy dragoon pistol, sergeant's grade, with plain brass mountings. Length, 13⅜ inches.
2. British light dragoon pistol, brass mountings—somewhat shorter than the heavy dragoon pistol.
3. Another British heavy dragoon model, also brass-mounted.

4. The American Committee of Safety model, copied after the British light dragoon pistol.

5. Another American-made dragoon pistol, this one has a maple stock and brass mounts.

6. An American pistol made at Rappahannock Forge.

7. The French model 1763–66 horseman's pistol as shortened in 1769–70 and used by Continental Light Dragoons.

8. The French model 1777, pattern for the first regulation United States pistol made after the war in 1799.

9. Pair of officer's pistols with sterling silver mountings, steel barrels—captured from the British. Length, 14 inches.

10. Pair of British officer's pistols, brass barrels and mounts. Length, 16½ inches.

11. American-made officer's holster pistols stocked in cherrywood. Length, 13½ inches.

12. American pistols of the Kentucky type with unusual shaped grips and using early British-made locks. Length, 18¼ inches.

While it is a pretty well-documented fact that carbines were almost nonexistent in most of the light dragoon regiments in the Continental Army, there were a few—and these, of course, were pieces captured from the British and the Hessian mercenaries. But it must have been a fact that each dragoon equipped himself with a carbine—or other suitable long arm—if it was at all possible.

The long arms shown in Figure 10 are some of those most likely to have been used by the American horsemen. Both sides of most of these pieces are illustrated in order to show the method of attachment to the shoulder carbine sling when one was used.

1. British light dragoon carbine, caliber .65, with 37-inch barrel. Over-all length is 4 feet 4½ inches.

2. British musketoon, about .65-caliber and with barrel about 26 inches long.

3. A late model (1780) British Elliott cavalry carbine with 28-inch barrel.

4. British flintlock blunderbuss with brass barrel and furniture. The ring and bar are not original and were added to carry the weapon on a carbine shoulder sling. Length, 2 feet 8 inches.

5. German rifled carbine of the type carried by Hessian dragoons. The bore is .75 and the barrel is 36 inches long. Over-all length is 4 feet 3 inches.

6. The model 1763–66 French carbine with brass mounts, caliber .65, and an over-all length of about 45 inches. This was a rifled carbine, much sought after by American horsemen.

7. French model 1777 smoothbore musketoon with an over-all length of 46 inches and bored for a .65 ball.

The short supply of captured carbines and musketoons made the issue of other types of long arms a necessity when the field commanders considered it necessary for their men to be so armed. Then muskets of all kinds, and even the long Pennsylvania rifles, were issued and used.

The variations in caliber made the continuous supply of ammunition a complicated problem. It appears that men armed with off-caliber weapons managed to equip themselves with individual bullet molds and in their spare time made paper cartridges to fit their personal long arms.

Those with standard-caliber pieces, usually .69, used the gang molds issued to squads or other groups and made the manufacture of cartridges somewhat of a cooperative affair.

HORSE EQUIPMENTS

Since there had been no army as such governed by a central colonial government, no means of procurement of military equipment existed when the Continental Army was organized and the war against the British began. True, there had been Americans in substantial numbers fighting for the British during the French and Indian Wars, but uniforms, arms, and equipments had been issued by the British. When the Americans were mustered out of the British service, their uniforms and their accoutrements were turned in to the British quartermasters. So in reality there was little for the Americans to arm and equip themselves with from British stores when hostilities started. No doubt some British stores were confiscated right at the start, but nothing in large quantities came into American hands except by capture.

Since no cavalry organizations were authorized by Congress as part of the Continental Army until mid-1776, the demand for horse equipments was light until that time. When the First Regiment of Continental Light Dragoons was formed, orders were written that prescribed their uniform and equipments, but uni-

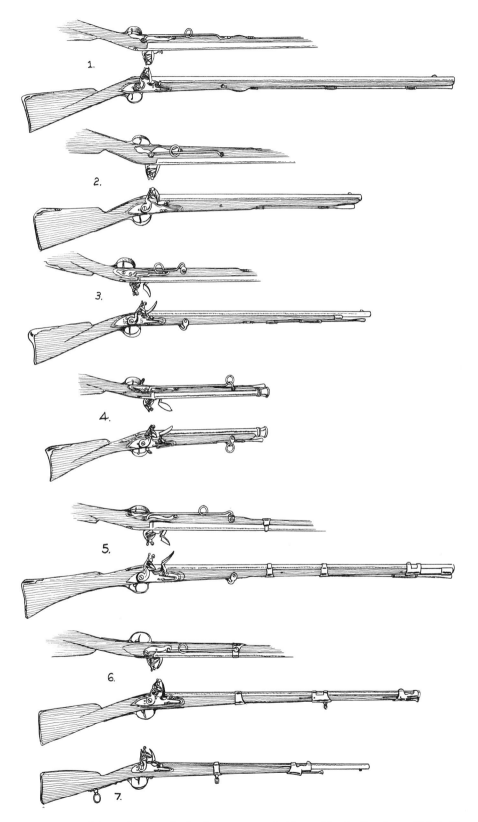

FIGURE 10. Some of the carbines and other long arms probably used by the Continental Light Dragoons.

equipped mostly with a large variety of converted riding saddles of types they were used to, for the largest majority of the men who made up the personnel of the dragoon regiments were from the southern colonies and had been expert horsemen all their civilian lives. Officers were required to furnish their own saddles and other horse gear, and I am satisfied that many of the rank and file also brought their own saddles and bridles when they enlisted as dragoons.

Figures 11 through 15 illustrate five different types of saddles that are known to have been used in the South as general riding and hunting saddles during the mid- and late eighteenth century. Originals and saddles that have been restored by expert saddlemakers at Mount Vernon and Williamsburg, Virginia, were the models for these illustrations. I have added only rings and staples as they would have been added to convert the originals for military use.

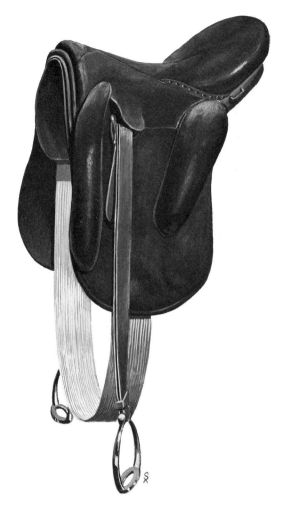

FIGURES 11–14. Saddles used during American Revolution by Continental Light Dragoons.

forms were not immediately available, and equipments, including saddles and bridles, had to be those items that were immediately obtainable and suitable for quick conversion to military use.

Civilian saddles of this period were not too unlike some European military saddles. Converting them for use by mounted soldiers meant attaching rings and staples at necessary points on cantles, pommels, and skirts for the securing of necessary equipment—holsters, saddlebags, valises or portmanteaus, carbine buckets, and so on.

While a certain number of captured British dragoon saddles must have been utilized in each of the four regiments of American light dragoons, they were

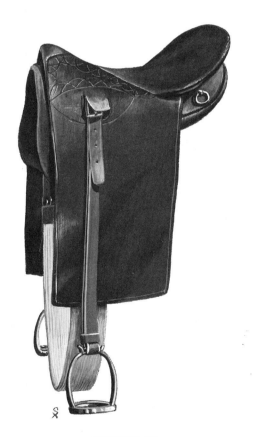

FIGURE 12

Figure 11 is an English-type saddle built on a wood tree reinforced with metal plates. It has a moderate-height cantle and solidly stuffed knee and thigh rolls sewed to the skirts for steadying the rider over walls and fences. This type was popular for riding to the hounds. Fitted with double skirts, the inner one to protect the horse from chafing by the girth buckles, this saddle was probably equipped with iron stirrups and a linen girth; neither was found with the restored model at Mount Vernon.

Figure 12 is the common riding saddle that was found throughout the colonies during the period of the Revolutionary War and was the model for later military saddles adopted by the young United States government.

Built on a wooden tree with slab sidebars, it has a moderately high cantle and a peaked pommel set over padded underskirts. The outer skirts are squared at the bottom and long enough to prevent interference

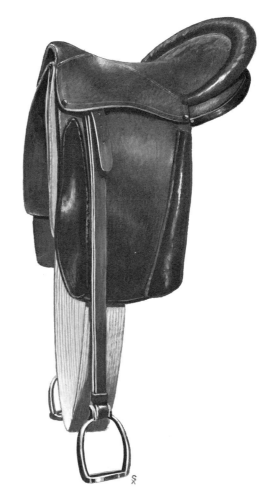

FIGURE 14

FIGURE 13

of the bottom edge of the skirt with the top of the rider's boots—a characteristic subsequent military saddles retained.

Neither girth nor stirrup irons had been preserved with the original at Mount Vernon, but it may be safely assumed that the girth was linen and the stirrups were iron similar to the pattern shown. The staple and ring on the rear bars were added to the drawing and were not present on the model.

The saddle shown in Figure 13 is another type of hunting saddle probably adapted for military service, but of a type 50 or more years older than the others already shown. The model used for this illustration had been expertly restored by artisans at Mount Vernon.

The cantle has about the same rise as the preceding saddles, but the pommel is much flatter and more rounded. Two separate sets of side jockeys afforded protection for the rider's legs from sewed seams and the fastening of the outer skirt to the bars of the tree. The bulky knee roll at the forward edge of the skirt steadied the rider over jumps. Double girth billets allowed a measure of girth adjustment when used with a single-buckle girth. Stirrups of iron are patterns used during that era.

The hunting saddle shown in Figure 14, also made on a tree with wooden sidebars, was, in all likelihood, a type used for dragoon service during the war. The model for this illustration, beautifully restored to almost usable condition, was found at Mount Vernon.

A roll around the edge of the cantle was to give added security to the seat, as were the knee and thigh rolls on the skirts. The position of the rolls on this saddle and the one shown in Figure 13 would seem to indicate that the seat used on both required the legs to be in near vertical position, thus the use of a long stirrup would have been required. And the military seat of that era was one with long stirrups, supposedly to afford steadiness to the rider when he rose in the stirrups to add power and strength to his sabre cuts.

The type of saddle shown in Figure 15 is one I have seen painted with seeming fidelity of detail on a number of horses in paintings contemporary with the period of the Revolution. While I am reluctant to use drawings and paintings as sources for my illustrations, the fact that this same type saddle was portrayed by more than one painter of that period, and by Howard Pyle, the meticulous illustrator of historical subjects during the latter part of the nineteenth century, seems to indicate that such a saddle did indeed exist and was constructed pretty much as these artists indicated.

The extremely high and almost vertical cantle must have been well reinforced with iron on the tree; otherwise, it would have been extremely susceptible to breakage. Stirrup leathers are not let through the outer skirts as is usually the case. Underskirts protect the horse from girth buckles, and stirrups were probably iron.

Figure 16 illustrates the type of saddle used by some American officers. Patterned after British officer saddles, those used in the light dragoons were either made up as custom orders by American saddlers or were captured British equipment. No doubt many dragoon

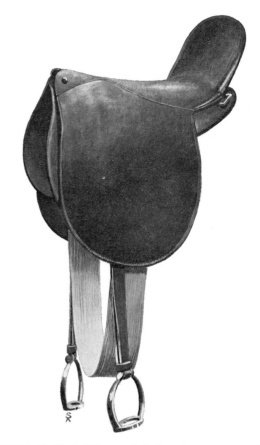

FIGURES 15–17. Saddles used during American Revolution by Continental Light Dragoons.

officers in the Continental service rode the same type of converted civilian saddle that their men used. But there *were* saddles of this type in the service, and their construction was over a wooden tree with sidebars, as is apparent from the view of the saddle shown here.

The roll-padded seat and forward part of the skirts were made chiefly of leather to withstand the wear. The skirts themselves, judging from photographs of British equipment of that period (*Horses and Saddlery*, by Major G. Tylden; J. A. Allen & Co., London, 1965) were covered with brocade cloth, or other heavy ornamental material. These saddles were made on wooden trees with seats of stretched webbing as a ground. The padded covers were fastened over this.

Figure 17 is a German saddle, and is based on the saddle used by Hessian General Johann Kalb during the Revolutionary War. It is shown here because it is the type of saddle that some American officers undoubtedly rode. The Kalb saddle is in the military history section of the National Museum.

Photographs of this saddle made while it was undergoing restoration a number of years ago show a wooden tree with very fine-quality heavy leather on the skirts and covering the bars. The seat, with the embroidered tapestry-like cloth removed, is the hammock type made of several layers of webbing stretched between pommel and cantle, and fastened to the arches with large-headed nails. Double billets under the outer skirts provide for fastening the girth, and large-size rolls just below the pommel afford steadiness to the upper front part of the legs. The saddle shown here differs only slightly from the Kalb saddle.

While it is almost certain that dragoons who dressed and equipped according to regulations were an exception, rather than a rule, I have chosen to show a number of Continental Light Dragoons dressed and equipped as the orders directed. If I were to show them as they probably appeared most of the time, little good would be derived from the illustrations and text as far as showing what Congress and the commander in

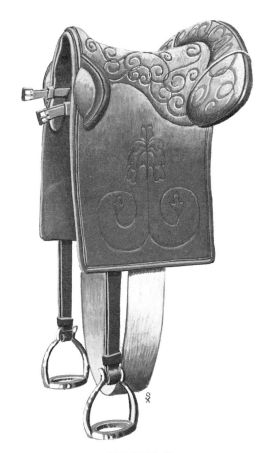

FIGURE 17

FIGURE 16

chief approved as official uniform and equipment. To know these illustrations represent dress and equipment as ordered will let each reader's imagination, tempered by an intimate knowledge of civilian dress of the period, picture for him the light dragoons as they must have appeared a large part of the time. That some did look as I depict them at least part of the time there can be little doubt, from the correspondence and contemporary paintings preserved. The existence of bits and parts of uniforms, including coats, boots, helmets, leather accoutrements, and so on, lends credence to the thought that some appeared as they were supposed to.

The light dragoon in Figure 18 is dressed as expected by Congress, and his equipment, both on his person and on his mount, show him ready for the march or battle. He is armed with a heavy horseman's sabre in a leather scabbard with metal mounts, sus-

FIGURE 18. Regulation dress and equipments for Continental Light Dragoons.

pended from his person by a shoulder belt passed through the loop on his right shoulder to hold it in place at all gaits. A 3-strap linen haversack hangs from the left shoulder. A pair of flintlock horseman's pistols are carried in the bearskin-covered holsters attached to the pommel of the saddle; a Pennsylvania rifle is suspended from the saddle by a heavy leather bucket supporting the butt stock. A strap buckled around the stock and barrel forward of the lock secures the upper part of the rifle against his thigh and to the pommel of the saddle.

Attached to his saddle, which is similar to the one shown in Figure 12, but with rounded skirt corners, are a mail pillion (for supporting wallet and blanket free of the horse's loins) and a crupper. A breast collar buckled to rings set in the forward edge of the saddle skirts aids the crupper in preventing the saddle from moving forward or backward, no matter how steep the terrain or fast the pace. A pair of two-strap saddle-bags such as shown in Figure 6 hangs behind the cantle, with a picket rope coiled under the buckled saddlebag cover straps. A wooden keg-type canteen hangs over the off saddlebag, suspended from a ring on the bars by its linen carrying strap.

An English-type halter with its lead strap tied to a ring at the near-side pommel lies under the double bridle with bit and bridoon on the horse's head. Not necessarily a military bridle, it is the general type used by both military and civilian riders.

The dragoon shown in Figure 19 wears much the same uniform as the trooper in the preceding illustration, but his equipment differs somewhat. The scabbard for his steel-hilted sabre is suspended from a shoulder belt, too. But he wears a wide carbine sling with its attached chain and toggle for attaching the carbine when he dismounts. His captured British carbine is attached to the pommel of the saddle by a buckled strap and rests against his leg, while the muzzle is supported in the leather British-style carbine bucket secured to a pommel ring by a buckled strap. The trooper's picket pin is carried on the carbine bucket, the point inserted in a ring attached to the bottom of the bucket and the shaft secured by a buckled strap.

The saddle shown here is the same one shown in Figure 12, while the bridle is a simpler one than the double bridle, having just a single pair of cheeks and a Pelham-type bit using double reins. The halter is a type common to both military and civilian use. The rest of the equipment is the same as that shown on the preceding figure.

The light dragoon captain shown in Figure 20 stands at the ready with his big flintlock pistol cocked, the frizzen rearward, the pan primed and prepared to fire! His rank is designated by the silver epaulette on his *right* shoulder. The quality and fit of his uniform coat and his buckskin breeches, along with his finer-

made brass-trimmed helmet with its scale chin strap, marks the difference between himself and the coarser-clothed enlisted dragoon. An ivory-gripped officer's-type sabre is suspended by a white buff shoulder belt, and a gilt sabre knot hangs from the steel hilt of the sabre guard.

The saddle this light dragoon officer rides is identical to the one in Figure 11. A mail pillion attached to the staples below the cantle support a valise and blanket. Saddle holsters on the pommel have leather covers and brass tips. A metal canteen is suspended from a cantle ring by a cord and toggle, and steadied at the bottom by a leather thong tied to a small **D** ring stitched to the rear edge of the off skirt. Crupper and breast strap are used to prevent the saddle from moving in either direction in steep country.

In typical military fashion of the day, a half-saddle blanket with decorative edge stripes is fastened to the skirts and bars of the saddle, protruding only *behind* the saddle. Bridle and halter are semimilitary type, with Pelham bit and double reins. The lead rein is tied to a pommel ring set in the leading edge of the near-side saddle skirt. A cloak, secured to the pommel of the saddle, over the holsters would complete this officer's outfit for all-weather field service. But it is probable he would wear a fringed linen hunting shirt if a prolonged march and stay in the field were pending.

The dragoon in Figure 21, wearing his *regimentals* (coat with its distinctive facings), is on picket duty, armed with a British carbine and brass-hilted sabre in a leather scabbard hung on a buff shoulder belt. A white buff sabre knot is attached to the hilt of his sabre. The black cartridge belt at his waist holds a leather cartridge box slightly curved to fit the contour of his body; it holds 12 paper cartridges for the .65-caliber carbine he holds at the ready. The carbine belt over his left shoulder is made of buff leather with brass buckle. The chain and toggle with which the carbine is slung dangles behind the butt plate of the weapon.

The saddle on this mount is the same as the one shown in Figure 13—a civilian saddle modified for light dragoon use. Valise and blanket form the cantle pack, while a pair of bearskin-covered holsters are hung at the pommel, steadied by a buckled strap around the martingale. The carbine bucket, suspended from a pommel ring by an adjustable strap, is the same type used by the British and most other European cavalry, being a heavy leather socket with its sus-

FIGURE 19. Regulation dress and equipments for Continental Light Dragoons.

FIGURE 20. Regulation dress and equipments for Continental Light Dragoons.

pension strap passing under the bottom and held in place by a strap at the mouth.

Crupper and martingale complete the equipment attached to the saddle. The bridle is a double one, with bit and bridoon, probably the same rig this trooper used at home when he rode to the hounds or to church. The halter is the type common to the times, with leather lead strap attached to the near side of the saddle.

Figure 22 portrays a hussar of the Lauzun Legion as it appeared upon its arrival on this continent in July, 1780. Actually a unit of the French Navy under command of Armand Louis de Goutant, duc de Lauzun, this colorful unit was a part of the French forces under General Rochambeau that came to help the Con-

tinental Army fight the British. The hussars, 300 strong, were the only French mounted forces to land on these shores, and they were mostly employed as mounted scouts and couriers. They brought their own horse equipment with them, but were mounted on American horses after their arrival. Half the mounted French contingent were lancers, according to Colonel John Womack Wright (page 60, *Some Notes on the Continental Army*), the other half serving as hussars, armed with sabre, pistols, and carbines.

The late Colonel Harry C. Larter, one-time president and Fellow of The Company of Military Historians, describes their dress thus:

The Cavalry were uniformed and equipped as hussars with sky blue dolmans, yellow cuffs and white lace loops, tall

FIGURE 21. Regulation dress and equipments for Continental Light Dragoons.

hussar bonnets with black fur pennants trimmed with yellow, sky blue pelisses lined with white sheepskin, edged with black, and decorated with white lace loops, and yellow breeches. Hussar officers wore the same dress as the men with the notable exceptions of a white cloth pelisse and red breeches.

Other writers say the pelisses were not brought from France—a small discrepancy. The hussar shown here is dressed substantially as Colonel Larter described. His brass-hilted sabre is encased in a brass scabbard, and the sabretache is sky blue trimmed in white, with the anchor and crown insignia of the legion. Waist belt, sabre slings, and the carbine sling carried in his hand are red-enameled leather. The sash around his waist is yellow with red trim.

The French horse equipment on his mount consists of a double-bridle-and-halter combination of black leather fitted with a bit and bridoon. The lead strap is tied to the pommel end of the hussar-type surcingle that holds the *schabraque* (shabrack) in place on the hussar saddle. A stripped saddle of the type used by these hussars and lancers lies on the ground.

Holsters are concealed under the pommel fold of the sky-blue *schabraque* with white and yellow lace trim around its perimeter, and a cloth valise is strapped to the high cantle peak. The carbine can be seen strapped to the off side. Breast harness and crupper are used to keep the saddle from slipping.

Without a doubt these French horsemen were the best and most completely equipped horsemen in the Continental service during the long struggle for independence from Great Britain.

FIGURE 22. Hussar of the French Lauzun Legion (ca. 1780).

Figure 23 shows a British subaltern who has been captured by some Continental Light Dragoons. This enemy officer belongs to the British Seventeenth Light Dragoon Regiment, one of the two British light dragoon regiments that saw service during the Revolution. His uniform is scarlet with white collar, lapels, cuffs, and coat-tail turnbacks. Lace trim on button-holes and tail of coat is silver, as are his buttons and epaulette.

His breeches are white and his boots black with white metal spurs. His red-horsehair-crested helmet is blackened brass with black fur trim around the black front plate with its white skull and cross-bones over a scroll bearing the words "OR GLORY."

His horse equipments are regulation for British horse. The white saddle cloth has a white lace border trimmed in black. The wreath in the rear corner is green with white letters in a red field. At the front corner is a gold crown with "GR" in red under it and the Roman numerals "XVII." Saddle, bridle, and reins, as well as halter, are brown leather; the lead rein buckled to the halter ring is white, which seems to have been traditional with the British mounted service.

FIGURE 23. A subaltern of the British Seventeenth Light Dragoon Regiment captured by an officer and enlisted men of a Continental Light Dragoon regiment.

The American captors are dressed in their regular regimentals. The officer at right is a lieutenant, with a single silver epaulette on his left shoulder.

Figures 24 and 25 show several types of punishment doled out to wrongdoers in the Continental Army. Discipline and punishment were severe and swift, for the Continental Army was made up of every type of human in the colonies, many of them hard cases who had never held much respect for law and order. The success of any military body was based primarily on instant obedience to an order, thus officers of the mob that formed the bulk of the Army were faced with an almost hopeless task of whipping them into units capable of fighting well-disciplined, crack British troops, taught to react to every command swiftly and without question.

Plundering was a common offense of the soldiers in the Continental Army. Washington ordered this to be met with swift severity—and flogging was the punishment ordinarily meted out for this and other derelictions that demanded a quick cure! It was a form of punishment that met with public approval in those times.

In the light dragoon regiments, the trumpeter of

FIGURE 24. Typical punishment in the Continental Army.

each troop was, by military tradition, delegated to wield the cat-o-nine-tails. Figure 24 shows a trooper tied to a stable broom crosspiece by the wrists, and the trumpeter awaiting the commanding officer's order to start the flogging. Generally the extent of the flogging —the number of lashes ordered—was in proportion to the seriousness of the offense.

The *wooden horse*, shown at the left of Figure 25, was often ordered for offenses of a minor nature. It was made as shown with a narrow-edged wooden

FIGURE 25. Typical punishment in the Continental Army.

plank supported by four stout wood legs. The culprit straddled the plank with his hands tied behind his back and a number of muskets tied to his feet to "keep him from being thrown."

The *picket*, at the right of Figure 25, was another common form of punishment for lesser infractions of army rules and regulations. A long post with a hook driven into it near the top was set firmly in the ground. The prisoner was forced to stand on a stool while one wrist was tied to the hook at the top of the post. Another small post with a blunt top was set in the ground at the base of the big post, as shown, and the heel of one foot was placed on the small post, then the stool pulled away. The man being punished was kept in that position for a specified length of time, again depending on the extent of his offense.

The *gantelope*, punishment for theft and other crimes directly affecting the men of the troop, was carried out in several ways. A later and perhaps more common term for this type of punishment was "running the gantlet." The first way of carrying out the gantelope was called the *running*, in which men formed two lines, each man holding a switch. The offender, naked to the waist, marched through the line behind a sergeant with a reversed sharpened pole to prevent the prisoner from moving too fast. As the prisoner passed, each man was permitted one stroke with his switch. By another system, the prisoner was lashed to a wagon wheel and the troop or regiment passed by, each man giving one stroke with a cat-o-nine-tail. This was pretty harsh treatment, but it served as a real deterrent. A man so punished once was not apt to commit the same offense the second time.

Deserters and those showing cowardice were summarily shot, usually in front of a large group of soldiers, who, needless to say, were effectively impressed.

Officers who committed grave offenses were cashiered—given a dishonorable discharge. There were several degrees of such discharges, the first being a simple discharge without fanfare and public disgrace. A second type rendered the officer incapable of ever serving again. The third, a *discharge with infamy*, degraded the offender from the rank of officer and gentleman. This sort of ceremony usually took place before the entire organization, whether it was the whole army, a brigade, regiment, or troop. The prisoner was brought to the front, his sentence read, and his commission as an officer publicly canceled; his sword was broken over his head, and his insignia of rank ripped from his uniform and thrown in his face. Then the man servant of the provost marshal, or another servant of equally low station, kicked him from the camp.

Chapter 7 of Colonel Wright's little book, *Some Notes on the Continental Army*, covers this subject of discipline and punishment rather thoroughly.

A few final statements concerning the Continental Light Dragoons will round out this brief picture of the hard-riding and hard-fighting men who came before the very first United States cavalryman.

The predominant hair style of the light dragoon was *clubbed* hair, that is, hair gathered at the back, then tied in a firm bundle, which was folded up and to the side where it was tied in a "club." Done in this fashion, it was likely to stay in place during the excitement and violent action of a mounted fight.

Much real concern was shown concerning the proper care of the hair. Orders stated that the Continental soldiers were to wear their hair short or plaited (braided) up; another order directed that the men's hair be "plaited or powdered and tied." Because of the lack of barbering facilities during those early days, it was not unusual for men to let their hair grow rather long. But most kept it arranged neatly on their heads, pulled back evenly and tied in a sort of queue. Officers were directed to set an example for their men. One order stated that the men

will not be allowed to appear with their hair down their backs loose and over their foreheads and down their chins at the sides, which makes them appear more like wild beasts than

soldiers. . . . Any soldier who comes on the parade with beard, or hair uncombed shall be dry shaved immediately and have his hair dressed on parade. (*Changes in the Uniform of the Army*, by Captain Oscar F. Long, A.Q.M., U.S. Army, Army and Navy Register. Washington, D.C., 1895, p. 30.)

This certainly refutes the contention of some of our rather slovenly present youthful population that their hair styles and facial hair are no different than those of the people who fought the original revolution to free this country from England's rule.

Officers were required to powder their hair for guard duty and ceremonies. In garrison the men were required to powder their hair every day and shave at least three times a week. Before a general inspection all arms were required to issue two pounds of flour and one-half pound of rendered tallow per one hundred men—for powdering and dressing the hair.

Mustaches and beards were forbidden for officers and men in all the corps. No pictorial evidence exists that shows facial hair, other than several day-old beards, on any man serving in the Continental Army —*except* some of the French hussars of the Lauzun Legion, and perhaps other French soldiers who came to this continent to help.

As mentioned at the beginning of this chapter, the Continental Light Dragoons suffered just as much for want of clothing and equipment as any of the rest of the "rag, tag, and bobtail" American Army. The illustrations show what they were *supposed* to wear and what they were *supposed* to use for arms and equipment. Bear in mind that they wore what they could obtain, and no doubt many a light dragoon rode into battle looking more like Ichabod Crane than a dashing cavalryman!

It is known that many who were unable to equip themselves with any kind of headgear to protect them against sabre blows sewed iron straps inside the usual civilian-type tricorn or round hat, with additional iron bands arcing over the skull, to protect their heads from lethal cuts and slashes from British and Tory blades.

It is also probably very true that more light dragoons rode against the British in ordinary shoes and high stockings than rode with booted feet in their stirrups. But then, this book is to show what was *supposed* to be worn—and it is the clothing and equipment prescribed by orders and regulations that will be shown and described throughout all its pages.

CHAPTER TWO

The United States Army Dwindles

1783–1812

AFTER THE CESSATION of hostilities, the Continental Army kept dwindling until Congress ordered its disbandment. On November 25, Washington, with the one regiment of infantry and two battalions of artillery that remained, marched into one end of New York City as the British under Sir Guy Carleton marched out of the other.

On January 3, 1784, Major General Henry Knox, Secretary of War, reported to Congress that only 700 rank and file remained in the army. The lawmakers believed that a standing army in peacetime was "inconsistent with the principles of republican governments and dangerous to the liberties of a free people," and might be used as an active agent in "establishing despotism." With this as their avowed attitude, they ordered all troops to be discharged except 25 men at Fort Pitt and 55 at West Point. These, with a proper proportion of officers, were to guard the stores and equipment left over from the war. This amazing piece of legislation was passed June 3, 1784.

The very next day, June 4, this astute body passed additional legislation that was indecisive in its context—calling out from the various states 700 men for twelve months. These men, with a proportionate number of officers, were to man the frontier posts to be abandoned by the British according to the terms of the peace treaty.

But such a short enlistment period proved completely impractical, for even such a small number of men could not be recruited—and Indian depredations on the frontier increased to an intensely serious situation.

For more than 2 years Congress fumbled around, until finally the combination of Indians, British, French, and Spanish on the frontiers made even the most pacific of the members realize that the Army *had* to be increased. On October 20, 1786, they authorized an additional 1,340 privates and noncommissioned officers. These, in addition to the 700 already authorized, were to be organized into a *legionary corps* consisting of two troops of cavalry, one battalion of artillery, one battalion of light infantry troops, and three regiments of infantry. But only two companies of artillery were ever enrolled. The total armed force of the new nation was less than a thousand men—and they were scattered along a chain of forts in the Northwest, in the South, and along the Atlantic Coast—no more than a frontier constabulary aimed at making the Indians behave and at protecting the arsenals and supply bases in the more populated sections of the country. (*The Beginning of the U.S. Army*, by James Ripley Jacobs; Princeton, Princeton University Press, 1947.)

On August 7, 1789, the War Department was created as one of the executive branches of the federal government. The Secretary of War was to perform any duties the President might assign to him in reference to army, navy, Indian affairs, or lands under grant for military services. He was to have a chief clerk to act in his absence. All employees of the department were compelled to take an oath "well and faithfully to execute the trust committed" to them. By 1792 they had grown to only 10, with an average yearly salary of $460. (*Military Laws of the U.S.*, by J. F. Callan, rev. ed., 85–86.)

With the creation of the Constitution, the President was made the commander in chief of the army, and Congress was made responsible for the nation's defense. It was under this new government that the War Department was created. All commissioned officers were appointed by the President and all persons serving in the army were referred to as "in the service of the United States." (*The History of the United States Army*, by William A. Ganoe; New York; D. Appleton-Century Co., 1942.)

Indian depredations in the Ohio Valley and a sound trouncing of poorly trained and equipped troops under General St. Clair during the winter of 1791 sent

Congress into a storm of legislative action. It authorized a substantial increase in the tiny Army, including a squadron of 4 troops of light dragoons. Each troop was to be commanded by a captain, with a lieutenant and a coronet under him; the dragoons were to serve dismounted when ordered. The monthly pay ranged from $166 for a major general to $3 for a private. These were the first regular mounted troops in the new United States Army.

After an attempt at organizing the Army into divisions and brigades, the War Department ordered that the legionary corps urged by the Secretary of War be formed. The state militia was to be divided into 3 corps, grouped according to age. The regular troops, 5,120 were to become a legion with 4 sublegions. The regiment as a unit of the Army was abandoned. There was to be no grade for officers between brigadier general and major. Each sublegion was to be composed of 1,280 men, commanded by a brigadier general, and was to be made up of 12 battalions of infantry, 1 battalion of riflemen, 1 company of artillery, and 1 troop of dragoons. A major general was given command of the whole legion. The legion organization was authorized in December, 1792.

In August, 1794, the dragoons, along with the infantry battalions, proved themselves against the Indians at the Battle of Fallen Timbers.

The uniforms worn by the light dragoons of each sublegion were slightly different in cut from those the Continental Light Dragoons had worn. Washington had settled on blue coats with red facings for all infantry and dragoons in 1782, and these same colors, along with white vests and breeches, were retained by the post-Revolutionary dragoon. But the falling collar was replaced by a high standing collar, and the horsehair crest on the leather helmets were replaced by a strip of bearskin covering the top of the billed leather jockey-style helmet, running from bill to back edge. Only the color of the turban around the base of the helmet distinguished a dragoon of one sublegion from a trooper of another. Colors of the 4 sublegions were white, red, yellow, and green.

Shoulder loops, first added to the uniform in 1787, are now seen on the dragoon's uniform for the first time. Each loop, or strap, buttoned to a small button on the collar, was edged with a narrow binding of red cloth.

Figure 26 shows a light dragoon of this period. He is armed with a sabre hung from a shoulder belt of the

FIGURE 26. Dragoon private (ca. 1794), in the uniform established for all cavalry and infantry in 1782. Only the color of the turban around his cap identifies the sublegion of which his troop is an integral part.

same type used by the Continental mounted soldier. The sabre, as yet not standardized by the War Department, could have been one of the many types with iron guard used by horsemen during the last years of the war.

The Whiskey Rebellion in August of 1794 led to additional legislation affecting the Army. A premium was placed on the re-enlistment of the trained soldier by raising the monthly bounty, clothing, and pay allowance to $9.00 for a sergeant major down to $6.66 for a private. When the dragoon officer or private furnished his horse, arms, and accoutrements, he was to receive 40 cents a day in addition to his pay; when the enlisted man furnished his own rations and forage, he was to receive an additional 25 cents a day. The pay in cash was to be raised $1.00 per month for all enlisted men, plus an initial bounty of $16.00 for those who re-enlisted and $14.00 for recruits. Congress had begun to realize that a decent pay was necessary to attract and retain decent men.

Early in 1795 legislation was approved that would increase the legion to its intended strength—4,800 enlisted men, with 3-year enlistments. And it was at this period that all persons in the Army were to receive a specific number of rations. This additional compensation ran from 15 for a major general on down to 1 for a private soldier.

A year later the legion was abolished and the Army was organized into 4 regiments of infantry, 2 companies of light dragoons, and the corps of artillerists and engineers, which had been combined.

In March, 1797, the General Staff was formed when the positions of quartermaster general and paymaster general were created; these, combined with the judge advocate and the one remaining brigadier general in the army, formed the first General Staff.

Early in 1798 it appeared as though there would be trouble with France, so Congress hastened to increase the size of the Army. By July it seemed that war was at hand, and additional increases were authorized, including 6 new troops of dragoons, who were to be "enlisted for and during the existing differences between the United States and the French Republic." A full regiment of light dragoons, the first *regiment* of cavalry authorized by the United States government, was to be organized from the 2 existing troops and the 6 new ones. Three more regiments of dragoons were authorized but never recruited.

Organization of the regular dragoon regiment was altered again by adding a cadet to each company and by dividing the regiment into 2 battalions of 5 companies each. The ranks of ensign and coronet were abolished and replaced by the grade of second lieutenant. As yet there was no grade of colonel in the Army. A general pay raise for the Army was authorized at this time.

Uniform regulations for January, 1799, prescribed a new uniform for the dragoons. It was to be a green coat with white buttons, lining, and facings, white vests and breeches, and helmet caps. But when the contractor who was to make these uniforms asked In-spector General Major General Alexander Hamilton for patterns so he could begin manufacturing the uniforms, it seems General Hamilton did not think much of white facings for field duty for dragoons—so he made a change on his own. ("The Green Coats of the Enlisted Light Dragoons, 1799–1801," by Detmar H. Finke and H. Charles McBarron, in the *Military Collector & Historian*, Vol. VI, No. 2, 36–37.)

When the pattern arrived at the office of the Secretary of War for approval, the green coat had facings of black velvet instead of white cloth as originally ordered. The pattern coat, as reconstructed by Finke and McBarron, was as follows:

Green coat with black collar, cuffs, and lapels. Standing collar three inches high with small button and blind button hole on each side. Cuffs three inches deep, indented at the upper part, having each three blind holes double and forming an angle with one button at the point, and one at each extremity of the sides. Each lapel to be four inches at the top gradually lessening to two and a half at the bottom, having seven buttons equidistant, beginning half an inch from the bottom of the collar with which the top of the lapels is to range in contact. On each shoulder a strap an inch wide edged with black, terminated by a small button in line with the bottom of the collar. The skirts to be of sufficient length fully to cover the seat, turned up on front on each side with black, three inches wide below and narrowing to a point at the bottom of the lapel, edged behind with black, terminated at the bottom by a button. On each skirt, three double blind button holes, forming an angle with the point below, and with the like buttons as above described, i.e., plain yellow, those of the extremities of the upper angle to range in a line with the buttons of the hips. The button holes to be yellow, the lining white.

This uniform is illustrated in Figure 27, which shows both front and back of the coat described above. The dragoon wears the leather cap with the bearskin roach, which was replaced within months by the type of helmet usually associated with the War of 1812 and pictured in the drawings that illustrate that period. The major difference between the helmet worn with this green coat with black facings and the later one is the brass plate with the charging horseman. It was changed to pewter about 1812.

According to Finke and McBarron, yellow epaulettes were worn with this uniform by the dragoon noncommissioned officers.

Washington's death and an end to the threat of war with France let Congress sink back into its feeling of security. Its first move was to tear down the military force it had established. In May, 1800 it discharged 3,399 men from the Army, retaining only the first 4

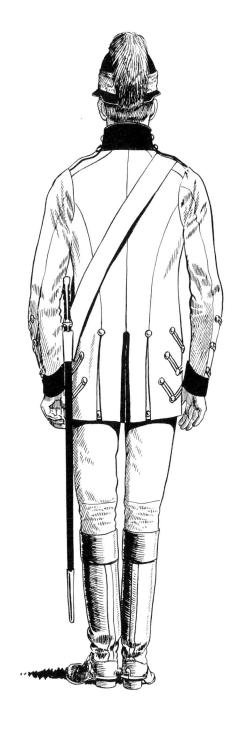

FIGURE 27. The 1799 dragoon short coat was green with black facings. The helmet shown here changed shortly to the type commonly associated with the light dragoons during the War of 1812, but with a brass plate on which was raised the familiar charging horseman—the same plate that was changed to pewter about 1812.

regiments of infantry, 2 regiments of artillerists and engineers, 2 troops of light dragoons, and the commanding general and his staff.

It was just a few months later that a manual of exercises and drills for dragoons was published by E. A. Jenks. This "exact set of cavalry exercises, an approved work" set forth a system of drills for the mounted arm, and explained the manual of the pistol and sword, the only weapons with which the dragoons were armed. In theory, at least, the dragoons of this period were to be armed with the cavalry sabre, Starr contract of 1798, shown in Figure 28, and the first pistol manufactured under contract to the United States, the North & Cheney .69-caliber U.S. Model 1799. This was patterned after the French Army pistol, Model 1777, and is shown in Figure 29. A total of 2,000 of these pistols were made for issue to the young army about 1800.

The Starr cavalry sabre was the first sword of any kind to be made under contract to the United States government. Harold Peterson, in *The American Sword, 1775–1945* (New Hope, Pennsylvania, Robert Halter, The River House, 1954), terms it the first official United States sword. Only 2,000 of them were made.

The design of this sabre is very similar to the popular type of Revolutionary War horseman's sabre. The blade is slightly curved with a single edge and a pronounced false edge that starts 7 inches from the point. The blade is stamped "N. Starr & Co." near the hilt, as shown on the drawing. The reverse side is stamped "US/1799" in two perpendicular lines. The grip is wood covered with leather and wound with twisted brass wire. The backstrap is iron and expands to form the flat pommel. The stirrup-shaped knuckle bow is a heavy bar of iron. The scabbard is leather with iron

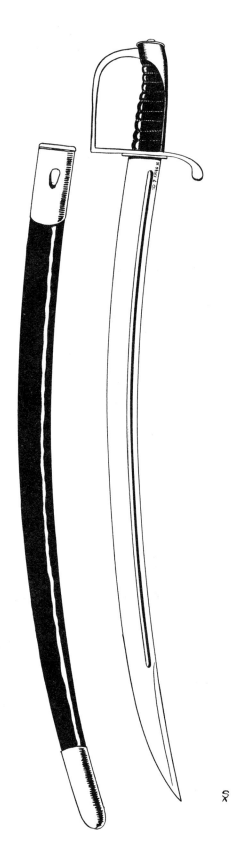

FIGURE 28. Cavalry sabre. Starr contract of 1798. This was the first edged weapon made under contract to the United States government following the winning of independence from Great Britain. The quillon and knuckle bow are iron, as is the backstrap and pommel. The grip is wood covered with leather wound with twisted brass wire. The steel blade is single-edged with a 7-inch false edge at the point. The blade is 33 inches long and 1½ inches wide at the hilt. The scabbard is leather, iron-mounted, with a stud at the throat for a shoulder-belt frog.

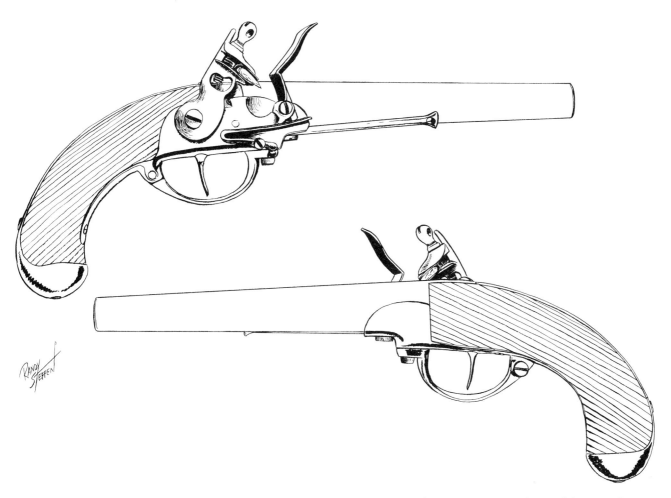

FIGURE 29. The North & Cheney U.S. Model 1799 pistol, caliber .69—the first pistol to be manufactured under contract to the United States government. This model was used to arm the U.S. Light Dragoons about 1800.

mounts. These sabres were made to be suspended from shoulder belts fitted with frogs to take the frog stud on the iron throat. The steel blade is 33 inches long and 1½ inches wide at the hilt. Two different specimens of the 1807 horseman's sabre made under contract by William Rose & Sons are shown in Figure 30. The one at the left is from the National Museum collection and has a 35⅛-inch blade. The sabre at the right is the one from the Phillip J. Medicus collection, described by Hicks (*Notes on United States Ordnance*, by Major James E. Hicks; Mt. Vernon, N.Y., privately printed, 1940). Both specimens have much the same specifications other than blade length, and there are specimens known in other collections with still different blade lengths. The guard and all other metal parts of the hilt are iron, and the grips are wood covered with leather wound with twisted brass wire. Scabbards are leather with iron mounts and are drawn from descriptions in correspondence between Purveyor of Public Supplies Tench Coxe and the Secretary of War of January 6, 1808.

Horse equipment as issued to the dragoons during this period is unknown, although it seems likely that it would be similar to the equipment procured for the Continental Light Dragoons during the last year of the Revolution. Most likely it consisted of an English-type saddle and double bridle with bit and bridoon, although it seems equally possible that the European hussar-type saddle could have been used in some form, since both these types were known to have been issued for service in the second war with Great Britain.

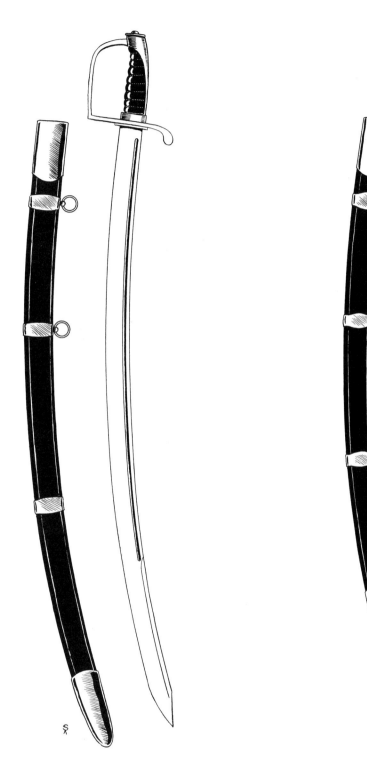

FIGURE 30. Two different specimens of the William Rose & Sons contract-of-1807 horseman's sabre. The one at the left is from the National Museum collection and has a 35⅛-inch blade. The sabre at the right is the one from the Phillip J. Medicus collection as described by Major James E. Hicks. Both specimens have much the same specifications other than blade length, and there are specimens known in other collec-tions with still different blade lengths. The guard and all other metal parts of the hilt are iron, and the grips are wood covered with leather wound with twisted brass wire. Scabbards are leather with iron mounts and are drawn from descriptions in correspondence between Purveyor of Public Supplies Tench Coxe and the Secretary of War of January 6, 1808.

Thomas Jefferson, President of the United States at the time, felt that the country should maintain only a force strong enough and large enough to protect the frontier from the Indians. He would not admit the necessity for an army large enough to meet the initial attacks of foreign troops in the event of another invasion and war. In actuality, only a body of well-trained and adequately equipped regulars could hope to perform both functions satisfactorily. But the President would not accept this point of view argued by the Secretary of War and the General Staff.

The 2 remaining companies of dragoons had been dismounted and were serving as infantry when the Act of March 16, 1802, further reduced the Army to a dangerously low number, and the mounted arm was eliminated completely! By June 1, 1802, the Army had a total of 172 officers and an authorized enlisted strength of 3,040—but according to the records of the War Department, considerably fewer than this number were actually present for duty.

But it was this same legislation that established the United States Military Academy at West Point, where thousands of future cavalry officers received the training that prepared them for 135 additional years of service with the mounted corps.

Not until the Act of April 12, 1808, were there any mounted regulars in the United States service. War with Great Britain was threatening and Jefferson realized the pitifully small Army had to be increased to insure the safety of the nation. In February he had sent a request to Congress for an additional 6,000 men.

Authorized were 5 additional regiments of infantry, 1 regiment of light artillery, and 1 regiment of light dragoons—all to be enlisted for 5 years.

Besides the regular officers, 2 cadets were assigned to each troop, and there were 8 troops authorized for the dragoon regiment instead of 10 (companies), as the other regiments had. But in spite of all good intentions, the Army still had only 2,965 men a year later (Ganoe's *History of the United States Army*, 113).

CHAPTER THREE

A Second War with the British and the Next Decade

1812–21

At the beginning of 1812 the several thousand regulars composing the United States Army were scattered throughout the forts protecting the frontier and serving as skeleton garrisons in the many coastal forts. The regiment of dragoons had been broken up and small detachments were serving as foot troops with the infantry.

On January 11 Congress, still fluctuating back and forth in its reduction and enlargement of the army, again authorized an increase. Among other units, 2 regiments of dragoons were supposed to be recruited, but it is doubtful that more than a fraction of these 2 12-company regiments was ever formed:

The purpose of this book, however, is not to repeat the successes and follies of the United States government and the armed forces it controlled, but to document the clothing and equipment furnished the mounted arm.

The Quartermaster Department, a vitally important entity throughout the remainder of this book, was also created by Congress during the flurry of legislative acts that sprang forth in the hysteria that prevailed with the threat of another war with the British. Confusion and inefficiency marked its inception, but at least it was a beginning of an organized supply department.

UNIFORMS

Uniforms of the United States Light Dragoons in 1812 were probably the same as those prescribed for dragoons when the general uniform change was authorized in 1808. In a letter to the author in 1962, Detmar Finke, historian in the office of the chief of military history and fellow of The Company of Military Historians, described these uniforms in detail:

The dress uniform worn by the light dragoon officers in 1812 seems to have been the same as that authorized for the regiment in 1808. A blue roundabout jacket with three rows of plated bullet buttons on the chest, trimmed with silver lace and cord; buckskin pantaloons and a helmet with a bearskin over the top. The undress uniform was a single-breasted blue coat reaching to the bend of the knee, with twelve bullet buttons on the chest and a laced collar with two blind button holes on each side. Four buttons on the sleeve and four on the pockets.

The enlisted men since the winter of 1810–1811 had been wearing a uniform consisting of a blue coatee with red collars and cuffs and white false button holes on the chest, hooked up the front; white overalls with a blue stripe down the side, white vests and leather caps like the officers, with a blue and white plume. The musicians wore a white coatee with blue collars and cuffs, trimmed with blue cord and lace, and white buttons. The same overall and caps as the enlisted men.

With the advent of the Second Regiment of Light Dragoons, commander Colonel James Burn, in June 1812 sent a description of the uniform prescribed for his regiment to the Secretary of War for approval and it was approved as the uniform to be worn by all personnel of both regiments. The dress uniform consisted of a short blue hussar jacket with three rows of silver bullet buttons and blind button holes of blue twist on the chest, and the blue skirt turnbacks also trimmed with blue twist. The collar and sleeves were trimmed with silver braid. Blue cloth pantaloons trimmed on the side seams and around the seat with silk braid. The undress coat was a blue single-breasted coat reaching to the bend of the knee, with silver bullet buttons and blue twist on the breast like the full dress coat. The skirt turnbacks were blue and united at the bottom of the skirt by a silver double fleur-de-lis; blind button holes of herringbone design on the cuffs and skirt turnbacks. The collars were trimmed with silver braid as in the dress uniform. White single-breasted vests and white or buckskin pantaloons for parade, and blue pantaloons for service. Dragoon boots with tops to cover the knees and white metal spurs. Black stocks. A leather helmet with blue feather tipped with white, nine inches long. The adjutant was distinguished by a white plume tipped with blue, the quartermaster by a green plume, and the paymaster by a blue plume with a red top. The surgeon and his mates wore the undress coat with black collar and cuffs and a black plume.

A blue hussar cloak with a cape trimmed with silver lace was worn by all officers. The housings were blue with two rows of silver lace on the border for field officers. The company officers' housings were bordered by a single row of silver

FIGURE 31. Officer, left, and enlisted men of the Second Regiment, U.S. Light Dragoons (1812–15). The officer and the private at the right are wearing the dress uniform, alike in cut, color, and decoration, except that the officer's lace on collar, cuffs, and breeches is silver, while the lace on the enlisted man's uniform coatee and breeches is white silk ferret. The private in the center wears the undress uniform with the coat skirts reaching to the bend of the knee. It is decorated like the dress short coat with the addition of 4 buttons and herringbone-design blind buttonholes on each sleeve and each skirt between the turnbacks. Officer undress uniforms are the same pattern as those of the men—only the lace is different, as in the dress uniform.

lace and distinguished by bars placed diagonally from the corners, captains three, lieutenants two, and cornets one. The medical staff had only a silver lace border on their housings. The holsters were of bearskin.

The enlisted men wore the same uniform except that they used silk ferret lace instead of silver lace.

This uniform was simplified in 1814 when the white ferret lace was ordered removed from the coats of the enlisted men. In this fashion the uniform was worn until the regiment was disbanded in 1815.

The uniforms described above, as approved by the Secretary of War for both regiments in the summer of 1812, are shown here in Figure 31.

The officer, at the left, with drawn sabre, is distinguished quickly from the enlisted men by his scale-and-bullion-fringe epaulettes. A closer glance would show that the braid, or lace, on collar and sleeves is silver instead of silk ferret, as used on collars and sleeves of the enlisted men's uniforms. Other than that, the pattern was the same. Jacket and pantaloons, as they are now called, are blue cloth—the cloth of the officer's uniform being finer than that of the enlisted man's.

This officer and the enlisted man at the right both wear the dress uniform with the short hussar jacket. The undress uniform worn by the dragoon in the center, oddly enough, is even more ornate than the dress clothing, for the skirts are longer and are ornately trimmed on the back, as shown in Figures 37 and 38. The sleeves on the undress coat are also embellished with 4 buttons and herringbone-design blind buttonholes.

The crested leather helmets shown on officers and enlisted men in all the drawings illustrating the 1812-period light dragoons are identical except for the white metal decorating the front, sides, and crest of the officers' helmets. Those for the men are reinforced at the sides with iron straps. The specimens in the National Museum, as shown in *United States Army Headgear to 1854*, Volume I, by Edgar M. Howell and Donald E. Kloster (Washington, Smithsonian Institution Press, 1969), are different from copies of photographs made by the author from prints Nos. 42 099 and 42 099A in the files of the Military History Branch of the Smithsonian in 1964. The 2 helmets are, without a doubt, for officer and enlisted man, and are identical to those in my drawings.

Chin straps on the officers' helmets terminate in a brass plate with a star stamped in its center. Enlisted men's helmet chin straps terminate in a small pewter button.

While those described in the above-mentioned Smithsonian publication undoubtedly lack *working* chin straps, as stated by Howell and Kloster, it is inconceivable to this writer that an unwieldy helmet of this type would be issued and worn by men trained and equipped to fight on horseback without a means of holding the helmet in place with a chin strap. The photograph of the officer's helmet referred to above shows a pewter-scale chin strap on a leather strap with a buckle in the center, adequately long to adjust under the chin.

The authors of the Smithsonian publication state, "The placement of the straps and their length indicate they would not meet under the chin of the wearer and were only decorative." A pewter-scale chin strap, made with the scales wired to substantial wine-colored leather straps and with a buckle in the center, is part of the writer's collection. It is the same type of chin strap shown in the Smithsonian photographs cited above, and it is reasonable to surmise that it came from an 1812 dragoon officer's helmet.

Another difference between helmets of officers and enlisted men is the pewter front plate. On the officer's helmet the plate is neatly stamped in an oval shape, with the raised border of the plate forming the edge. The enlisted man's helmet is stamped with a border having squared edges at corners and sides, and with punched holes through which heavy thread passes to attach the plate to the front of the leather helmet. The visor on the officer's helmet is bound with a neat pewter molding, while the visor for the men is plain and unbound. The crest on all helmets is made of long white horsehair arranged in small hanks and held firmly between the two halves of the helmet.

Boots on the dragoons in Figure 31 are black leather with tops that cover the knees. Spurs are white metal, of the usual military pattern.

The officer wears a shoulder sabre belt, and my drawing was made from a specimen on display in the National Museum. Waist-type sabre belts such as those worn by the enlisted men were drawn from specimens in the Colonel Johnson collection at West Point in 1964. They are made of white buff leather, as is the officer's shoulder belt. This shoulder belt is shown in more detail in Figure 36.

ARMS

The officer in Figure 31 is armed with a contract-of-1807 sabre made by William Rose. While the fuller on this blade is different from that on the ones illustrated in Figure 30, it is drawn from an 1807 sabre in the National Museum. It is evident there were some transition models between the pattern of 1807 and that of 1812, for the sabre in the Smithsonian has an iron scabbard with the same very small drag as used on the 1812 scabbard. Scabbards for the 1807 sabres were normally leather with iron mounts.

Both enlisted men in Figure 31 are equipped with 1812-pattern sabres. Figure 32 shows both the Rose and Starr sabres of the 1812 pattern; these are very similar in appearance. The hilt of the Starr sabre at the left, has the hilt attached to the blade at more of an angle.

In the *Military Collector & Historian* for June, 1953, H. Charles McBarron describes an officer's Model 1812 sabre in his collection (Vol. V, No. 2, 53). The photo accompanying the description shows that it is exactly the same pattern as the regular-issue Starr sabre except for the silver plating of the hilt, checkering of the highly polished wood grips, and the decorative bands of Sheffield silver plate on the scabbard. McBarron's research revealed from commissary general correspondence with Nathan Starr that these sabres were delivered between August 3 and November 26, 1814, and cost $20 each, as compared to a cost of $8 for the standard sabre. The government was reimbursed for the extra cost by the officers who received them.

As with all dragoons in the service of the Continental Army during the Revolution and in subsequent service with the young United States Army, regulations called for each officer and man to be armed with a pair of pistols in addition to the sabre. These pistols were intended to be carried in holsters attached to the saddle, and were termed "horse" pistols mainly because of their intended use by mounted men.

Figure 33 shows one pistol known to have been used by the U.S. Light Dragoons during this period. The United States Pistol Model 1805 shown here had the distinction of being the first pistol to be manufactured at an armory operated by the federal government. At least 2,000 pairs were authorized to be made at Harpers Ferry, and this pistol has long been acclaimed as the most beautiful American martial pistol ever made. Its smooth clean lines and its brass furniture contrast smartly with its polished stock. These pistols were carried butt forward in heavy-jacked leather holsters with bearskin covers. Five tin cylinders encased in leather were located under the holster covers on each side for carrying paper cartridges. These holsters are shown in Figures 34, 35, 36, 37, 38, and 39.

These were big pistols, having an over-all length of just under 17 inches, and were bored to shoot the then standardized .69-caliber bullet. The Light Dragoons were armed with these single-shot muzzle-loading flintlock pistols until the mounted service was discontinued a few short years after the second war with the British terminated.

HORSE EQUIPMENTS

Dragoons recruited for service during the first decade of the nineteenth century undoubtedly were furnished with horse equipment made under contract to the new United States government, but this writer has been unable to uncover any definite information on such issues in more than 9 years of intensive research. As pointed out in the last chapter, it seems likely that either an English-type military saddle was in use, or the hussar type popular in Europe and used to some extent by the French on this continent during the Revolution—or both!

Contracts in the Quartermaster section of the National Archives clearly point out the type of saddles made especially for the U.S. Light Dragoons before hostilities started, and later. One such contract is that between the United States (through the agency of Tenche Coxe, purveyor of public supplies) and James Walker, a saddlemaker of Philadelphia. Since the contract itself describes the saddle and accompanying equipments so completely, it should be published here in its entirety.

Know all Men by these Presents, That it is hereby mutually agreed, by, and between the United States (by the agency of Tenche Coxe, Purveyor of Public Supplies and James Walker of Philadelphia, Saddler, that the said James Walker, of Philadelphia, Saddler, shall and will manufacture, and deliver within three months from the date hereof two hundred sets of horse equipments, not inferior to the patterns; and fit for effective military service, as follows viz: One strong horsemans or troopers saddle, lined with stout undyed twilled cotton serge, stuffed with hair, with a brass head and cantle, improved stirrup irons, two girths (worsted webbing therefor to be furnished by the United States). One leathern breast plate, iron rings and staples to saddles, One valise pad with straps to secure it to saddle, One valise of Ravens Duck painted, with leathern buckle straps, loop straps, and straps to secure it on the pad. One troopers leathern halter, One double bridle bit

FIGURE 32. At right is the Rose contract-of-1812 cavalry sabre. Five hundred of these blades were made for the purveyor of public supplies. The hilt is similar to previous Rose contract sabres, except that the leather grip covers are not wound with brass wire. The scabbards are iron, japanned black.

The sabre at left is the Nathan Starr contract-of-1812–13 sabre, second type, with the wider space between grip and knuckle guard. Otherwise its parts are similar to the Rose pattern, except the blade, which has a sharper curve.

Blades on both patterns are about 33½ inches long. Officers' sabres are generally identical to those of the men, except that the hilts are silver-plated for some officers.

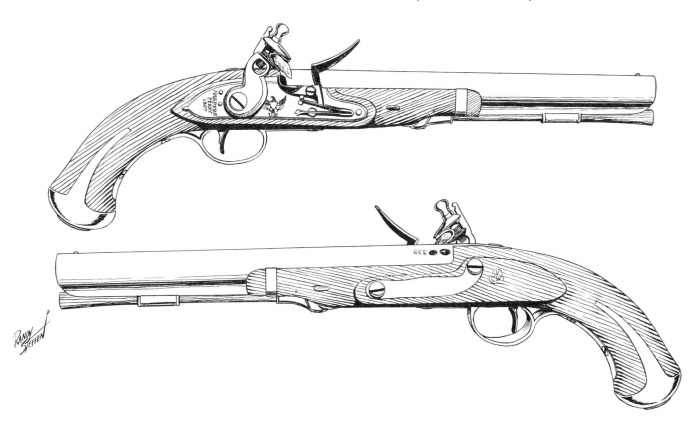

FIGURE 33. Harpers Ferry single-shot muzzle-loading flint-lock holster pistol, Model of 1805, with which the U.S. Light Dragoons were armed until the mounted service was discontinued a few short years after the second war with the British terminated. This pistol, shooting a .69-caliber ball, had the distinction of being the first model of pistol to be made in a United States arsenal. Drawn from a specimen in the West Point Museum collection.

and bridoon, One pair of holsters, One pair of holster covers of bear skin, one leathern circingle [*sic*] of bridle leather, which horse equipments are to be delivered at the public arsenal of the United States on Schuylkill river.

It is further agreed, that the price of the said equipments for complete set is and shall be fifteen dollars sixty six and an half cents money of the United States payable to the amount of each and every parcel delivered, on demand, after a strict inspection by a person or persons to be appointed for that purpose by the United States, and after such inspector shall certify that the said horse equipments have each, and all been so by him inspected and found similar and not inferior to the patterns & thoroughly fit for effective Military service.

It is expressly conditioned that no member of Congress is, or shall be admitted, to any share or part of this contract or agreement, or to any benefit to arise thereupon.

Witness the hand of the said Tenche Coxe, Purveyor of Public Supplies and the hand and seal of the said James Walker this 9th day of May Eighteen hundred & Twelve.

sealed and delivered   Tenche Coxe (signature)
  in presence of us   James Walker (signature)
Jas. Sidney Coxe
James W. Weatherby

The saddle shown at the top of Figure 34 is a reconstruction of the saddle as described in the Walker contract. General shape and type are also based on the British hussar saddle of 1805. While the contract description of the James Walker saddle is vague as far as specific details are concerned, I believe this *reconstruction* to be a reasonably accurate one. On page 131 of Major Tylden's *Horses and Saddlery*, he describes the adoption of the British hussar-type saddle and states that a similar saddle was used by the American dragoons in 1812.

The saddle shown at the bottom of Figure 34 is a literal copy of the European hussar saddle, as it was used by Lauzun's Legion during the Revolutionary War and by some units of U.S. Dragoons during the second war with the British. Some of McBarron's plates in The Company of Military Historian series of prints, *Military Uniforms in America*, show various militia organizations of this general period equipped with this type of hussar saddle, which came from the

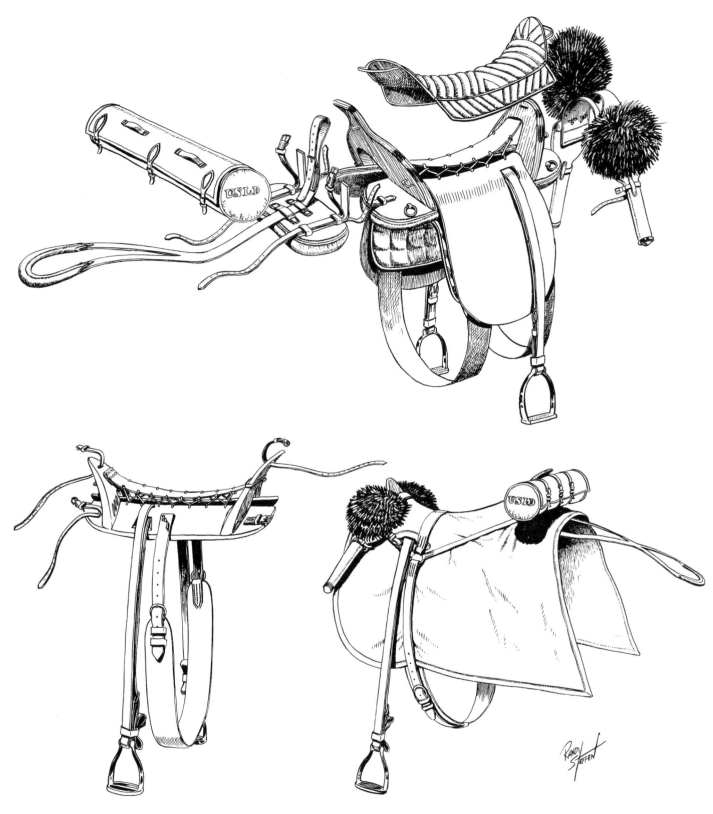

FIGURE 34. Horse equipments used by U.S. Light Dragoons in 1812.

Hungarians, and probably from the Mongols before them.

Both saddles, the American version at the top and the European at the bottom of Figure 34, are constructed on a tree most likely made of beech, with a rawhide seat nailed to cantle and pommel and laced to the top edges of the bars with leather thongs. Both have slots for the stirrup leathers mortised into the sidebars, and both have high-peaked pommels and cantles, the purpose of which is to support the cloak and valise high enough to clear the horse's back. The Walker-contract saddle uses, in addition to the high cantle, a valise pad (commonly called a mail pillion in those days), on which the valise and wallet were supported.

A removable padded and quilted seat is shown on the Walker saddle, patterned after the British 1805 saddle in its construction and manner of fastening with loops to pommel and cantle. The U.S. Model 1841 dragoon saddle, described in the Ordnance Manual of that year, had a similar seat secured to the tree in much the same way. The Walker saddle specifications also included a padded underskirt to protect the sides of the horse from the girth buckles. And in contrast to the European-type saddle at the bottom, the Walker saddle was equipped with two girths—considered important by some cavalry experts of the period.

Some sort of covering was necessary for use with the European saddle, and most always a *schabraque* was used with the type of surcingle shown to keep the housing and the packed saddle from shifting. The American saddle made by Walker was designed for use without a housing, having outer skirts long enough to protect the rider's legs from horse sweat and girth buckles.

No specimen of the Walker contract saddle exists today, and I want to stress again that the saddle shown in Figure 34 as the Walker saddle is a *reconstruction* based on the contract and the author's knowledge of contemporary horse gear. I believe it reasonable to assume that the saddle made under this contract closely resembled my drawing.

The European-type hussar saddle at the bottom of the illustration was drawn from actual specimens at the West Point Museum and from photographic illustrations copied from European military equipment pictured in Major Tylden's book, and from drawings in Captain McClellan's report on his European study

and in J. Roemer's *Cavalry, Its History, Management, and Uses in War* (New York, D. Van Nostrand, 1863).

During the last year of the second war with Great Britain, a small book with an enormous title was published in Philadelphia. The title page of the copy in the West Point Library is reproduced here:

A

HAND BOOK FOR CAVALRY;

CONTAINING

THE FIRST PRINCIPLES

OF

CAVALRY DISCIPLINE,

FOUNDED ON RATIONAL METHOD;

INTENDED

TO EXPLAIN IN A FAMILIAR AND PRACTICAL MANNER,

THE

MANAGEMENT AND TRAINING OF THE HORSE,

AND THE INSTRUCTION, DISCIPLINE, AND DUTIES

OF

U. S. LIGHT DRAGOONS:

CONFORMABLE TO

THE ESTABLISHED ELEMENTARY DISCIPLINE OF INFANTRY

FOR THE

UNITED STATES' MILITARY FORCE,

AND

THE LATEST IMPROVEMENTS

IN THE MODERN ART OF WAR.

BY COLONEL WILLIAM DUANE,

ADJUTANT GENERAL IN THE ARMY OF THE UNITED STATES.

PHILADELPHIA:
PRINTED FOR THE AUTHOR.
1811.

Colonel Duane, then the adjutant general of the U.S. Army, obtained one of the first copyrights for this little book, which he had printed privately. Not written as an official handbook or manual for instruction of U.S. Light Dragoons, it did, nevertheless, set forth specific instructions for the training of the dragoon, the discipline of the horse, the training of the dragoon on the trained horse, and the methods of evolution peculiar to cavalry. I am sure the book was written and published with hopes that its principles would be adopted not only for the instruction of all United States mounted troops, but also for the education and training of the mounted militia forces in the several states. These volunteer groups were far more numerous than the dragoons under the jurisdiction of the federal government.

The section on horse accoutrements contained a detailed list of parts of the saddle and its related equipments, and a similar list of parts making up the bridle and halter. The curb bit, which the author describes as being the best form for the dragoon curb and other equipments described by the author are not illustrated. The lack of these plates is explained in the last two paragraphs of the author's introduction. It seems the current Secretary of War considered the work with all its plates too voluminous, so the book was printed with only a fraction of the original illustrations. As luck would have it, those picturing the saddle, halter, and bridle are among the missing ones. Therefore it became necessary once more to reconstruct the saddle Colonel Duane describes as intelligently as a lifetime with saddles and 20 years of research on horse gear would permit. The saddle shown in Figure 35 is such a reconstruction.

The saddle shown in Figure 35 shows a definite advance from the hussar type hastily contracted for in 1812. This one is built on a typical English tree—a combination of wood reinforced with iron at the pommel. The seat is formed of stretched webbing, called strainings, over which a heavy leather ground is fastened by saddler's tacks at pommel and cantle.

Padded underskirts protect the horse from girth buckles, and the outer skirts are long enough to prevent interference with the tops of the rider's boots. Staples, buckles, and rings are fastened to skirts, pommel, and cantle, on which the necessary dragoon appurtenances are hung and secured. A pouch, strap, and buckled strap on the near side of the rear sidebars accommodate horseshoe nails and an extra fitted shoe. A "pad," or valise pad, or mail pillion, is provided for carrying the valise and wallet so as to prevent injury to the horse's back.

Crupper and breast strap are combined to hold the saddle in place. Holsters are fastened to a ring at the pommel by means of leather thongs. The holster pipes are secured to the breast plate by buckled straps, and loops on the fronts of the holsters allow the passage of the surcingle to keep them firmly in place.

The bit illustrated in Colonel Duane's handbook is shown here in detail and on the bridles shown on the horses. Bridles and halters are *reconstructed* from the lists of parts and descriptions.

The carbine bucket shown on the horse equipped for field service at the top of Figure 35 is *not* listed in this handbook, since dragoons at this time were usually armed with pistols and sabre only. It merely illustrates the type of carbine bucket used by those few dragoons armed with long arms.

Another clue that seems to substantiate the fact that the saddle shown in Figure 35 did exist during the last year or two of the War of 1812, and probably until the mounted service was abolished in 1815, is the description of the saddle considered best for dragoon service in Hoyt's *Rules for Cavalry*, published in 1816.

Epaphras Hoyt, a cavalryman during the Revolution, used his experience to recommend horse equipment, arms, accoutrements, and tactics to the militia troops for which his book was intended. While the saddle described in this treatise coincided closely with the saddle described by Colonel Duane and shown in Figure 35, Hoyt considered the bridoon bit as "superfluous," and answering no valuable purpose. "It fills the horse's mouth and embarasses him in his movements," he wrote.

Hoyt also considered a means to link up the horses when dismounting and fighting afoot a very important appendage, and suggested the use of a strap or leather thong for this purpose. But not until the McClellan equipments were adopted in 1859 was such a link listed as a part of the cavalry outfit.

Hoyt urged the universal use of a good sabre knot, ". . . made of pliable leather, capable of shaping itself to the wrist, and should be attached to the hilt, through which the right hand is thrust when the sword is to be drawn." And, of course, this was in general use during the War of 1812 and is shown on the officers and dragoons in the following illustrations.

Rules for Cavalry urged the adoption of the carbine for cavalry, and mentions a breech-loader of some kind as being the ideal. Hoyt pointed out that in wooded country, such as the kind that covers much of the eastern United States, fighting dismounted with the carbine would place men armed in this fashion on even terms with infantry.

COLOR PLATES

COLOR PLATE I. Bugler (left) and sergeant, First Regiment, U.S. Dragoons, ca. 1839, in dress uniforms and equipped for mounted parade. The sergeant is armed with the Model 1836 Hall carbine; Model 1833 dragoon sabers are slung from the belts of both dragoons.

COLOR PLATE II. Private, Regiment of Mounted Rifles, ca. 1846. Except for the dark blue trousers with the distinctive black stripe edged with yellow cord, this rifleman would be hard to distinguish from a dragoon in field dress of the same period. He is armed here with the Model 1840 heavy saber, and holds in his hands the issue Ringgold saddle with which the regiment was equipped.

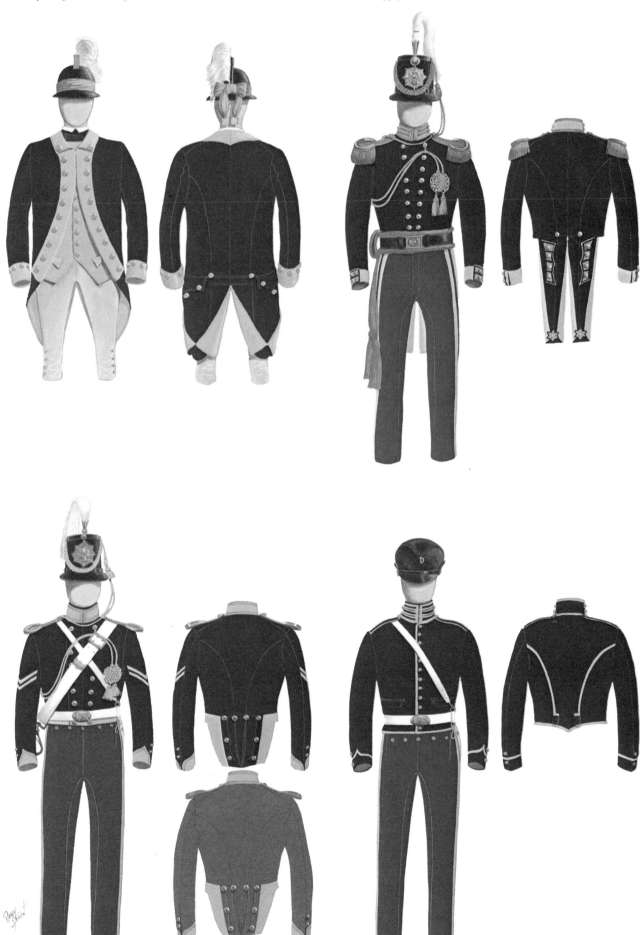

A. 1780–83, Second Regiment Continental Light Dragoons

B. 1833–51 Dress Uniform, Subaltern, U.S. Dragoons

C. 1833–51 Dress Uniform, noncommissioned officers, Privates, and Buglers (red), U.S. Dragoons

D. 1833–51 Field Uniform, noncommissioned officers and Buglers, U.S. Dragoons

UNIFORM COLOR PLATE I

A. 1833–39 Undress Coat for Officers

B. 1833–51 Great Coat for Officers and Enlisted Men

C. 1833–51 Shell jacket for Officers

D. 1839–51 Frock Coat and Forage Cap for Officers

E. 1839–51 Forage Cap for Enlisted Men

F. 1851–   Uniform for Enlisted Men

G. 1851–   Uniform for Officers

UNIFORM COLOR PLATE II

A. 1851 Officer's Overcoat   B. 1851 Officer's Stable Jacket   C. 1851 Musician   D. 1854 Musician

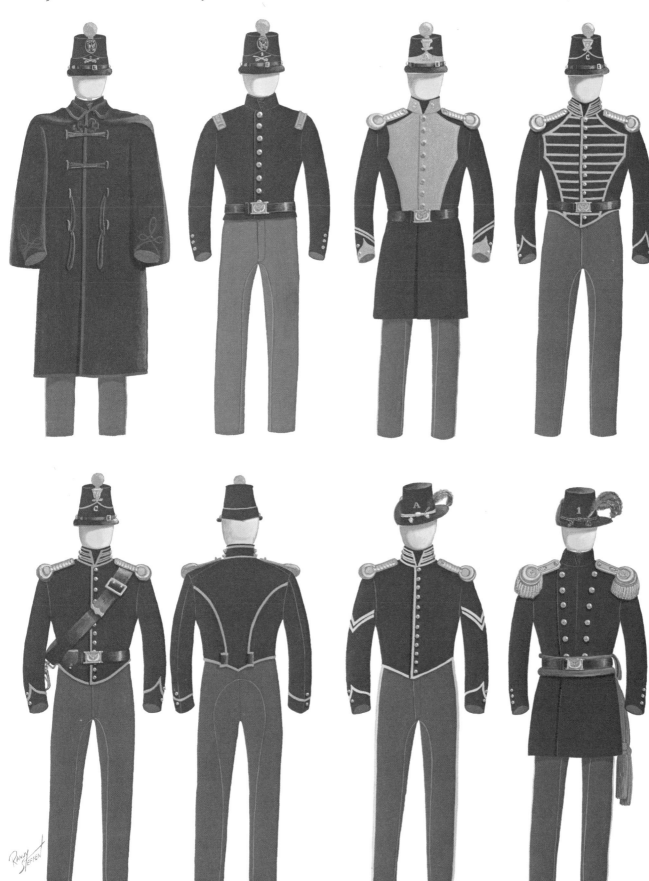

E, F. 1854 Dragoon Jacket and Cap for Enlisted Men   G. 1855 Cavalry Enlisted Man   H. 1855 Cavalry Officer

UNIFORM COLOR PLATE III

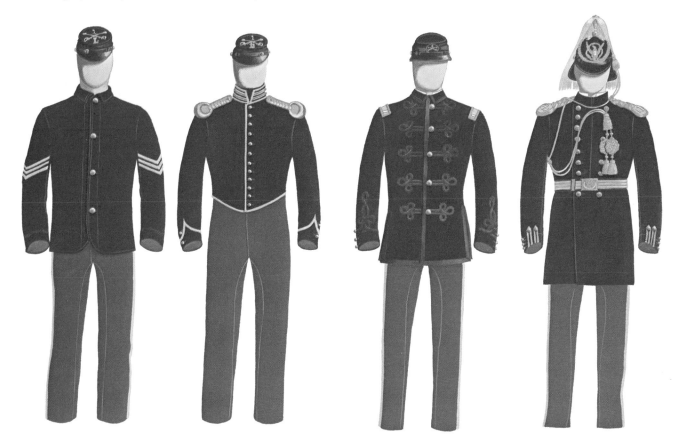

A. 1861–72 Enlisted Man's Fatigue, or Sack, Coat

B. 1861–72 Enlisted Man's Shell Jacket

C. 1872–75 Officer's Undress Coat

D. 1872–79 Officer's Dress Coat 1872–81 Officer's Dress Helmet

E. 1872–81 Enlisted Man's Dress Helmet 1872–84 Dress Coat

F. 1872–84 Musician's Dress Coat 1872–84 Enlisted Man's Dress Helmet

G. 1872–84 Enlisted Man's Dress Coat

UNIFORM COLOR PLATE IV

A. 1872 Officer's Overcoat

B. 1872 Plaited Blouse

C. 1874 New piped 5-button Blouse for Enlisted Men

D. 1875 Sack Coat for Officers, without Braid and Slashes

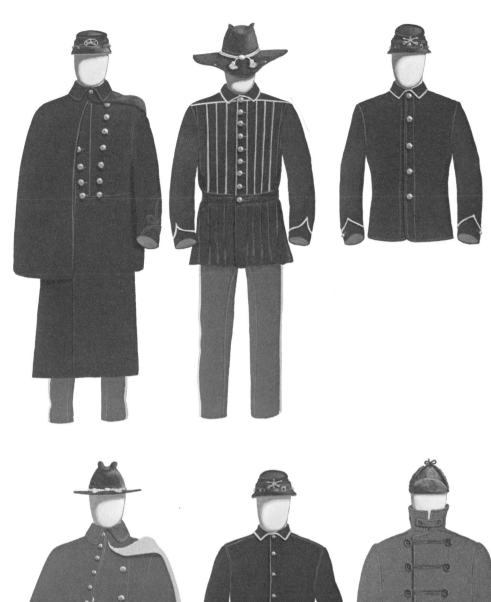

E. 1879 Enlisted Man's Overcoat Cape Lined with Yellow Cloth 1883 Chevrons below elbow on Overcoat

F. 1881 Piped Blue Shirt for Enlisted Men

G. 1883 Blanket-lined Canvas Overcoat

H. 1884 Gold-Lace Chevrons and Service Stripes for Enlisted Men's Dress Coats

UNIFORM COLOR PLATE V

A. 1884 Officer's Ulster Overcoat

B. 1888 New-Pattern Dress Coat for Enlisted Men

C. 1889 Officer Undress (Optional)

D. 1889 Officer Undress (Optional)

E. 1890 Full Dress, Indian Scouts

F. 1890 Overcoat, Indian Scouts

G. 1892 Officers' Undress Coat

H. 1895 Officer's Undress Coat and Forage Cap

UNIFORM COLOR PLATE VI

A. 1899 Blue Field-Service Blouse for Officers

B. 1899 Khaki Field-Service Uniform for Officers

C. 1899 Field-Service Uniform for Enlisted Men

D. 1901 Officer Field Dress, Summer

E. 1901 Enlisted Man Field Dress, Summer

F. 1902 Mounted-Dress Uniform, Enlisted Man

G. 1902 Mounted-Full-Dress Uniform, Officer

UNIFORM COLOR PLATE VII

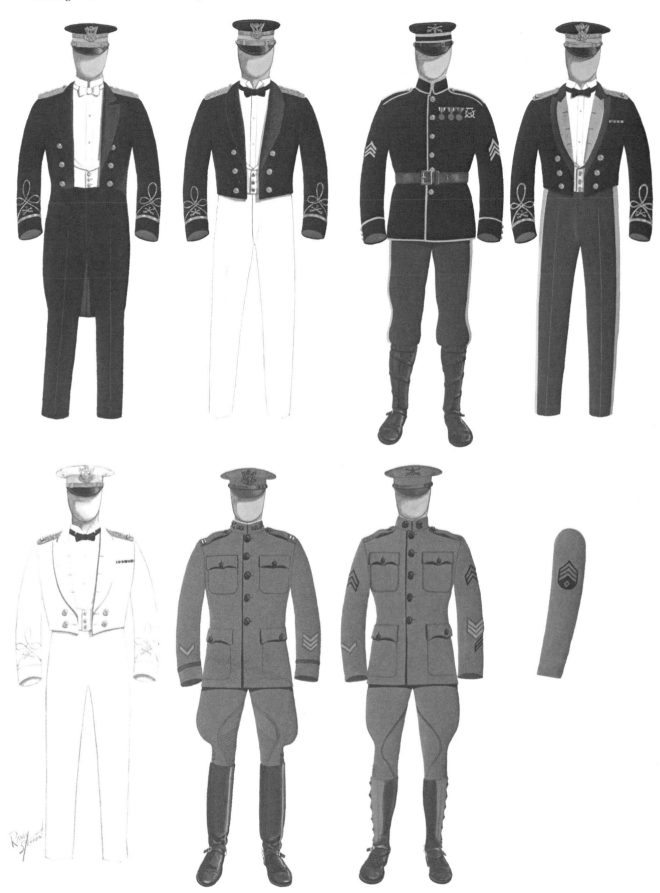

A. 1902 Officers' Uniform for Evening Wear

B. 1902 Officers' Mess Jacket

C. 1907 Dress Trousers for Mounted-Dress Uniform, Enlisted Men

D. 1912 Blue Mess Jacket, Officer

E. 1912 White Mess Jacket, Officer

F. M1912 Service Coat and Breeches, Officer
1918 War-Service and Wound Chevrons

G. M1912 Service Coat and Breeches, Enlisted Man
M1917 Leggings; 1918 Service and Wound Chevrons

H. 1918 Sleeve Insignia for Warrant Officers and Enlisted Men who had Commissions during the War

UNIFORM COLOR PLATE VIII

A. 1924 Officer's Service
Uniform

B. 1924 Enlisted Man's Service
Uniform

C. 1937–38 Officer's Blue Mess
Uniform

D. 1937–38 Officer's Special-
Evening-Dress Uniform

E. 1938 Officer's Full-Dress
Uniform

F. 1938 Officer's White Dress
Uniform (without belt)

UNIFORM COLOR PLATE IX

FIGURE 35. Horse equipments of U.S. Light Dragoons in 1812.

FIGURE 36. Lieutenant colonel, First Regiment, U.S. Light Dragoons (ca. 1812), in full-dress uniform. His saddle is the hussar type popular with dragoon officers and is equipped with the full housing and distinctive surcingle generally used with the hussar equipments. His bridle is of the same general pattern as the regulation one, except that it is more ornate and made of better materials. He is armed with the same weapons as his junior officers and the enlisted dragoons, his sabre being the more ornate officer pattern.

The officer shown in Figure 36 wears the dress uniform as described earlier in this chapter. His collar reflects the extreme reached in American military styles, when the collar was required to reach the tip of the ear, yet be no higher in front than would permit turning the head. He wears the jacked-leather officer's helmet described in the section "Uniforms," and a white buff shoulder-type sabre belt, on which is hung the officer's model of the Nathan Starr contract-of-1812 sabre.

His saddle is the European-type hussar saddle popular with light dragoon officers, and his saddle cloth with its two rows of silver lace on a dark blue field show him to be of field grade. His dragoon boots are fitted with white metal spurs of the type that are screwed to the heel, without spur straps. A letter written in 1813 by a quartermaster inspector to the commissary general revealed that a large number of spurs with screws, along with a few officers' sabres, some pistols, and sabres for enlisted men, would be delivered soon.

His bridle, more ornate than those of the dragoon enlisted men, is fitted with scales of metal over the crown piece to protect the horse's head from sabre blows. The curb bit, while the same type as those used by the troopers, is ornamented with a decorative boss.

In Figure 37, a captain of U.S. Light Dragoons (Second Regiment, as indicated by the numeral 2 on his valise) is dressed in the undress uniform prescribed for dragoons in June, 1812, and is equipped for field service. His saddle is the improved English type shown in Figure 35, and is girthed *over* the saddle cloth marked with a single row of silver lace and three silver bars in the corners to designate his rank. The officer's cloak described by Finke is strapped to the pommel under his holsters. He uses the standard-pattern halter and bridle for field duty. A leather loop, buttoned to the crownpiece of the bridle by a brass stud, holds the halter in place near the horse's poll. Octagonal rosettes, similar to helmet side buttons used later, are shown on the brow band of these bridles, and are drawn from specimens in the author's collection.

The sergeant of the First Regiment of U.S. Light Dragoons shown in Figure 38 wears the undress uniform prescribed for marches and campaigns and is armed and equipped for field duty. He rides the 1812 Walker contract saddle, with a folded blanket for padding, pommel and cantle packs consisting of cloak under his holsters, and valise with wood canteen suspended from the valise by its carrying strap. Bridle and halter are regulation. The lead strap here is folded up and wrapped in the same manner as was customary in the United States service through most of the nineteenth century.

This private of the Second Regiment of U.S. Light Dragoons, Figure 39, wears the dress uniform prescribed in 1812 and rides the Walker contract saddle fitted with a dress *schabraque*, or housing. For garrison duty his horse is fitted with the bridle without the halter. His Harpers Ferry Model 1805 pistol is held at the ready as he challenges a visitor to the camp. He is also armed with the Starr dragoon sabre, contract of 1812. As was the custom during this era, he uses only the curb rein, with the snaffle rein carried looped over the holsters on the pommel of the saddle.

The record of the U.S. Army in the so-called War of 1812 was not exactly one to brag about. True, the war did not end in defeat for the Americans, but if the British had not been distracted so thoroughly by France on the Continent, the outcome of this little war might have been drastically different. The part played by the dragoon regiments is hardly worth mentioning. They had not been fully recruited at any time since the two regiments were authorized in 1812, and those that were uniformed, equipped, and mounted were deployed on miscellaneous assignments as couriers and aides.

Finally, in March, 1814, the two regiments were combined into a single regiment consisting of 8 troops. Each troop had a captain, a first lieutenant, a second lieutenant, a coronet, 5 sergeants, 8 corporals, 1 riding master, 1 master of the sword, 2 trumpeters, 1 farrier, 1 blacksmith, 1 saddler, and 96 privates.

Seven years later the mounted arm ceased to exist, and the U.S. Army was without mounted troops until 1832, when some mounted rangers were called up for emergency duty on the frontier!

In the interim, however, there were those who were only too aware of the shortcomings of an army without cavalry, and in 1822 Pierce Darrow, a lieutenant colonel of volunteers in the Connecticut Militia and a military instructor, published his *Cavalry Tactics*. Darrow was aware that some uniform system of cavalry training and maneuvering for the militia units of the various states was a real necessity. His book was aimed at fulfilling the void he felt existed.

In 1824 William Theobald Wolfe Tone, a lieutenant in the First Regiment of U.S. Artillery, wrote another manual proposing a school of cavalry for the Cavalry of the United States, which, of course, did not even exist then as a branch of the Army.

Lieutenant Wolfe Tone, formerly of the French army, was educated in the Imperial School of Cavalry of St. Germains and served under Napoleon in the French light horse and on the staff. His book was the result of his experience and was written after General Macomb, of the U.S. Engineers, commissioned him to compile such a work out of the regulations and prac-

FIGURE 37. Captain, Second Regiment, U.S. Light Dragoons (ca. 1812), in undress uniform and with one of the issue dragoon saddles packed for service in the field. The saddle cloth is worn under the saddle for field duty. The officer is armed with a pair of single-shot flintlock muzzle-loading holster pistols and the officer's model of the Starr 1812-contract dragoon sabre.

FIGURE 38. Sergeant, First Regiment, U.S. Light Dragoons (ca. 1812), in undress uniform and with the Walker contract saddle packed for service in the field. He is armed with a pair of U.S. Model 1805 single-shot muzzle-loading flintlock holster pistols, made at Harpers Ferry, and the Starr 1812-contract dragoon sabre.

FIGURE 39. Private, Second Regiment, U.S. Light Dragoons (ca. 1812), in dress uniform and with the parade housing over his 1812 Walker contract saddle. He is armed with a pair of U.S. Model 1805 single-shot muzzle-loading flintlock Harpers Ferry pistols and the Starr dragoon sabre, contract of 1812.

tice of the several armies of Europe. The object was to adapt it to the use of the Military Academy, under Macomb's jurisdiction as head of the Engineers, and to present a uniform system of training for the volunteer cavalry within the United States.

This author's recommendations for uniform, arms, and equipment may have been heeded, in part, by the War Department almost a decade later when the U.S. Regiment of Dragoons was authorized and recruited —to become the first unit of this country's permanent cavalry arm. A copy of this book (*School of Cavalry; or System of Organisation, Instruction, and Manoeuvres, Proposed for the Cavalry of the United States*; Georgetown, James Thomas, 1824) may be found in the West Point Library.

CHAPTER FOUR

The United States Mounted Ranger Battalion

1832–33

THE COMPLETE ABOLITION of the cavalry arm in 1821 was not the only drastic change suffered by the U.S. Army. Congress, always with its awareness of where the votes came from, as usual had its ear tuned to the public clamor for a further reduction of the Army! In spite of the urgent need for more soldiers along the ever-expanding frontier to protect the settler, the trader, and the trapper, Congress listened to the public, who scorned all military men, and further reduced the Army. In spite of the demoralization caused by the subsequent shuffling of the regiments and the abolishment of the Ordnance Department, the little Army went right on with surprising spirit.

A drastic change in uniform style took place at this time. For the first time, blue was prescribed as the national color for military uniforms, and for the first time the laced bootee, or modern-type shoe, was issued to all enlisted men. Better weapons, more accurate and with greater range, were issued to the soldier.

Cavalry having been eliminated from the service, the maneuvers of a mounted arm had to be kept up to date by publishing regulations for the volunteers. In the fall of 1826, the Secretary of War appointed a board to draw up a cavalry tactics manual. Major General Scott was made president, while militia generals from several states served under him. The new manual covered the care and training of mounts, nomenclature and use of the sword and pistol, drill in one or two ranks, formations of a regiment of four squadrons in order of battle, schools of the trooper and squadron, and elaborate maneuvers corresponding to those of the current infantry tactics. (Ganoe's *History of the United States Army*, 165.)

Unrest on the part of the wild Indians living along the Red River in what is now the southeastern part of Oklahoma resulted in the marching of more infantry to that area. Less than a year later, more Indian uprisings along the Mississippi called for concentrating an entire infantry regiment at Jefferson Barracks to

discipline the Sac and Fox Indians under Black Hawk, and other companies of soldiers were stationed at points above and below St. Louis at trouble spots. These movements of troops further weakened the small Army, and Congress, under administrative changes, finally realized that something had to be done to meet the increasing threat to the frontier and the rest of the nation.

The Ordnance Department, which had been abolished 11 years earlier, was re-established in the early spring of 1832, and the topographical engineers were made a regular bureau of the War Department.

Now Black Hawk and his warriors became so hostile that Washington realized a large force would be necessary to overpower them, so the Sixth Infantry and 900 volunteers from Illinois were concentrated at Dixon's Ferry. At about the same time, June 15, 1832, Congress authorized the raising of 600 mounted rangers—the first federal mounted force since 1821. Working with unusual alacrity, the government expedited the red tape required for this force, so that by July 23 an official regulation authorizing the United States Mounted Ranger Battalion was a part of the official regulations of the Department of War (Ganoe, p. 171). The 6 authorized companies were raised by the appointed company commanders in different sections of the frontier. Henry Dodge was appointed major commanding the battalion. Among others, Nathan Boone, son of Daniel Boone, received an appointment as captain commanding one company. Pay for enlisted rangers was $1.00 per day, but included allowances for clothing, arms, equipment, horse, and forage for the horse.

Company commanders started recruiting for their respective companies during the summer, but it wasn't until November 1 that a set of regulations governing the equipping, dress, and activities of the mounted rangers appeared in a general order (National Archives, *General Orders*, 1832):

84

General Order   Head Quarters of the Army
  No. 99   Adjutant Generals Office
             Washington   1st November, 1832

ORDER

The General-in-Chief has received from the War Department the subjoined Regulation, which is published for general information.

War Department
November 1st, 1832

Regulations respecting Mounted Rangers

I. Under the Regulations of the Department of War of the 23rd of July, 1832, the rank and file of the Mounted Rangers are to forage their horses at their own expense. They will therefore habitually provide the forage themselves, without the intervention of a public agent; but where it shall become necessary, under pressing circumstances, to obtain forage from the United States, the officers of the Quarter Masters Department shall issue it on the requisition of the commander of the troop or detachment, and shall furnish him with a certified abstract of the issues to each individual, showing the cost of the forage supplied, which shall be noted on the muster roll for stoppage at the next ensuing muster.

II. Baggage Wagons are not to be allowed to the Mounted Rangers under any circumstances, unless in such extraordinary cases, as may be considered as exceptions to the spirit of this Regulation, where an officer of the rank of Colonel may direct otherwise. And, in such cases, the officer so interfering, shall make an immediate report to the Commanding General of the circumstances requiring the procedure.

III. The character of a mounted corps, as well as the nature of the service on which they are employed are opposed to the encumbrance of Wagons. On long marches on the remote frontiers, a limited number of pack-horses, to be proportioned upon the responsibility of the officers authorizing the same, to the nature and probable length of the expedition, will be allowed; but in their ordinary movement they must depend upon the resources of the Country, and the supplies which they can carry along with them.

Lew Cass
(signed)   R. Jones
Adjt. Genl.

The Mounted Ranger Battalion was made up of young, hardy hunters, trappers, and other outdoorsmen, who were required to furnish their own horses and horse equipment, weapons, and dress. They were completely without uniforms or insignia of rank of any kind, although contemporary writings reveal they did have buglers. Recruiting rules specified that they be clothed in the "hunting dress of the day."

Captain Jesse Bean raised one of the companies of mounted rangers, and these men were mustered into the service at Fort Gibson, Arkansas Territory, in

mid-September. Early in October, Bean's company was ordered on a reconnaissance tour between the Arkansas and the Red rivers. On the sixth of that month the 80 rough-looking rangers started on their tour of the country to the west. A week later the newly appointed Indian commissioner, Henry Ellsworth, an English traveler by the name of Latrobe, and the American novelist Washington Irving caught up with the mounted rangers and rode with them to observe whatever contact they might make with the Indians.

In *A Tour of the Prairies*, Washington Irving wrote a number of passages that describe the dress, equipment, and conduct of this company of rangers better and more completely than any other official or unofficial document. The following are verbatum excerpts from this book, with interpretive comments in brackets:

Chapter II

On arriving at the fort [Gibson], however, a new chance presented itself for a cruise on the prairies. We learnt that a company of mounted rangers or riflemen had departed but three days previous to make a wide exploring tour from the Arkansas to the Red River, including a part of the Pawnee hunting grounds where no party of white men had as yet penetrated....

As we should have a march of three or four days through a wild country before we could overtake the company of rangers, an escort of fourteen mounted riflemen [*sic*], under the command of a lieutenant, was assigned to us.

*   *   *   *   *   *   *   *   *   *   *   *

Chapter III

Here was our escort awaiting our arrival: some were on horseback, some on foot, some seated on the trunks of fallen trees, some shooting at a mark. They were a heterogeneous crew; some in frock coats made of green blankets; others in leathern hunting shirts, but the most part in marvelously ill-cut garments, much the worse for wear, and evidently put on for rugged service.

*   *   *   *   *   *   *   *   *   *   *   *

Chapter IV

The long drawn notes of a bugle at length gave the signal for departure. The rangers filed off in a straggling line of march through the woods.

*   *   *   *   *   *   *   *   *   *   *   *

Chapter VIII

In a beautiful open forest . . . were booths of bark and branches, and tents of blankets, temporary shelters from the recent rain, for the rangers commonly bivouac in the open air. There were groups of rangers in every kind of uncouth garb. Some were cooking at large fires made at the feet of trees; some were stretching and dressing deer skins; some were shooting at a mark, and some lying about on the grass. Venison, jerked and hung on frames, was drying over the embers in one place; in another lay carcasses recently brought in by the hunters. Stacks of rifles were leaning against the trunks of trees, and saddles, bridles, and powder horns hanging above them, while the horses were grazing here and there among the thickets. . . .

We were received in the frank, simple hunter's style by Captain Bean, commander of the company; a man about forty years of age, vigorous and active. His life had been chiefly passed on the frontier, occasionally in Indian warfare, so that he was a thorough woodsman and a first-rate hunter. He was equipped in character; in leathern hunting shirt and leggings, and a leathern foraging cap. . . .

While we were conversing with the captain a veteran huntsman approached . . . his dress was similar to that of the captain, a rifle shirt and leggings of dressed deerskin, that had evidently seen service; a powder horn was slung by his side, a hunting knife stuck in his belt, and in his hand was an ancient and trusty rifle, doubtless as dear to him as a bosom friend. . . .

The party was headed by a veteran bee hunter, a tall, lank fellow in homespun garb that hung loosely about his limbs, and a straw hat shaped not unlike a bee-hive; a comrade, equally uncouth in garb, and without a hat, straggled along at his heels, with a long rifle on his shoulder.

* * * * * * * * * * * *

Chapter X

They were mostly young men, on their first expedition, in high health and vigor, and bouyant with anticipations. . . .

The cooking was conducted in hunter's style; the meat was stuck upon tapering spits of dogwood, which were thrust perpendicularly into the ground, so as to sustain the joint [meat] before the fire, where it was roasted or broiled with all its juices retained in it in a manner that would have tickled the palate of the most experienced gourmand. . . .

Many of them were neighbors of their officers, and accustomed to regard them with the familiarity of equals and companions. None of them had any idea of restraint and decorum of a camp, or ambition to acquire a name for exactness in a profession in which they had no intention of continuing.

* * * * * * * * * * * *

Chapter XI

. . . the men in every kind of uncouth garb, with long rifles on their shoulders, and mounted on horses of every color. . . .

The whole scene reminded me of the description of bands of buccaneers penetrating the wilds of South America, on their plundering expeditions against the Spanish settlements. . . .

. . . The lads of the West holding "shot-guns," as they call the double-barrel guns, in great contempt.

* * * * * * * * * * * *

Chapter XIII

They looked not unlike banditti returning with their plunder, and the wild dell was a retreat worthy to receive them. The effect was heightened after dark, when the light of the fires was cast upon the rugged looking groups of men and horses; with baggage tumbled in heaps, rifles piled against the trees, and saddles, bridles and powder horns hanging about their trunks. . . .

I [Captain Bean] must issue written orders, that no man shall hunt without leave or fire off a gun, on pain of riding a wooden horse with a sharp back. I have a wild crew of young fellows unaccustomed to frontier service. It will be difficult to teach them caution. [This seems to refute the popular conception that most of these young rangers were frontiersmen.] . . .

The bugle sounded the signal to mount and march. The troop filed off in irregular line down the glen, and through the open forest, winding and gradually disappearing among the trees, though the clamor of voices and the notes of the bugle could be heard for some time afterward. The rear guard remained under the trees in the lower part of the dell, some on horseback with their rifles on their shoulders; others seated by the fire or lying on the ground, gossiping in a low, lazy tone of voice, their horses unsaddled, standing and dozing around, while one of the rangers, profiting by this interval of leisure, was shaving himself before a pocket mirror stuck against the trunk of a tree.

* * * * * * * * * * * *

Chapter XXII

In his hurry and worry he [one of the young rangers] had put on the saddle the hind part before! [This indicates beyond a doubt that some of the saddles were left-over dragoon saddles from the War of 1812 and later, with high pommels and cantles—saddles that would make such an error easy in the excitement of an alarm.]

The above quotations from Irving's narrative reveal much about the dress and equipment of the mounted rangers, and the lack of discipline stemming from the cordial terms on which officers and men had been before their enlistment. That Captain Bean—and the other commissioned officers of the battalion—were functioning under difficult conditions is a gross understatement.

A final word about dress and equipment of this organization: Each man equipped himself and his horse with the type of clothing, arms, and horse gear that suited his personal preference. There is little doubt that every type of saddle in use for the past three decades—both civilian and military—was found in the battalion. The same is true for weapons; they must have ranged the full gamut of calibers, from old military pieces to the latest Pennsylvania rifles, from the plainest to the most ornate.

The term of enlistment for the rangers of the battalion was for a period of one year. The Army soon saw that a disciplined and trained mounted force was necessary for effective action against the Indians, and that a more colorful display than the nondescript mounted rangers was needed to impress the finery-loving Plains people, now more of a threat to the frontier trade than ever.

FIGURE 40. Ranger, U.S. Mounted Ranger Battalion (ca. 1832), with his Mexican saddle and other civilian horse equipments that he furnished. He is armed with his personal weapons—a short, heavy-barreled flintlock rifle, long knife, and fighting belt ax. The led horse is equipped with a dragoon saddle left over from the War of 1812, a pair of holster pistols, and the owner's choice of accoutrements fastened to the saddle according to his individual taste.

CHAPTER FIVE

The United States Dragoons

1833–50

THE UNITED STATES Regiment of Dragoons was authorized on March 2, 1833. Recognizing the need for a trained mounted corps that would be dressed colorfully enough to impress the Indians then making trouble on the frontier, Congress was persuaded to abolish the rag, tag, and bobtail mounted ranger force of 685 officers and men and replace them with an impressive full regiment of outstandingly uniformed and equipped dragoons.

Aware of the time needed to raise, clothe, and equip such a regiment, the Mounted Ranger Battalion was not dismissed from the Army until at least a nucleus of the dragoon companies had been recruited and were ready for duty.

The U.S. Regiment of Dragoons constituted in the spring of 1833 was to be the first unit of permanent cavalry in the U.S. Army; it retained its designation as dragoons until 1861, when all mounted units became "cavalry."

On March 6, 1833, the Adjutant General's Office in Washington issued General Order No. 14 that made public the list of officers appointed by the President to administer the regiment. Major Dodge, commanding the Mounted Ranger Battalion, was promoted to the rank of colonel and was given command of the new regiment. Stephen Watts Kearny was appointed lieutenant colonel, and Richard B. Mason became a major.

Most of the ranger captains went to the new regiment, and among the dragoon lieutenants were Jefferson Davis, later President of the Confederate States of America, and Phillip St. George Cooke of Virginia, later the father-in-law of J. E. B. Stuart and commander of the federal cavalry bureau during the American Civil War.

This same general order ordered the organization of the Regiment of Dragoons to be completed "from such officers of the Battalion of Mounted Rangers as may be deemed qualified for the service." It further ordered the Mounted Ranger Battalion to continue in service until it was formally relieved by regular cavalry, which would be a portion of the 10 companies of dragoons authorized for the new regiment.

General Order No. 15, dated 5 days later (March 11, 1833), ordered Colonel Dodge to remain in command of the rangers and to return to the frontier, where the battalion was to be held ready for service until relieved by the dragoons. In this order, Jefferson Barracks was designated as the station for concentration of dragoon recruits enlisted for the regiment, and Lieutenant Colonel Kearny was ordered to superintend the recruiting. He was ordered to depart immediately for this post, along with the other officers appointed, and to recruit only "citizens of good character, not under 20 or over 35."

Lieutenant Colonel Kearny and Major Mason immediately jumped into the task of outfitting the dragoons. A letter from Kearny to an assistant quartermaster at the Philadelphia Clothing Bureau is reproduced here, from a photocopy of the original in the National Archives, showing the concern of this officer for the type of materials to be used in the dragoon horse equipments.

Head Qr. Regt U.S. Dragoons
New York   April 22 1833

Sir

    Yours of the 18th was this morning received. Spurs made of Brass, plated in Iron will be more serviceable, & cheaper than others, & I prefer them   The Plate may wear off in time; but that is less objectionable, than the liability of Brass spurs to break

    Dark Blue will be a good color, for the girths & Surcingles. We want a thousand Breast Bands, for our Saddles, of the same material & buckles, as the girths,—They should be sewed in the center thus   , that they may lay smoothly on the Horses Breast   I have written to Major Mason, of the Dragoons, now at Washington, to inform you, of the color of them—I want them of the same, as the facings of our uniform

Very Respectfully
Your ob. Servt
S. W. Kearny
Lieut Col. Dragoons
Com'Q

Lieut C. A. Waite
A.Q.M.
Phil-a
P-a

On the same date, April 22, 1833, Major R. B. Mason submitted an estimate for the number of arms, accoutrements, horses, horse equipments, forage, and miscellaneous items to the quartermaster general's office for approval. Because of its value in establishing specific items as articles of issue to the dragoons, it is reproduced here in its entirety:

Estimate of the No. of Arms & Accoutrements, Horses and Horse Equipments, Forage, etc., etc., for the U.S. Regt. of Dragoons.

715 Guns according to pattern.
715 Cartridge Boxes & Belts, according to pattern.
715 Swords
 44 do. for officers
715 Pistols, same size bore as the Guns
715 Dragoon horses.
715 Saddles, with stirrups, girths, surcingles, cruppers, breast band & Blanket, with bearskin cover for saddle.
715 Saddlebags.
715 Bridles, double reined
715 Curry combs
715 Holsters with bearskin cover.
715 Halters.
715 Nosebags & Straps with leather bottoms.
200 Pack mules with packsaddles, cruppers, breastbands, halters & pack ropes—Spanish packsaddles are best.
915 Pickets, for picketing horses, ———— inches long, shod with iron
  6 Brass 3 pounders, mounted on light carriages, equipped complete for either horse or foot artillery—As horse artillery each gun equipped for 2 horses.
  3 Light 3 pounder cassons [sic], to contain about 250 rounds each. Each casson [sic] equipped complete for 4 horses.
Ammunition, one half to be musket balls made into grape, the other to be roundshot. All to be fixed and sent with the cassons [sic].
  1 Travelling forge, light as possible, with implements complete, equipped complete for 4 horses.
 64 Axes, 6 to each company, 1 to each field officer. 1 to Regt. Staff.
 64 Spades, 6 to each compy. 1 to each field officer, 1 to Regt. Staff.
 64 Grass Scythes, 6 to each compy. 1 to each field officer, 1 to Regt Staff.
108 Wall tents, flies & poles, 6 for the field officers, 2 for Regt Staff, 16 for each company and its officers.
    Independent of this allowance, tents will be required for the medical officers & Hospital.

62,448 Bushels of Oats for 6 months	}	Ea. horse 12 qts of oats
or		or
41,632 do of corn for same period		8 qts of corn per day

1,166 tons of hay, for six months. This is at the rate of 14 pounds to each horse, per day, but of the Prairie Hay, a horse will require more.

As the Dragoon horses will subsist during their summer excursions entirely upon grass, this estimate of forage has been made for only six months. but as they will have to be foraged from the date of their purchase more forage will be required for the first year.

715 Cords, 15 feet long, for carrying grass to horses, when picketed at night.
 10 setts [sic] of shoeing tools—1 for each company. Each compy. should have some saddler's implements for mending and repairing Bridles, Girths, Saddles, etc.
9,606 pounds of Iron, for horse shoes & nails—This for one year.
Stabling for officer's horses, Dragoon & pack horses.
Store houses for forage.
Clothing, same as to other troops.
Straw, Books, Stationary [sic], same as to other troops.
Camp Kettles & Mess pans, same as to other troops.
Small quantity of spare rope to replace lost or broken halters.
Large Bearskins to go over the ammunition packs to protect them from rain.
Leather Sacks for packing dried Buffalo Meat. These can be obtained in the Buffalo country.
915 Leather or rawhide hobbles, for horses when turned loose to graze.

In the report made by Lt. Col. Kearny and myself to the military board, all recommended that there should be with the Regiment of Dragoons, 6 brass 3 pounders. I have therefore embraced them in the above estimate, but upon conversing with the Ordnance officers, and much reflection on the subject since, I am clearly of the opinion that it would be advisable to substitute *Three* light Brass 6 pounders, in lieu of the six 3 pounders. Two 3 pounders require 4 horses. A six pounder requires 4 horses. Two 3 pounders and their carriages are heavier, the two together, than a six pounder and its carriage: It is therefore evident that 4 horses can take a six pounder wherever 2 horses can a 3 pounder. The six pounder has the greatest range & will do more execution than both the 3 pounders put together. *Three light brass sixes, mounted upon light carriages,* can be taken with facility over any country that the Dragoons can march, and will present a much more powerful battery than *six 3 pounders.* From the six pounder the shrapnel shell can be thrown, filled with musket balls, the explosion of which is very destructive, and would produce a wonderful effect on Indians. The 3 pounder is too small for this kind of projectile. The shrapnel shell is as easily thrown from the six pounder as a round shot. It is fixed to the cartridge like a round shot, all put into the gun together, and rammed home at the same time. If the six pounder be adopted, they should be equipped complete for either horse or foot artillery, a casson [sic] to each gun—the ammunition all to be fixed—the whole to be shrapnel shell and grape.

R. B. Mason
Maj. Dragoons

Washington, D.C.
22 April 1833

23 Bugles
2 Standards for the Regt. and one Guidon for each compy.

The 200 mules to be disposed of as follows:

Field officers, 2 each	6
Regtl. Staff	2
Offrs. of a compy, 2	20
Artillery & Ammunition	35
Transp. of Company baggage 4	40
Hospital	3
Qr. Master	4

90 mules will transport 16 days rations (for 715 men) weighing about 22,880 pounds, allowing about 250 pounds to each pack _____ 90
_____
200

R. B. Mason
Maj. Dragoons

Following established protocol, the quartermaster general, Brigadier General T. S. Jesup, submitted the estimate to the Secretary of War, Lew Cass, for his approval. The Honorable Secretary, always aware of the need to adhere to fiscal budgets, immediately reduced the number of pack mules to be allotted to the dragoons to 100, half the number requested in Mason's estimate, and passed the responsibility for approval and procurement of other items on the estimate to the officers in charge of the other specialized bureaus of the War Department. His views of strict economy are reflected in his letter to the quartermaster general, which follows:

Department of War
April 30, 1833.

I approve the estimate of Supplies for the Regiment of Dragoons, prepared by Maj. Mason, and accompanying this, with the following limitations.

But one hundred pack mules, with their equipments, will be allowed, until it is ascertained that the nature of the Service requires a greater number.

The ordnance and Ordnance Stores will be the subject of a special report from the Colonel of Ordnance, before the ultimate arrangements respecting them are made.

The subject of the tents is referred for the special consideration of the Quarter Master General, who will submit his opinion thereupon, after which a decision will be made. The same course will be taken with respect to the propositions for Stables and stone-houses.

The officers in charge of the several bureaux [sic] will take such measures as respectively belong to them, for procuring the supplies alluded to. Each will submit his views to the Secretary of War, in relation to his own branch of Service, previously to any arrangement being made. The object will be,

1. To procure the necessary supplies, in season, of good quality, and upon the most economical terms.
2. To take care that the horses and mules are not procured faster than they are actually wanted, as their keeping will be attended with much expense.
3. To proportion the forage, and all the other supplies to the probable demands as they may arise from time to time, so as not to keep on hand an unnecessary number of articles liable to injury.

The corps, with the best management, will be an expensive one. The most rigid economy ought, therefore, to be exerted, and will be expected, as well in organizing as in maintaining it.

The officer in charge of the Clothing Bureau will be furnished with a copy of the regulations, this day adopted, establishing the uniform of the Regiment of Dragoons. And he will prepare and submit, without delay, the necessary estimates for the clothing.

(Signed) Lew Cass.

Genl. Jesup
Quar. Mr. General.

Regulations for the uniform, dress, and horse equipments of the Regiment of Dragoons referred to in the above letter were published to the Army by the Adjutant General's Office in the form of General Order No. 38, dated May 2, 1833. It set forth in some detail the description of clothing and equipment for officers, noncommissioned officers, privates, and buglers as follows:

Head Quarters of the Army
Adjutant General's Office
Washington, 2 May, 1833

Order.

The General-in-Chief has received the following Regulation from the War Department and commands that the uniform as herein established be scrupulously observed:

DRESS OF THE DRAGOONS.

COAT.—Dark blue cloth double breasted, two rows of buttons, ten in each row, at equal distances, after the fashion of the coat described for the Infantry, except that the buttons are to be gilt, the lace gold, the collar, cuffs, and turnback, yellow, the skirt to be ornamented with a star, instead of a bugle, and the length of the skirt to be what is called THREE QUARTERS.

The slash flap in the skirt and sleeve to correspond with that of the Infantry; the slash on the sleeve to designate rank in the same manner. The collar to be framed with lace, two loops on each side the collar, with small uniform buttons at the back end of the loops.

EPAULETTES.—According to the established rule where the button is yellow and according to rank; the strap to have no number on it.

BUTTON.—Gilt, convex, device a spread eagle, with the letter "D" on the shield.

TROUSERS.—For the company Officers, blue grey mixture of the same color as that for the Infantry, with two stripes of yellow cloth, three fourths of an inch wide, up each outward seam, leaving a light between.

Field Officers and Adjutant, dark blue cloth, with two stripes of gold lace up each outward seam, three fourths of an inch wide, leaving a light between. For the summer, all officers to wear plain white drilling.

CAP.—Of the same material as that for the Infantry, but according to a pattern furnished; to be ornamented with a gilt star, silver eagle and gold cord; the star to be worn in front, with a drooping white horse hair pompon; the Field Officer to have a SMALL strip of red hair, to show in front of their pompons.

AIGUILLETTE.—Of twisted gold cord, with gilt tags, to be worn under the epaulettes of the right shoulder, will distinguish the Field Officers and Commissioned Staff.

BOOTS.—Ankle.

SPURS.—Yellow metal.

SABRE.—Steel scabbard half basket hilt, gilt with two fluted bars on the outside; fish skin gripe bound with silver wire, and of the pattern deposited with the Ordnance Department.

KNOT.—Gold cord, with acorn end.

SASH.—Silk net, deep orange color, and like that of the Infantry, as to shape and size, to be tied on the right hip, to be worn only when in full dress, or when directed by the Commanding Officer.

WAIST BELT.—Black patent leather, one and a half inch wide, with slings, hooks and plate, like those of the general staff, omitting on the plate the letters U.S., and inserting the letter "D" within the wreath.

STOCK.—Black silk.

GLOVES.—White.

UNDRESS

COAT.—Dark blue cloth, cut after the fashion of citizens coat, with nine buttons on each breast, one on each side of the collar four on the cuff, four along the flaps, two on the hips, one on the bottom of each skirt, and two, one and a half inches apart, about midway of each skirt. Epaulette strap on each shoulder. This coat will habitually be worn when not in full dress, and may be worn (without epaulettes according to orders) upon all duty done by detail, where the Officer is not required to be in full dress.

Officers upon ordinary stable duty, marches, or active service, will be permitted to wear a shell or stable jacket, corresponding with that of the men.

GREAT COAT.—Blue grey mixture like that furnished the men, double breasted, with sleeves, stand up collar, cape to meet and button all the way in front, and reach down to the upper edge of the cuff of the coat.

TROUSERS.—Same as the full dress with the exception of the stripes.

FORAGE CAP.—Black Leather, same as those furnished to the men.

HORSE FURNITURE

HOUSING.—Blue cloth with gold lace border for the Field Officers and commissioned Staff, one and a half inches wide and yellow cloth border of the same width for Company Officers.

BRIDLE.—Black leather.

MOUNTING.—All metallic mountings, stirrups, bits, &c, of saddle and bridle, to be of yellow metal.

NON-COMMISSIONED OFFICERS, BUGLERS AND PRIVATES OF DRAGOONS.

COAT.—Dark blue cloth short coat, double breasted, with yellow collar, cuffs, turnbacks, and brass shoulder knots of the exact cut and fashion, of the one furnished the clothing bureau. Sergeants to wear chevrons of three-bars, points towards the cuff on each sleeve, above the elbow; Corporals, two bars. The collar of the chief musicians and sergeant's coats, to be trimmed with yellow worsted binding, after the style of the officers. Musicians coats to be of red cloth, yellow turnbacks and cuffs, yellow buttons.

TROUSERS.—Same material as for other corps, but cut and made after the style and fashion of a pair furnished the clothing Bureau. Sergeants to have two yellow stripes, three fourths of an inch wide up each outward seam, leaving a light between. Corporals and Privates, one yellow stripe up each outward seam. The stripes to be in advance of the seam.

JACKET.—Blue cloth for winter, white cotton for summer; stand up collar trimmed with yellow worsted binding like Sergeants coat; single breasted, one row of buttons in front. These jackets are to be made of cloth of the quality used for the old uniform coats.

CAP.—Same material as for other Corps, but the pattern, ornaments and trimmings, like the one furnished the Clothing Bureau. Drooping white horse hair pompon.

GREAT COAT.—Same material as for other Corps. Stand up collar, double breasted, cape to reach down to the cuff of the coat, and to button all the way up.

BOOTS.—Ankle.

The Non-commissioned Staff to wear Aiguilettes on the left shoulder, like those for the Artillery.

Non-commissioned Staff and First Sergeants of Companies, wear yellow worsted sashes.

FORAGE CAP.—Black leather, like pattern furnished Clothing Bureau.

The following parts of the 1832 Regulations for Uniform and Dress of the Army, even though they are not specifically worded for dragoon officers, apply to the wearing of the dragoon uniform:

OFFICERS OF REGIMENTS OF ARTILLERY AND INFANTRY.

There is no distinction of dress and undress for officers of Artillery and Infantry.

The sash is to be worn on all occasions where the officer is in full dress.

The frock coat, as here established, may be worn as a common morning dress in quarters and on certain duties off parade; to wit: inspections of barracks and hospitals—courts of inquiry and boards—inspections of articles and necessaries—working parties and fatigue duties—orderly duty and upon the march.

The waist belt is to be worn over the frock coat, and when the officer is engaged on duty of any description the sash is to be worn.

The swords of mounted officers will be suspended from the belt by slings of the same materials as the belt, with a hook attached to the belt, to suspend the sword more conveniently when on foot.

GENERAL REMARKS.

Mustachios, long whiskers or beards, are not to be worn.

The hair to be short, or what is generally termed cropped—the whiskers not to extend below the tip of the ear.

Vests are not described, as they form no part of the military dress. When worn, however, by General or General Staff officers, they may be of buff, blue or white, to suit season and climate, with the small uniform button; for Regimental officers, the same, with the exception of the buff.

The Forage Cap may be worn off duty with the Frock Coat and with the Shell Jacket—in winter, the Forage Cap, in cold climates, will have a temporary band of black fur, two and a half inches wide, attached to the bottom, to unite in front by a tie of black ribbon.

Regimental officers, not serving with their Regiments, nor doing duty in the line, may wear cocked hats of the same description as those prescribed for General Staff officers, except that the loop will be of black silk; the eagle yellow, the tassels to conform to the color of the button.

Cocked hats may be either open or formed so as to shut like the hat which has heretofore been designated chapeau de bras.

Even though regulations governing the dress of the dragoons were published in May, and those concerned were commanded to "observe scrupulously" these articles, evidence points to the fact that uniforms were not issued until 1834. H. Charles McBarron, in a letter to Theodore B. Pittman dated August 1, 1954, stated:

The First [sic] Dragoons did not receive their uniforms until after their expedition through the prairies with Col. Dodge. In 1833 they had a motley appearance. In one company, (A) for instance, they all had sabers but some were worn on shoulder belts, some on the waist. They had 46 rifles, 33 of them Harpers Ferry half-stocked, the rest had only pistols. Most of them were in the clothes they had worn on enlistment.

While I do not know what the primary source of this information was, McBarron is one of the most meticulous researchers in the field of military history, and I do not question his statement. It seems logical that a considerable period must have passed between the establishment of a set of regulations for dragoon uniforms and the manufacture and issue of such clothing and equipments.

But since the primary purpose of this work is to show the regulation uniform, arms, accoutrements, and horse equipments, we shall pass over such deviations lightly. To describe in great detail all such irregular garb and equipment would make the compiling of this book a never-ending task.

Therefore, let it suffice to say that General Order No. 69, dated August 14, 1833, spelled out in detail the time schedule for mustering out the noncommissioned officers, musicians, and privates of the Mounted Ranger Battalion—on the day their one-year term of enlistment was completed. The third lieutenants and other officers who did not want to be transferred to the Regiment of Dragoons were to be discharged on the first day of October, 1833. The brevet third lieutenants were transferred to the dragoons as brevet second lieutenants, and they were ordered to report to the senior officer of dragoons immediately.

Six additional brevet second lieutenants were transferred from infantry regiments to the new dragoon regiment with the same rank. Two of these junior officers were sent directly to Boston for recruiting service, while the remaining 4 were ordered to proceed directly to Jefferson Barracks.

UNIFORMS

1833–36

Contemporary illustrations of dragoons during the first decade of their existence are, for all practical purposes, nonexistent. In an article written for *The Guidon* (Vol. I, No. I), the journal of the Cavalry Collectors Association, Lieutenant Colonel R. T. Huntington remarked, "One of the many mysteries of our early dragoon history is the almost complete absence of contemporary illustrations of dragoons in the period 1833–40. . . ."

This lack of pictorial representation of dragoons and their equipment is true, as well, for official publications originating from the Army. Fortunately there is a comparative abundance of descriptive material that enables one to illustrate accurately most of the

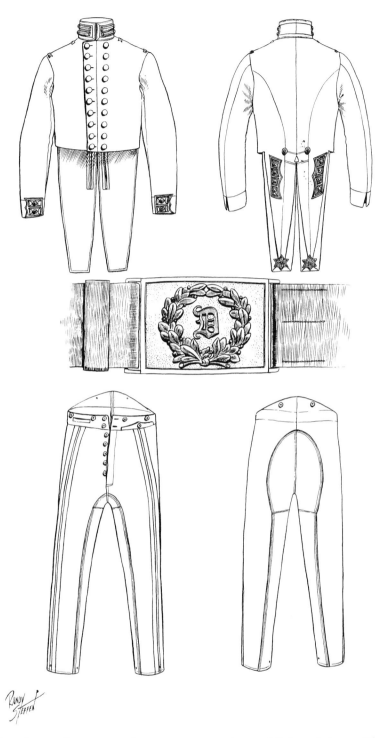

FIGURE 41. Dragoon-officer dress-uniform coat and trousers, 1833 pattern. Stripes on trousers were gold lace for field grade officers and yellow cloth for company officers. Gold lace slashes on the coat cuffs indicated rank: 4 for field grades, 3 for captains, and 2 for subalterns. The belt plate, center, is cast brass with raised silver laurel wreath and old English "D." Uniform and plate regulation until 1851. Drawn from a specimen in the State of California collection.

dragoon equipment and clothing when used with existing specimens of these items found in museums and private collections. Such has been the case with the illustrations for the early dragoon period in this book.

Figure 41 shows the coat, trousers, and belt plate as described in the regulations, Dress of the Dragoons, given above. It will benefit the reader to refer often to the regulations throughout this chapter when examining corresponding illustrations.

Figure B of Uniform Color Plate I shows this same dress uniform in its correct colors.

The author was fortunate in locating, quite by accident, what seems to be the only existing specimen of a very early dragoon officer's dress uniform, as worn by James Clyman from 1834 to 1836, in the historical collection belonging to the State of California. Packed away for years in a box, it was finally uncovered and brought to the author's attention by Norman Wilson and Jack Dyson of the California Division of Beaches and Parks. In remarkably fine condition, the uniform was complete with coat, trousers, sash, and cap complete with gilt cords, bands, and white horsehair plume. These drawings were made directly from the dozens of color and black and white photographs and sketches made in Sacramento.

The coat shown in Figure 41 was for a subaltern or lieutenant, there being no difference in the slashed flaps on the sleeves that designated rank between first and second lieutenants. Referring back to the dragoon dress regulations, you will notice in the second paragraph that "the slash flap in the skirt and sleeve to correspond with that of the Infantry; the slash on the sleeve to designate rank in the same manner." Corresponding regulations for infantry officers referred to the regulations for artillery officers, and this section of the regulations describes rank designations thus: "... loops and small buttons on the slashed flap of the sleeve, four for field officers, three for captains, and two for subalterns, to be placed at equal distances."

Epaulettes on both shoulders were worn with the dress uniform. Rank distinctions of epaulettes were the size of the bullion fringe, both in diameter and length, and the presence of rank insignia on the strap. The following excerpt from the 1832 uniform regulations, then in effect for the rest of the Army, give details of the rank distinctions for all grades as concerns epaulettes, as well as the regulations governing the wearing of aiguillettes by staff officers. Epaulettes for a lieutenant are shown on Figure 44.

BADGES TO DISTINGUISH RANK. EPAULETTES.

OF GENERAL OFFICERS—as described above.

OF A COLONEL—bright bullion, half an inch diameter, three inches and a half long; plain lace strap, ornamented with an embroidered spread eagle; the number of the Regiment to be embroidered within the cresent; cresent solid; eagle and number to be silver where the bullion is gold, and gold where the bullion is silver.

OF A LIEUTENANT COLONEL—the same as the Colonel, omitting the eagle.

OF A MAJOR—the same as a Lieutenant Colonel as to shape and size; the strap to be of silver lace, where the bullion is gold, and of gold lace where the bullion is silver; the number on the strap to correspond in color with the bullion.

OF A CAPTAIN—plain lace straps and solid crescent; bullion smaller than that of a Major's, and two and a half inches deep; regimental number on the strap to be gold embroidered where the bullion is silver, and to be silver embroidered where the bullion is gold.

OF A LIEUTENANT—the same as for a Captain, except that the bullion is smaller.

The bullion of all epaulettes to correspond in color with the button of the coat.

All officers having military rank, to wear one epaulette on each shoulder.

The number on the strap of the epaulette being intended to denote the Regiment, it will be worn by Regimental officers only.

Epaulettes may be worn either with pads or boxes.

AIGUILLETTES.

Staff officers, General as well as Regimental, except the Topographical Engineers, will be distinguished by Aiguillettes.

AIGUILLETTES OF GENERAL STAFF OFFICERS— twisted gold cord, with gilt engraved tags, worn on the right shoulder, under the epaulette.

The General Staff is to include—

> The Adjutant General,
> The Inspectors General,
> The Aides de Camp,
> The officers of the Quartermaster's Department,
> The officers of the Subsistence Department,
> The officers of the Pay Department,
> The officers of the Medical Department,
> The Commissary General of Purchases.

AIGUILLETTES OF REGIMENTAL STAFF OFFICERS —twisted gold and silver cord, with gilt tags, worn under the epaulettes of the right shoulder.

Officers' trousers were made, even during the earliest period, with a regular button fly front. Trousers for enlisted men had a drop front for the first few years, and later the same type of fly front as those for officers. Trousers for both officers and enlisted men were high-waisted, for the same issue was used for wear with both the dress uniform and the

94

fatigue short jacket. Double layers of cloth formed a *reinforce* down both legs, on the seat, and in the crotch, as shown on the drawing.

Suspenders were worn under the coat. A watch pocket and a side pocket closed with a buttoned flap were provided on the front of the trousers. No pockets were allowed in the back.

Another look at the front view of the officer's coat will reveal the slash pockets in the skirts.

The belt plate was drawn from a specimen in the National Museum. It is of cast brass with a silver wreath and Old English letter "D," and is 1½ inches wide. As specified in the regulations, the belt is black patent leather with black patent leather slings fitted with gilt spring swivel snaps for attaching the sabre (as shown in Figure 44).

Another detail not to be overlooked are the button threads on both outside and inside of the end of each trouser leg. These were for attaching leather or cloth straps that fit under the arch of the boot to keep the trouser legs from rising when in the saddle. The buttons themselves were on the inside of the trouser legs where they were not visible.

The dragoon cap illustrated in Figure 42 is shown with worsted yellow cords and bands as worn by enlisted men of the dragoons, but was drawn from the officer's cap in the California State Collection in Sacramento. Officer and enlisted caps were made from identical patterns, the difference being in the quality of patent leather on the top, the lower band, the visor, and the chin strap, as well as the quality of the wool felt that forms the body of the cap. Undersides of all visors were lined with green leather.

Of course, the cords and plaited three-strand bands of the officer cap were of metallic-gilt cord, as were the oval-shaped plaited forms above the tassels and the tassels themselves. On the officer's cap the base of the white horsehair plume is trimmed in a distinctive manner, while the base of the enlisted man's plume is perfectly plain.

To my knowledge the officer's cap in the California capitol is the only existing specimen, and few military historians have had an opportunity to examine it. At the time Edgar M. Howell and Donald E. Kloster wrote *United States Army Headgear to 1854,* published by the Smithsonian Institution in 1969, the existence of this cap was unknown to the staff of the National Museum. A label inside the crown of the cap carries the maker's name, "Russel & Co., Philadelphia," and "Superfine."

The grenade supporting the horsehair plume is without the flame that characterizes the enlisted man's grenade and has a larger sphere at the bottom and more finely detailed leaves on the top section that encloses the base of the plume. The metal ring encircling the base of the plume is gilt, as is the eight-pointed ribbed star behind the silver eagle that forms the distinctive dragoon cap plate. This plate is shown in Figure 43. The inset in Figure 42 shows the grenade and the base of the officer's plume in detail.

The cap plate (Figure 43) is identical in pattern for both officers' and enlisted men's caps, the difference being in the finish. Officer cap plates have a gilt star with the eagle in silver, while that on the enlisted man's cap has a brass star with an eagle made in a less valuable white metal. The eagle on the cap plate is basically a Napoleonic eagle, but differs in having a wreath superimposed over the breast. Eagle and star are fastened to the body of the cap by brass wires soldered to the back of the star.

The plaited bands and cord are fastened to the helmet at the top by being looped through rings in the metal discs fastened to the leather top by brass wires through both leather and body felt.

Figure 44 shows clearly the manner in which the cap cords were worn by officers with dress uniform. The two slides on the cord limited the drape of the cords around the collar. A loop on a fixed collar above the plaited flat ends of the cords is fastened to the top left coat button and allows the flat braids and tassels to hang in the proper position on the breast.

This illustration shows two young subalterns of the Regiment of Dragoons properly dressed and equipped for service with troops in dress uniforms. The deep orange silk-net sash is worn correctly on the right side with the knot above the right hip. Length of the orange silk-net sash with the James Clyman uniform in Sacramento is 44 inches with an 8½-inch tassel at each end.

The sabre suspended from the slings of the belt is the 1833 dragoon sabre, officer's model. A detailed description of this sabre will be found in the section under arms later in this chapter.

An additional detail of officer uniforms important in distinguishing rank, as clearly spelled out in the regulations for dragoon dress, is that trousers for company officers—lieutenants and captains—were blue-gray in color. Those worn by field officers—colonels, lieutenant colonels, majors, and adjutants, no matter what their rank, were of dark blue cloth. Stripes on

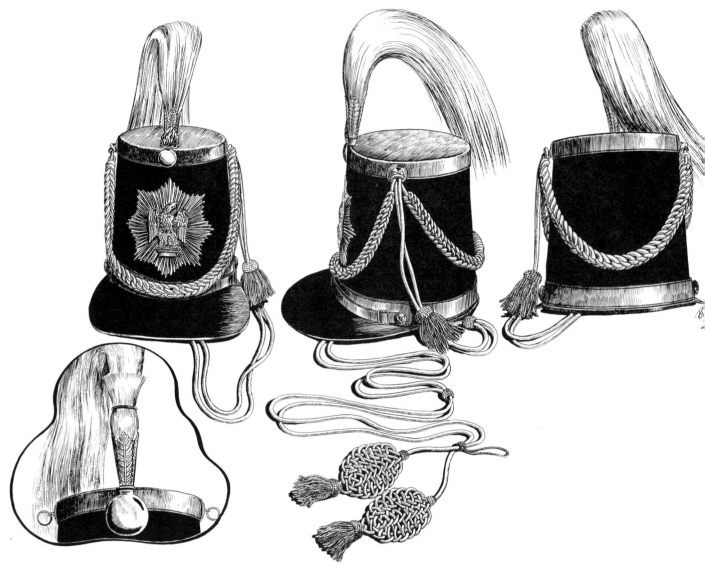

FIGURE 42. The 1833 dragoon cap for enlisted men. Officer caps are identical in pattern, but metal ornaments are gilt instead of brass; cords, bands, tassels, and flat-braided ornaments are gold instead of worsted. Horsehair plumes for field grade officers have a small strip of red hair in the front of the plume, the base of which is cut in a manner distinctive from the enlisted plume (see inset).

company-officer blue-gray trousers were ¾-inch yellow cloth; stripes on the dark blue trousers for field officers and adjutants were ¾-inch gold lace.

White trousers, plain and without stripes, were worn with the dress coat in summer by all officers. The pattern, except for stripes, was identical to the wool trousers worn in cooler weather.

In text describing his dragoon plate in Volume I, No. 1 of the *Military Collector & Historian*, McBarron says, "Full dress had its uses on the frontier in impressing visiting Indians, and it was often worn."

Buttons on both officers' and enlisted men's uniforms were of identical pattern, but differed slightly in size, as indicated in the caption for Figure 45. As shown, both large and small buttons were convex in shape, and according to the published regulations were gilt in finish. The national eagle with spread wings and a letter "D" inside a shield was the standard

FIGURE 43. The 1833-pattern dragoon helmet plate. This Napoleonic silver eagle on a gilt star, as described in the regu- lations, lasted until the uniform change in 1851. Drawn from a specimen in the author's collection.

design on dragoon buttons from 1833 to 1857, when a slight change occurred.

The earliest buttons for dragoons had a hollow back, as shown in Figure 45, with the type of attachment shown. Somewhat later, buttons were made with a hollow back in two pieces, much as they are made today.

A single difference that allows the earlier 1833–40 button with the hollow back to be distinguished from the 1840–60 two-piece buttons is the design of the shield on which the letter "D" is superimposed. The earlier-type shields are flat with no raised rim, while the later design incorporates a shield whose rim is in low relief.

Dragoon dress regulations specified ankle boots for both officers and enlisted men. Figure 46 illustrates one type known to have been worn by officers of this period; a specimen, from which this drawing was made, is in the West Point Museum and was known to have been worn by a cadet during the 1830's. It is made of fine leather, is black in color, and has a fairly high leather heel. The laces, through a single hole on each side of the heel piece, are of cord with the ends stiffened by some kind of sizing or glue.

The spurs in the illustration are one type popular with officers of this period; they fasten to the heel as shown. The spurs on the officers in Figure 44 are of a different pattern and were more common for officer wear. They were fastened permanently to the heel by a screw through a hole in each side of the heel band and were either polished brass or gilt in finish.

The fatigue uniform, prescribed for wear by officers for "ordinary stable duty, marches, or active service" under the heading of "UNDRESS" in the dragoon dress regulations for 1833, is shown in Figure 47. The shell jacket shown here conforms to the pattern of

FIGURE 44. Subalterns of the recently organized Regiment of U.S. Dragoons (ca. 1834). They wear the officer dress uniform, and the two slashes on the sleeves indicate they are lieutenants. Captains rate three slashes, and field officers, four. Collar, cuffs, and coat turnbacks are yellow, as are trouser stripes. The sash is orange silk net.

FIGURE 45. Button pattern for officers and enlisted men, 1833–57. Buttons for mounted riflemen had an "R" within the shield. After 1855, cavalry buttons had a "C" within the shield. Officers' buttons: large—⅞ inch; small—½ inch. Enlisted men's buttons: large—¾ inch; small—.55 inch. (Drawn from specimens in the author's collection.)

several existing specimens, with the collar trimmed with gilt lace similar to the collar on the dress coat. Other later specimens I have seen have plain collars without trim of any kind. (See also Figure C on Uniform Color Plate II.) Breast pockets are edged with gold lace cord. There is no other trim on the jacket, made of dark blue wool. These jackets were made both lined and unlined.

Until 1836 no shoulder straps were authorized for wear by dragoons, even though officers of other branches were required to wear them. After 1836, when regulations specified shoulder straps to be worn with the *frock coat*, it is generally conceded that this mark of rank was also worn on the dragoon shell jacket. A special shoulder strap for dragoons was prescribed in 1839.

Figure 47, showing two subalterns dressed for a march in the field, would be correct for the 1833–36 period dressed and equipped as they are shown, but *without* the shoulder straps. After 1836, and until 1839, they would appear as in the drawing.

Trousers for wear with the undress, or field, uniform were like those for the dress uniform but *without stripes*! That is, field officers and adjutants would be wearing dark blue trousers, while company officers would wear blue-gray ones.

The second lieutenant on the left, identified by a shoulder strap with no rank insignia, and the first lieutenant, with a single bar on his straps, both wear the regulation-pattern spur over their trouser arch straps. Spur leathers are black.

On their heads are the pattern-of-1833 leather forage caps for officers, with the gilt embroidered six-pointed

star that was the dragoon's distinguishing insignia, the same type of star that embellished the tails of his dress coat.

Figure 48 shows this forage cap in more detail, and includes the detachable 2½-inch-wide strip of black fur on the folding ear flaps that was prescribed for wear by officers and enlisted men by the 1832 uniform regulations, to which the 1833 dragoon dress regulations had been added. Under the heading of "General Remarks," this paragraph reads, in part, "...in winter, the Forage Cap, in cold climates, will have a temporary band of black fur, 2½ inches wide, attached to the bottom, to unite in front by a tie of black ribbon."

According to *United States Army Headgear to 1854* by Howell and Kloster, the dragoon caps were made of black morocco leather for enlisted men, and a good grade of goatskin for officers and cadets at the Military Academy. The dragoon caps were a little different pattern from the infantry and artillery patterns, in that the visors were wider, and the caps did have the folding neck cape, or hood, which let down 6½ inches to protect the neck and ears. The visor width at the center is about 4 inches. The crown is about 7½ inches high and 7½ inches in width. The cap was made so it could be folded flat, and all seams of the crown are welted. The sliding brass chin-strap buckle slide on the officer's cap is more decorative than the plain rectangular leather slides or brass wire buckle and leather slide on the caps for enlisted men.

A description of the officer's undress coat is found in the 1833 regulations for dragoon dress, but to my knowledge no specimen of this coat exists. My drawing in Figure 49 is, therefore, a reconstruction from the regulations; it is, I believe, essentially correct. Since the regulations do not specify otherwise, I must assume that the cord binding around the tails of the coat and the slashes on the top part of the skirts bordering the four buttons on each side were dark blue, of the same material as the coat itself. (See Figure A on Uniform Color Plate II.)

Epaulettes are shown on both officers in the illustration, but the regulations clearly state that this coat may be worn *with* or *without* epaulettes, according to orders.

A similar undress coat is in the West Point collection. Dragoon-type six-pointed stars are sewed to the point on the tails where the turnbacks meet, and I assume it must be a militia officer's undress coat. But the cut is the same, after the fashion of the civilian's coat of the 1830's. Button placement on the skirts is

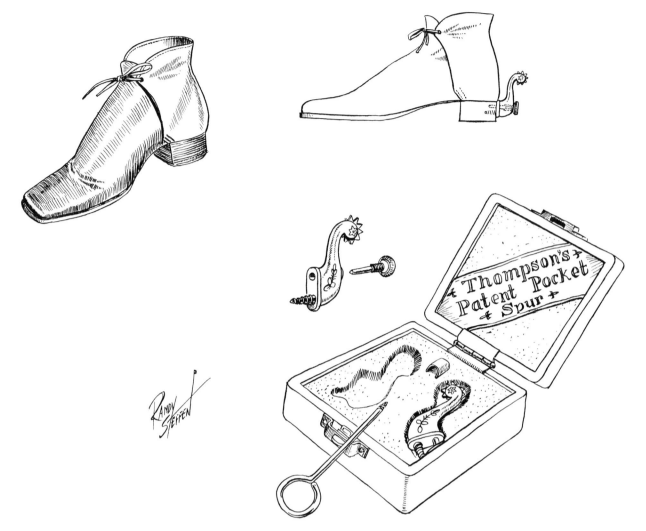

FIGURE 46. Officer's ankle boot and one type of patent pocket spur popular with dragoon officers for dress and ceremony (ca. 1833).

different than the description in the regulations. The cut of the coat in the drawing is patterned after the cut of the West Point specimen.

Undress trousers in the drawing are without stripes, as prescribed by the regulations, and for these company officers are blue-gray.

An important detail often misrepresented by modern illustrators is the strictly adhered-to regulation in the 1832 uniform series that prohibits the wearing of "mustachios, long whiskers or beards" by any army personnel, whether officer or enlisted man. In addition, under "General Remarks" officers and men are directed to wear their hair short, or what is generally termed cropped—the whiskers not to extend below the tip of the ear." Not until 1841 did regulations allow mustaches to be worn—and then only by dragoons.

The pattern for the enlisted man's dress uniform is shown in Figure 50. Colors of the coat, coat facings, cap cords and bands, trousers, and trouser stripes, as well as chevrons signifying noncommissioned rank, are shown on Figure C of Uniform Color Plate I. As described in the 1833 regulations for dragoon dress, the double-breasted short coat is faced with yellow cloth. The private's coat in Figure 50 has the prescribed collar, yellow trimmed with yellow worsted binding on the edges only.

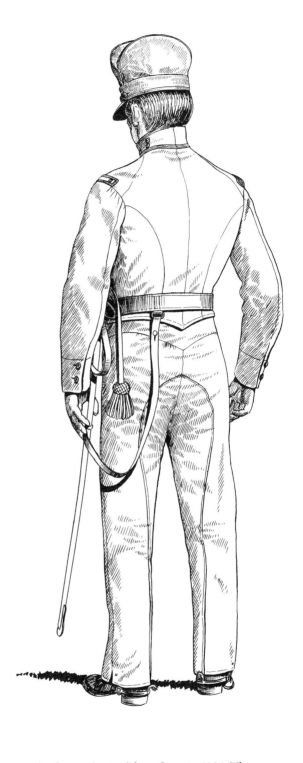

FIGURE 47. Shell jacket prescribed for dragoon officers, 1833–51, for wear on marches and for fatigue duty. Shoulder straps for officers, as shown here, were first prescribed in the 1836 regulations. White linen or cotton jackets for summer wear were also first authorized for officers in 1836. They were identical in pattern to the jackets shown above, but were without trim on collar and pockets.

FIGURE 48. Officer's forage cap, 1833–39, with the detachable 2½-inch strip of black fur attached to the headband for cold-weather wear.

Trousers are high-waisted, similar to those worn by officers, but with a drop front like the more recent Navy bell-bottom trousers had . . . with buttons in front and back for suspenders, or braces, as they were called then. A laced opening at the rear of the trousers allowed the dragoon to adjust the waistband so he could keep his trousers in place even without braces if his physique allowed. A reinforce of the same blue-gray material on the inside of the legs and seat compensated for normal wear in the areas that contacted the sides of the horse and the saddle when on horseback. Buttons attached to the insides of the trouser legs at their extremities provided for attachment of the straps that were worn under the arch of the ankle boot to prevent the trouser legs from rising when the dragoon was mounted.

In order to prevent confusion concerning the design of dress-coat collars for sergeants, as prescribed in the

regulations, let me add that these collars were identical to the collars shown on the officers in Figure 44, complete with two small buttons on each side, but with yellow worsted lace instead of gilt lace forming the blind button holes, as this particular style of trim was then called in military nomenclature.

The red musicians' (buglers') coats were identical in pattern and trim to the dragoon coats, eliminating the chevrons on the sleeves. Not until later was the rank of chief musician authorized. (See Figure C on Uniform Color Plate I.) Trousers for musicians were the same as for all corporals and privates—blue-gray in color and with a single ½-inch stripe of yellow cloth.

As a matter of interest, uniform regulations during this period called the garment commonly known as "trousers" by two other names in various parts of the regulation texts—*pantaloons* and *overalls*. It would be well to keep this in mind later in this and subsequent chapters when studying uniform regulations for specific periods.

There are two important details to remember when examining the enlisted dragoons portrayed in Figure 51. First, it is probable that the dragoon sabre belt as issued *before* 1837 or 1838 *had no shoulder strap*! In a letter to the author dated December 26, 1967, from Lieutenant Colonel R. T. Huntington, a recognized authority on early dragoon equipments, the following pertinent information was given:

> From the Board of Ordnance report in 1837, and from the 1834 and 1839 regulations, I am rather certain that the leather saber belts of the pre-1839 pattern did not have shoulder straps. This is principally because the 1834 regulations specify shoulder straps for the web saber belt only; the wording of the 1837 Ordnance Board report implies, too, that the shoulder strap was an addition to the saber belt.

A white webbing sabre belt 2 inches wide, with 1-inch slings and 2 1-inch shoulder straps, was listed in the 1834 regulations. This was probably an experimental belt issued in limited quantities either as an emergency measure or for test in the field. One of Catlin's paintings of the dragoons meeting the Comanches shows such a belt with the shoulder straps crossing in the back. On the other hand, this painting could have been meant to show a single shoulder strap over the right shoulder and a *narrow* carbine sling over the left shoulder. Huntington also theorizes that the 1833–34 carbine sling probably was a 1¼-inch-wide white buff-leather sling, similar to the rifle slings

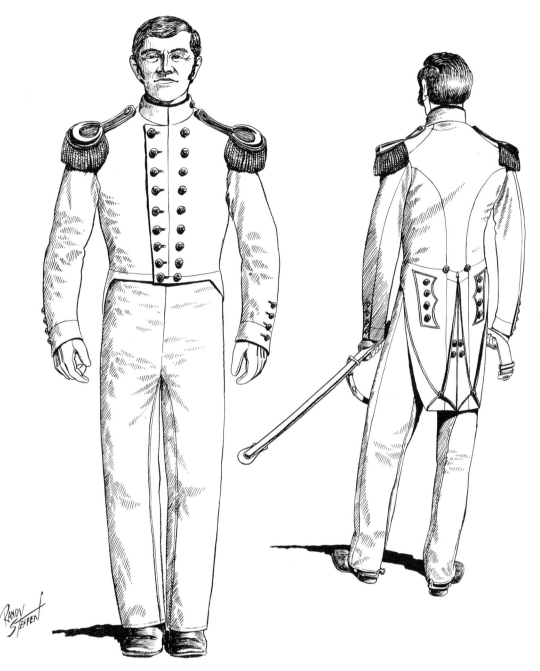

FIGURE 49. Undress uniform for officers, 1833–39, to be worn on all occasions when the full dress uniform was not prescribed, except for campaigns, marches, and stable duty.

This undress coat was replaced in the 1839 regulations by a less ornate frock coat.

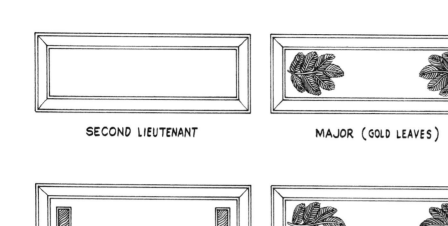

SECOND LIEUTENANT   MAJOR (GOLD LEAVES)   BRIGADIER-GENERAL (SILVER STAR)

FIRST LIEUTENANT (GOLD)   LIEUTENANT COLONEL (SILVER LEAVES)   MAJOR-GENERAL (SILVER STARS)

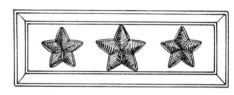

CAPTAIN (GOLD)   COLONEL (SILVER EAGLE)   GENERAL-IN-CHIEF (SILVER STARS)

FIGURE 49A. Shoulder-strap rank insignia (1x3½ inches) were first specified for commissioned officers in the 1836 regulations. In 1839 special shoulder straps were designated for dragoon officers. These were shaped like the epaulette strap with a large gilt crescent attached. The same rank insignia was worn on the dragoon straps as those shown here. The special dragoon straps were replaced in 1851 by larger (1⅜x4 inches) straps with the same rank designations shown in this drawing, which remained unchanged until the ranks of general and lieutenant general were added to the Army. From 1863 to 1872 a general's shoulder straps had 4 silver stars, and a lieutenant general's, 3. In 1872 the general of the Army's shoulder straps were changed to 2 silver stars with the arms of the United States in gilt embroidery between them. All shoulder straps remained unchanged until World War II (except for second lieutenant—single gold bar), when the rank of general and general of the Army were made two separate grades, with the latter's insignia a circle of stars, while the rank of general was designated by 4 silver stars, as it had been from 1863 to 1872. In 1872 the gold bars for first lieutenants and captains were changed to silver bars.

of the period, with a simple brass sling swivel to support the carbine.

Cost of the carbine sling listed in the 1834 regulations was 8 cents, with the sling swivel listed at 25 cents, in contrast to the sling listed at 18 cents in the 1839 regulations, and $1.25 for the new-pattern iron swivel.

Therefore, to make this illustration absolutely correct for the 1833–39 period, these dragoons should be shown *without* the shoulder strap on the sabre belt, and with a narrow 1¼-inch-wide carbine sling. I show them with the later belts and slings to make them do for the later dragoon period—up to the 1851 uniform change. Huntington's article in *The Plains Anthropologist* (Vol. XII, No. 38, [1967 series]) sets forth his findings and theories in detail.

That there were also *black* sabre belts issued to the Regiment of Dragoons is a well-documented fact. On

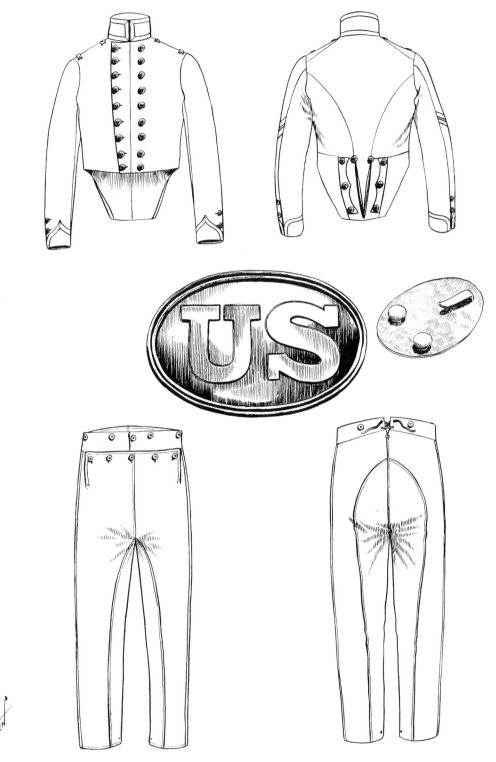

FIGURE 50. The 1833-pattern dress coatee and trousers (overalls, or pantaloons) for dragoon privates and corporals. Sergeant's collars were trimmed with yellow worsted lace like the collars on the officer dress coat, as were the collars on the chief musicians' coats. Cuffs, collars, and turnbacks on the skirt were yellow. Musicians' coats were red faced with yellow. The belt plate, center, is a lead-filled brass stamping, and was regulation until 1851.

FIGURE 51. Sergeant and private, Regiment of Dragoons (ca. 1839), in dress uniforms that were regulation from 1833 until the uniform change in 1851. The sergeant is recognized by his chevrons, the yellow lace, blind button holes on his collar, and his yellow worsted sash. Both dragoons are armed with the 1833 dragoon sabre. The private's 1833 breech-loading percussion Hall carbine, developed especially for the new regiment of dragoons, is suspended from its sling and swivel over his shoulder and back.

page 53 of *Regulations for the Government of the Ordnance Department*, dated May 1, 1834, the following list is found:

Component parts of cavalry accoutrements:

Sabre Belt (white leather) 2 in. wide, with 2 sling straps, ¾ in. wide with brass mountings _____1.00
Sabre Belt (black leather) 2 in. wide with 2 sling straps, ¾ in. wide with brass mountings _____ .75
Brass Belt-plate, for the above _____ .14
Sabre Belt (white webbing) 2 in. wide, with 2 sling and 2 shoulder straps, each 1 in. wide with brass mountings _____2.00
Pistol cartridge Box, carrying 12 rounds _____ .65
Holsters, pair, with hair seal-skin or patent leather, carrying 10 rounds _____ 3.00
Carbine Cartridge Box, carrying 30 rounds _____ .80

Unfortunately no pictorial reference or actual specimens of the early belts, carbine sling and swivel, or other leather accoutrements issued to dragoons in the 1833–39 period exists. It is therefore impossible to represent these items with documented certainty. Thus, it is necessary that I point out that Figure 51 shows the dragoon enlisted man as he appeared in 1839 and later. The uniform itself is correct for the period beginning in 1833, if dress uniforms were actually issued by the end of that year, or, with more certainty, as of 1834—and lasting until the uniform change in 1851.

Drawings of the dress uniform coat, cap, and trousers were made from specimens in the collections of the National Museum and the West Point Museum.

The brass shoulder knots on the men in Figure 51 and on Figure C of Uniform Color Plate I are made of polished brass stampings assembled with solder. They attach to the uniform coat by a flat brass piece on the underside of the knot that slides through a pair of metal staples sewed to each shoulder of the coat, and are locked in place by a flat swivel key through a slot in the knot at the end closest to the collar. The same-pattern shoulder knot, called shoulder scales after 1851, was regulation until several years after the close of the American Civil War.

The jacket shown in Figure 52 was drawn from a specimen in the Military History study collection in the National Museum, and it conforms precisely with the description in the 1833 regulations for dragoon dress. See Figure D on Uniform Color Plate I for color definition of jacket cloth and worsted binding. The two small bolsters on the back of the jacket at the termination of the binding on the back panel are for supporting the weight of the sabre belt with its heavy load of sabre and cartridge boxes.

While executing the illustrations for this book, I experimented with an 1854 dragoon jacket, identical to the 1833 pattern except for the cut of the sleeves and the height of the collar, with a loaded sabre belt, to check the effectiveness of the bolsters on the back of the jacket. Without a shoulder strap on the belt I found that the belt with the sabre, filled carbine cartridge box, and filled pistol cartridge box stayed in place well with the aid of the bolsters *only* if the belt was drawn up very tightly around the waist. Both on foot and on horseback the belt was extremely uncomfortable pulled up as tight as necessary to keep it from slipping down out of place, and I am of the opinion that it would chafe the wearer severely on a long march in hot weather. I can certainly appreciate the addition of a shoulder strap to help support the heavy weight of the sabre and ammunition. I am surprised that a period of three to five years elapsed before the shoulder strap was added.

The small pockets on the front of the jacket were certainly placed there for a definite purpose, and not for the convenience of the dragoon in carrying personal effects, for throughout the history of the soldier, here or abroad, loaded pockets have been forbidden. It is logical, therefore, to speculate that these pockets served a purpose vital to the functioning of the dragoon as a fighting man. The only practical surmise points to their use as containers for percussion caps. It is a matter of record that the Hall carbines with which the dragoons were furnished from 1833 through the early 1850's had some sort of brass primer boxes. Not until 1845 was a leather cap pouch officially approved and issued. I am certain, although I must admit that logic and not documentary evidence prompts my theory, that the brass primer boxes mentioned in contemporary correspondence concerning the Hall carbines must have been of a suitable size and shape to fit in these small pockets. No identified specimens of the brass primer boxes seem to exist, so there is no way to confirm this theory. The round, flat musket-percussion-cap dispensers usually associated with a slightly later period may have had their beginning with the adoption of the Hall carbine, for they do fit these pockets nicely, stay in place well, and provide a means for placing a cap on the nipple of the carbine quickly and without juggling loose primers in the hand. I

FIGURE 52. Dragoon jacket, pattern of 1833. Trimmed with yellow worsted binding around collar, cuffs, bottom of the jacket, edges of the shoulder straps, and on the back seams. The collar for an enlisted man is trimmed like the sergeant's collar on the dress coat. Pockets in the front are to hold a supply of percussion caps. This jacket was regulation until the uniform change in 1851. A similar jacket was authorized in 1854 and was worn until 1872.

would be almost willing to bet this was the type of primer box that was issued with the dragoon carbine!

Figure 53 shows the dragoon's summer jacket and trousers made of white cotton. This drawing was made from a jacket and trousers in the National Museum study collection (Military History Branch of the Smithsonian Institution, headed by Edgar M. Howell). Except for the absence of binding on the collar, cuffs, and seams, this jacket is of the same pattern as the blue wool jacket trimmed with yellow. Trousers, too, are of the same pattern as the blue-gray wool ones worn with the dress and field uniforms, but are made from white cotton and without stripes.

The forage caps shown on the dragoons in Figures 53 and D of Uniform Color Plate I are the 1833 pattern described earlier in the section on officers' uniforms. Identical in pattern to the officers' model, the enlisted man's cap is worn with the letter of his company fixed to the front panel, slightly below the looped welt, as shown. The company letter is a brass stamping 1 inch high, attached by brass wires through the leather of the cap.

Throughout this book reference will be made constantly to *ankle boots* and *Jefferson boots*, or *Jefferson shoes*. Figure 54 shows the difference between these two articles of footwear, and, while ankle boots only are mentioned in the early dragoon regulations for dress, it is reasonable to speculate that Jefferson shoes were issued for wear in garrison during the early periods, since specific mention is made in later regulations of issue of this shoe to dragoon and cavalry troops for nonmounted use. The Jefferson *bootees*, or shoes (they were called both) were issued to enlisted men of infantry and artillery for all wear.

Ankle boots for enlisted dragoons were almost identical in pattern to those worn by their officers, but were of coarser material and less meticulous workmanship. During this period ankle boots and shoes were made to fit either right or left foot. Boots and shoes made in rights and lefts were not manufactured for Army use, for officers or enlisted men, until several decades later.

All dragoon footwear was made of black leather, and a mixture of grease and stove blacking was used to black and polish them. A little later, lampblack and linseed oil was more commonly used, according to early ordnance manuals.

The Jefferson bootee is described in the 1816 uniform regulations for riflemen as "rising 2 inches above the ankle joint and not higher."

Webster's dictionary defines *ankle boot* as "boot reaching only to the ankle."

The pattern for the dragoon greatcoat was the same for officers and enlisted men. Made of a blue-gray cloth, kersey for the men and a finer material for officers, it was double-breasted with 2 rows of 6 large buttons on the coat. The cape, sewed to the coat under the collar, reached the upper edge of the cuff on the sleeve, and was closed with 12 small regulation uniform buttons. (See Figure B, Uniform Color Plate II.)

The greatcoat shown in Figure 55 was drawn from a specimen in the West Point collection, and was known to have been worn in the Seminole War in Florida. It came from the collection of Stanley J. Olsen of Tallahassee, Florida. The pattern of the greatcoat for mounted men changed little until it was abolished shortly after the turn of the century, when army blue was replaced by khaki and olive drab.

While not mentioned in the 1833 regulations for dress, contemporary writings mention dragoons in stable frocks grooming their horses. Because all stable frocks issued to mounted troops have been essentially the same, I made the drawing in Figure 56 to represent the pattern I feel sure must have been used. Made from a coarse, inexpensive, undyed material, like its later counterparts, it closed in front with a minimum number of plain buttons (probably bone). Worn over the field uniform, it protected the dragoon's clothing when he was performing jobs likely to soil his regular dress without the protection of such a covering.

Guidons and standards were listed on Major Mason's estimate of equipment sent on April 22, 1833, to the quarter master general. The 1834 ordnance regulations described the dragoon guidons, saying, "The guidons ought to be half red and half white, dividing at the fork, the red above . . . on the red the letters U.S. in white, and on the white the letter of the Company in red." But before these regulations were published, on September 2, 1833, the Secretary of War directed that the word "Dragoons" be added in red on the white half of the guidons. The West Point Museum has a specimen in their collection, and the drawing in Figure 57 of the 1836 guidon of the Second Regiment of U.S. Dragoons was made from this relic.

Prior to the authorization of the Second Dragoons, it is entirely probable that the guidons of the original regiment had the company letter in the white field as specified. Only after the addition of another regiment was the guidon redesigned, as shown in Figure 58.

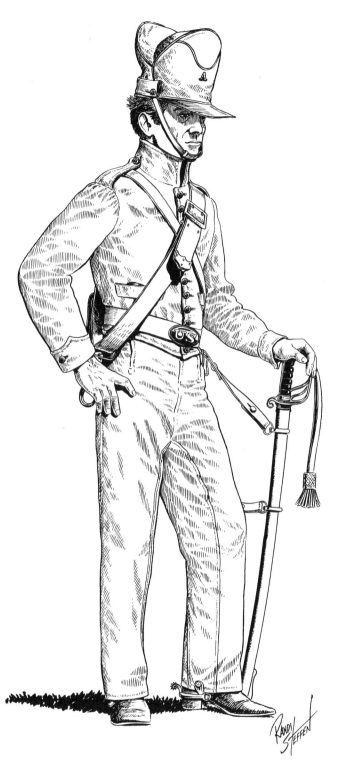

FIGURE 53. Dragoon white summer dress, 1833–51. Jacket and pantaloons for fatigue and field service were made identical to the woolen undress clothing, but from white cotton. This dragoon's forage cap is the leather pattern of 1833, regulation until replaced by the 1839 cloth forage cap.

This guidon pattern continued in use until the stars-and-stripes guidon was prescribed in 1863.

I have not been able to document the exact pattern of the standard for the U.S. Regiment of Dragoons from 1833 to the date when the Second Regiment was formed in 1836, but evidence points to use of the same design, except for the wording on the scroll, which probably read "Regiment" in the left scroll, "U.S." in the center, and "Dragoons" on the right-hand scroll.

1836 REGULATIONS FOR DRAGOON DRESS

The only change in the regulations governing the dress for dragoons since the 1833 regulations were published was in the wearing of the *undress coat*. Pattern of the coat itself remained identical to the coat prescribed in the 1833 order.

If you will refer back to the 1833 dress regulations near the beginning of this chapter you will find under the heading of "Undress" the statement that the undress coat "may be worn (without epaulettes according to orders) upon all duty done by detail where the Officer is not required to be in full dress."

The 1836 regulations expand further on this statement. The following is a direct quotation from this same paragraph: "This coat will habitually be worn (*with or* without epaulettes, according to orders), and upon all *drills* where the *troops* are not in full dress." The words in italics indicate the change in wording and meaning.

The following excerpts from the 1836 Regulations for Dragoon Dress also apply to the wearing of certain articles of dress and equipment for dragoon officers:

19. OFFICERS OF ARTILLERY, INFANTRY, AND DRAGOONS.

The sash is to be worn on all occasions where the officer is in full dress. The frock coat may be worn as a common morning dress in quarters and on certain duties off parade; to wit: at drills—inspection of barracks and hospitals—courts of inquiry and boards—inspections of articles and necessaries—working parties and fatigue duties —and upon the march; on all such occasions to be buttoned, and hooked at the collar.

The sword-belt is to be worn over the frock coat, and when the officer is engaged on duty of any description, except that of the stable, the sash is to be worn.

The swords of mounted officers will be suspended from the belt, by slings of the same materials as the belt, with a hook attached to the belt, to suspend the sword more conveniently when on foot.

FIGURE 54. Ankle boots, left, and Jefferson boots, or bootees, as they were called at times in the regulations. The ankle boots were issued to dragoons and cavalry, while the Jefferson boot, actually an ankle-height shoe, was issued to all arms. The mounted arms wore the ankle boot until late in 1859, when boots were issued to some regiments.

---

20. GENERAL REMARKS.

The hair to be short or what is generally termed cropped; the whiskers not to extend below the lower tip of the ear, and in a line thence with the curve of the mouth.

Vests are not described, as they form no part of the military dress. When worn, however, by general or general staff officers, they may be of buff, blue, or white, to suit season and climate, with the small uniform button; for regimental officers, the same, with the exception of the buff.

The forage cap may be worn off duty, with the frock coat and with the shell jacket—in winter, the forage cap, in cold climates will have a temporary band of black fur, two and a half inches wide, attached to the bottom, to unite in front by a tie of black ribbon.

Regimental officers not serving with their regiments, nor doing duty in the line, may wear cocked hats of the same description as those prescribed for general staff officers, except that the loop will be of black silk; the eagle yellow, the tassels to conform to the color of the button.

Cocked hats may be either open or formed so as to shut like the hat which has heretofore been designated chapeau de bras.

All officers are permitted to wear a citizen's blue coat, with the button designating their respective corps or stations, without any other mark on them; such a coat, however, is not to be considered as a dress for any military purpose whatever.

Note.—Non-commissioned officers and privates, as well as musicians, who shall have served faithfully for the term of five years, shall be permitted, as a mark of distinction, to wear a chevron on the sleeves of their coats, above the elbow, points up; and an additional chevron on each arm for every additional five years of faithful service. And those who served in the war, shall have the addition of a red stripe on each side of the chevron.

The above paragraph concerning service chevrons marks the beginning, for the dragoons and later cavalry, at least, of distinctive insignia signifying service in peace and war.

1839 REGULATIONS FOR DRAGOON DRESS

In 1839 a number of changes were instituted that affected the dress of officers only.

The first made more specific the spacing of the stripes on the trousers of the officer's dress trousers:

FIGURE 55. Dragoon greatcoat, worn by both officers and enlisted men from 1833 to 1851, when the pattern for officers was changed. Except for minor changes, the greatcoat remained virtually the same until 1902, when army blue gave way to khaki and olive drab.

". . . leaving a light of ¼ inch between [the stripes]. . . ."

Scabbards for officers' sabres were to be *browned*.

Third, a new *frock coat* replaced the 1833 *undress coat* (as shown in Figure 60 and Figure D on Uniform Color Plate II), with the following description in the published regulations: "FROCK COAT—dark blue cloth, cut after the fashion of that described for the artillery." The description for the artillery officers' frock coat from the same regulations follows:

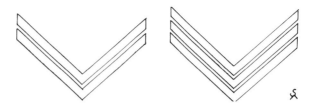

FIGURE 57. Pattern-of-1833 chevrons for noncommissioned officers of dragoons. Until 1847 only the ranks of corporal and sergeant were specified for the noncommissioned chevrons. These chevrons were used on dragoon dress coats right up to the uniform change in 1851, in spite of the points-up chevrons for five different grades that were authorized for wear on fatigue jackets in 1847. Musicians during this period wore red coats faced with yellow, and chief musicians, in addition, had collars trimmed with worsted lace after the fashion of sergeants' and officers' dress coat collars. First sergeants of companies and the noncommissioned staff were identified by their yellow worsted sashes.

FIGURE 56. Stable frock, 1833 issue. This rough white overgarment changed little, except in minor details, in more than a hundred years.

skirt, one of which at the hip, and the other at the bottom of the fold of the pocket, making four buttons behind; lining of the coat blue.

Another change from 1833 in this set of regulations is the shoulder strap authorized for dragoon officers. The strap shown on the officers in Figure 60, as well as Figure D of Uniform Color Plate II, is described:

SHOULDER STRAPS FOR DRAGOONS

Formed like the strap of the epaulette, and made of blue cloth, edged with gold lace like an epaulette; solid gilt crescent, with the number of the regiment embroidered within. The strap of the colonel to have on it a silver embroidered eagle; that of the lieutenant colonel *two* gold leaves at the points, where the crescent joins it; that of the major *two* silver leaves; that of the captain two gold bars; that of the first lieutenant one bar; that of the second lieutenant plain.

The 1839 regulations also prescribed a new white shell jacket for wear by officers of artillery, infantry, and dragoons.

Officers of regiments and posts will be provided with Shell jackets, to be worn in summer, during the extreme heat of the season, the Shell Jacket to be of the following pattern: white cotton or linen, with standing collar; cuff two and a half inches deep round the wrist, to open at the lower seam, where they will be buttoned by two small uniform buttons. A row of nine small uniform buttons down the front at equal distances; the front and rear of the jacket to come down in a peak.

. . . dark blue cloth, single breasted; with not less than eight nor more than ten (depending on the size of the officer) large regimental buttons down the front at equal distances, and two small regimental buttons at the fastening of the cuff; plain stand up collar; two large buttons at each pocket in the

FIGURE 58. Guidon and regimental standard (ca. 1837) for the Second Regiment of Dragoons. The regimental standard remained essentially unchanged until 1887, when the field was changed from dark blue to yellow. Even though regulations did not provide for regimental numbers after the Second Regiment of Dragoons was organized, existing specimens and quartermaster correspondence prove that most guidons were issued from the clothing bureau with regimental numbers from shortly after 1836. The guidon pattern was changed in 1863 to a swallowtail stars-and-stripes design.

The commanding officer will determine in orders, when the Shell Jacket is to be worn by the officers and men, according to the state of the weather. On duty the Sash will be worn with the shell Jacket.

A similar white shell jacket had been prescribed for officers in the 1836 regulations, but with 3-inch cuffs. No specific mention was made in these regulations concerning its wear by dragoon officers, although I am sure such was the intent. So it can be safely assumed, I believe, that the white summer shell jacket for officers came into general use shortly after the 1836 dress regulations were published. I have not made a drawing of this jacket, worn with the white drilling trousers prescribed by the 1833 dress regulations.

A new-pattern forage cap was introduced for officers and men of all branches in 1839. Figures 60, 61, 62, 64, and 65 show this cap, and Figures D and E of Uniform Color Plate II wear the officer and enlisted-man patterns as well.

United States Army Headgear to 1854 by Howell and Kloster contains a wealth of information, including a number of photographs of specimens in the Smithsonian collection. The above illustrations were made from sketches and photographs using these and an additional officer's cap in the West Point Museum collection as models.

This pattern of forage cap was worn by the Army until the uniform change in 1851. Some contemporary paintings and illustrations, especially of the Mexican War period, show bands of yellow cloth on the caps of dragoons. It is true that original specifications for the new caps called for colored bands, but no photographs or other documentary proof exists that would confirm the actual use of colored bands by any personnel *except* the band of the First Regiment of Dragoons, whose commanding officer had authorized *two bands* of yellow cloth around the cap, with the number of the regiment in front on a blue ground. I personally doubt that yellow bands were worn on dragoons of the line, since, as Howell and Kloster mentioned in their book, the folded cape on the enlisted man's cap would hide the band except for a narrow area directly in front of the cap.

Caps for enlisted men were made in two types, and both types are shown on the figures in the illustrations. Officer caps, on the other hand, probably were made in a number of different styles, all conforming in general to the prescribed pattern. I have seen photographs of officers with several different types, as compared to the

only authenticated existing specimen, the one at West Point.

Enlisted men's caps were equipped with a permanently attached folding neck cape. When folded it was held in place by black ribbons at each corner, which tied together at the front of the cap, and a buttonhole in the corner of the cloth just below the ribbon, which buttoned to the chin-strap button.

Officers were authorized to wear a detachable strip of black fur on their caps in winter. Exactly how this was attached is not known, although I feel sure it must have been held in place by stitches at regular intervals —stitches that could be removed easily when the weather cleared in the spring. Figure 62 shows an officer's cap with the strip of fur attached in this manner.

The following paragraphs from the 1839 Regulations for Uniform and Dress of the Army also apply to dress of the dragoons, and impart pertinent information for the period:

20. GENERAL REMARKS.

The hair to be short, or what is generally termed cropped; the whiskers not to extend below the lower tip of the ear, and a line thence with the curve of the mouth; moustaches will not be worn by officers or men on any pretence whatever.

Vests are not described, as they form no part of the military dress. When worn, however, by general or general staff officers, they may be of buff, blue, or white, to suit season and climate, with the small uniform button, and made with standing military collar; for regimental officers, the same, with the exception of the buff.

The forage cap may be worn with the frock coat and with the shell jacket; in winter, the forage cap, in cold climates, will have a temporary band of black fur, two and a half inches wide, attached to the bottom, to unite in front by a tie of black ribbon.

Regimental officers, not serving with their regiments, nor doing duty in the line, may wear cocked hats of the same description as those prescribed for the general staff officers, except that the loop will be of black silk gimp, the eagle yellow, the tassels to conform to the color of the button.

Cocked hats may be either open or formed so as to shut like the hat, which has heretofore been designated chapeau de bras.

All officers are permitted to wear a blue plain coat, with the button designating their respective corps or stations, without any other mark upon them; such a coat, however, is not to be considered as a dress for any military purpose whatever.

When not on military duty, black scabbards with gilt mountings may be worn by officers whose service scabbards are of metal.

FIGURE 59. Enlisted men, Second Regiment of U.S. Dragoons (ca. 1839). These men wear the short jacket trimmed with yellow worsted binding, and the 1833-pattern leather forage cap. They are armed with the 1836 Hall percussion breech-loading single-shot carbine and the 1833 dragoon sabre. Each is also equipped with a single-shot percussion muzzle-loading pistol, which is carried on the saddle. They wear the ankle boot prescribed for dragoons and light artillery.

FIGURE 60. The frock coat authorized for dragoon officers in 1839 for wear on most occasions, except stable duty, when full dress was not prescribed. This frock replaced the 1833 undress coat.

FIGURE 61. Pattern-of-1839 forage cap (1839–51). The officer pattern, left, is without neck cape, or havelock. The enlisted man's cap has a folding neck cape 4 inches wide. This cap was manufactured in two distinct styles, the second being the cap with the flatter, rounding visor—shown at top between the two men. The first lieutenant, left, wears the shell jacket prescribed for campaign wear in the 1839 regulations, and the new dragoon-officer shoulder strap.

23. BANDS.

A band will wear the uniform of the regiment or corps to which it belongs. The commanding officer may, at the expense of the corps, sanctioned by the council of administration, make such additions in ornaments as he may judge proper.

Color Plate I shows a sergeant and bugler of dragoons, ca. 1839, in dress uniforms and equipped for a mounted parade.

On May 23, 1836, Congress passed an act authorizing the raising of an additional regiment of dragoons. This regiment was designated the *Second Regiment of U.S. Dragoons*, and the original regiment, whose official designation had been the *Regiment of U.S. Dragoons* was redesignated the *First Regiment of U.S. Dragoons*. Uniforms and equipment were the same.

In August, 1842, Congress, always eager to cut costs in the military, ordered the Second Dragoons dismounted and reorganized as a regiment of riflemen.

General Order No. 21, dated March 8, 1843, ordered: ". . . in the meantime and until the new one can be supplied the Regiment (riflemen) will continue to wear the dress of the late Second Dragoons." But some change of heart caused the august body to order the Second remounted in March, 1844.

In May, 1846, after the outbreak of war with Mexico, Congress, in its usual fashion, hastily took steps to increase the size of the Army, and authorized the creation of a Regiment of Mounted Riflemen. The original purpose for raising this new mounted force was to send them to guard the Oregon Trail, taking the place of regular troops called to serve in Mexico. But the regiment joined Taylor's army in October.

On June 4, 1846, the Adjutant General's Office in Washington published General Order No. 18, which prescribed the dress for both "Engineer Soldiers" and the "Regiment of Mounted Riflemen." That part which pertains to mounted riflemen is as follows:

VI. The "undress" of the United States "REGIMENT OF MOUNTED RIFLEMEN" shall for the present, be the same as that for the Dragoons—except:

1st. That the BUTTONS and waist belt plate, shall bear the letter R. instead of the letter D.

2nd. The TROUSERS of dark blue cloth, with a stripe of black cloth down the outer seam, edged with yellow cord.

3rd. The FORAGE CAP to be ornamented with a gold embroidered spread eagle with the letter R. in silver on the shield.

4th. The sash to be crimson silk.

5th. Wings for coat according to pattern (to be provided). The "Undress" will be the only uniform to be required to be worn by the regiment until further orders.

The second article of the above order pertained to both officers and enlisted men of the mounted rifles. The other 4 articles were for officers only, except that first sergeants wore a sash of crimson worsted material, and all enlisted men wore the letter of their company on their forage caps, the same as dragoons. Actually, the only part of the mounted rifleman's (enlisted man's) uniform that distinguished him from a dragoon in "undress" was his dark blue trousers with the black stripe edged with yellow cord.

Color Plate II shows a private of mounted rifles in the prescribed uniform.

In February of 1847, General Order No. 7, published by the Adjutant General's Office, changed the *frock coat* for *field officers* of dragoons from a single-breasted frock to a *double-breasted* coat with two rows of seven buttons on a side. This same change was made for field officers and officers of the other corps of the Army, as well as for the general staff.

Paragraph 1292 of the 1841 regulations for dress of the Army contains an interesting and *important* ruling that affected the appearance of dragoons until the beginning of the American Civil War—as contrasted with the rest of the Army. This paragraph reads as follows:

1292. GENERAL REMARKS.
The hair to be short, or what is generally termed cropped; the whiskers not to extend below the lower tip of the ear, and a line thence with the curve of the mouth; mustaches will not be worn (*except by Cavalry regiments*) by officers or men on any pretense whatever.

The above order makes it clear that dragoons were free to wear mustaches . . . *but no other man in the Army,* from the General in Chief to the lowest private!! I can think of no logical reason for this! No-

FIGURE 62. Officer's forage cap, 1839–51, with the detachable 2½-inch strip of black fur on the headband for wear during cold weather.

where have I been able to find even a hint of why this order came into being.

The 1847 regulations for the uniform and dress of the Army announced few changes that affected the mounted regiments.

Figure 63 shows the pattern of the new chevrons that were prescribed in the regulations that incorporated all the other changes made since 1841. Why the chevrons were to be worn with points up must remain a mystery. They must have proved unpopular, for, even though they were to be worn only on undress, or field, jackets, the regulations concerning dress that came out in 1851 ordered all chevrons to be worn once more with points down.

But the new chevrons do reveal that additional non-commissioned ranks had been authorized for the Army, including, of course, the mounted corps. Prior to this time the rank of *first sergeant* had existed, but there was no distinctive chevron for this grade. A first

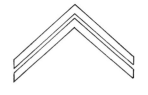 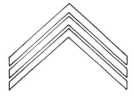 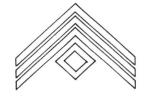 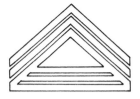 

CORPORAL	SERGEANT	FIRST SERGEANT	QUARTERMASTER SERGEANT	SERGEANT MAJOR

FIGURE 63. Pattern-of-1847 chevrons for noncommissioned officers to be worn only on field jackets. The regular 1833-pattern chevrons were worn on the dress coats, points down, as before. The above points-up pattern lasted only until the uniform change in 1851, when all chevrons for all corps were once more points down.

sergeant was recognized in full dress by a yellow worsted sash, but in the undress uniform his three stripes on each sleeve made him look no more important than any other sergeant. Now the three stripes with the lozenge set him apart from the others at a glance. But the grades of *quartermaster sergeant* and *sergeant major* were new, and their sleeve insignia with the extra bars and arcs made them recognizable instantly.

The following excerpt from the 1847 regulations affecting brevet rank was the only other deviation besides the changes already noted:

OFFICERS OF DRAGOONS, ARTILLERY, INFANTRY, &C.

Colonels of regiments or corps, having the brevet rank of Generals, may wear the uniform of their respective regiments or corps, or that of General officers according to their brevet rank, with the exception of the plume, which is to be worn only when commanding, according to their brevets. They will wear the plume of their respective corps.

All other brevet officers will wear the epaulettes distinctive of their highest rank according to their arm.

ARMS

For centuries the arm considered most essential to cavalry had been the sabre. Oddly enough, the U.S. Army, from its beginning, has rarely seen fit to emphasize the training of its mounted men enough to make them sufficiently proficient with the *arme blanche* to be deadly swordsmen in battle. Of course

there were sabre exercises in the dragoon and mounted riflemen regiments, but these were hardly on a level with the training European cavalrymen experienced. In spite of the general disenchantment with the sabre as an effective cavalry weapon, all the mounted units of the U.S. Army, from the Continental Dragoons to the modern cavalry, were armed with one type of sabre or another, until that weapon was finally discontinued as a cavalry weapon in 1934.

The Regiment of U.S. Dragoons was armed with a new sabre in 1833 and 1834. Designated the Model 1833 dragoon sabre, it was manufactured principally by N. P. Ames in Springfield, Massachusetts, but other firms made quantities of this weapon, as well, including W. L. & M. Sargent.

The 1833 dragoon sabre was patterned after the British Model 1822 light cavalry sabre, according to the display caption on a specimen exhibited at the Smithsonian Institution in 1967. The sabre on display there was one made by W. L. & M. Sargent.

Several variations of this sabre were made. The enlisted man's model was fairly standard, with few variations, but a number of different officers' models can be seen in the study collection at West Point. The guards on most officers' sabres are gilt, in contrast to the plain brass guards on the issue specimens. One officer's sabre at West Point has a brass scabbard; another has brass bands, sling rings, and drag; another has a regulation *browned* all steel scabbard. Some have fishskin grips, others, twisted-brass-wire-wrapped leather grips.

120

FIGURE 64. First sergeant and first lieutenant, the Regiment of Mounted Riflemen (ca. 1846) in the undress uniform prescribed for them until the uniform change in 1851. Only their dark blue trousers with black stripes edged in yellow cord distinguished them from dragoons in the dragoon undress uniform.

Figure 67 shows the standard pattern of the 1833 dragoon sabre fitted with the white buff-leather sabre knot that was used by officers and enlisted men in the field. Figures 51, 53, 55, and 66, as well as Color Plate I, show enlisted men with this sabre and sabre knot.

The dress sabre knot for officers was prescribed as "gold cord, with acorn end." This dress knot is shown in Figures 44, 60, and 66. The white buff sabre knot commonly used in the field by both officers and enlisted men is shown on officers' sabres in Figure 47.

FIGURE 65. Officer and enlisted man, the Regiment of Mounted Riflemen (ca. 1850), showing the cap insignia authorized for them that year. The officer's trumpet is embroidered in gold on a dark blue background; the enlisted man's insignia is stamped from sheet brass, and was evidently discontinued the following year, for there is no mention of it in the 1851 uniform regulations.

The original description for the sabre issued to dragoons did not specify the finish of the steel scabbards, but the 1834 Ordnance Department regulations described it as a *browned* scabbard, as did all subsequent regulations for dragoon dress—until it was replaced by the new heavy cavalry sabre in 1840.

On page 38 of *Army Life on the Western Frontier: Selections from the Official Reports Made Between 1826 and 1845 by Colonel George Groghan,* edited by Francis Paul Prucha (Norman, University of Oklahoma Press, 1958) Groghan, inspector general of the Army in reporting on the dragoons stationed at Fort Leavenworth in August, 1838, wrote:

> . . . the swords are bad, in truth the blades of many of them are entirely unserviceable, being so soft that it may be questioned whether or not the skull of an Indian might not prove too hard for them. . . . aside from the blade of the present sword, the scabbard is too thin and easily indented.

Based on this and general criticism of the 1833 dragoon sabre by officers of the Army, the War Department selected the French light cavalry model of 1822

(*The American Sword, 1775-1945,* by Harold Peterson; New Hope, Pennsylvania, 1945), and from Colonel Groghan's comments on his inspection of dragoons at Fort Leavenworth in July, 1840, it is apparent that the Ordnance Department imported a quantity of this model from France before authorizing manufacture of a copy in the United States. Groghan's report concerning these sabres is as follows:

> Swords. In some of my former reports I have spoken of the swords furnished by Ames as being of little account. There are, however, in the hands of some, perhaps a majority of the men French swords that are in every respect of the first order. They are of the number of 300 sent out by the Chief of Ordnance Department to Colonel Kearny some short time since. I wish most sincerely that they may be substituted for our own manufacture throughout.

Apparently sword makers in the United States were unable to supply an appreciable quantity of the new-pattern sabres at an early enough date, for the Ordnance Department issued a contract to Schnitzer & Kirschbauer, sword makers in Slingen, Prussia, on

FIGURE 66. Dragoon corporal, left (ca. 1847), in full dress uniform with the new but short-lived points-up chevrons on his sleeves. The major, First U.S. Dragoons, center, wears the double-breasted frock coat authorized in the 1847 regulations for field-grade officers, which permitted them for the first time to wear the cocked hat, or chapeau, instead of the usual full-dress cap, on occasions of ceremony. The colonel, right, wears this headgear.

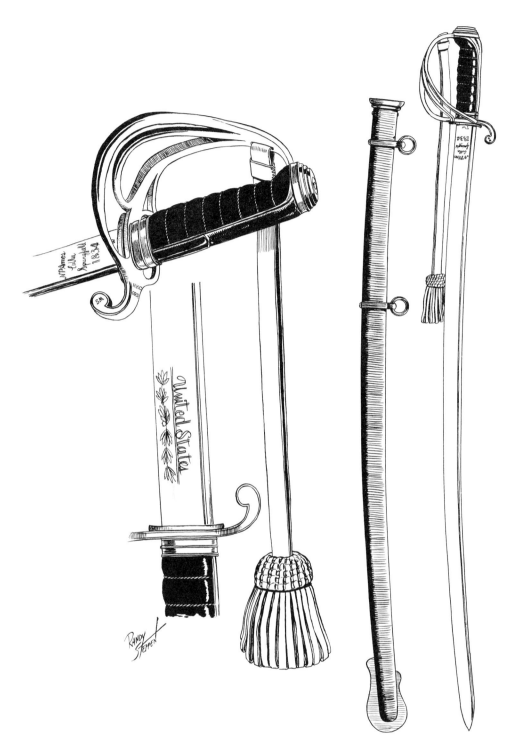

FIGURE 67. The 1833 dragoon sabre made principally by N. P. Ames, Springfield, Massachusetts. The sabre shown here is the enlisted man's model. The officer's sabre is identical in pattern, but with a gilt hilt. Some officers' sabres were furnished with brass scabbards (such a specimen is in the West Point Museum collection), but most had browned-iron scabbards, the same as those for enlisted men. This sabre was patterned after the 1822 British Light Cavalry sabre (N. P. Ames correspondence). The date on the blade indicates the year of manufacture. The blade is slightly more than 1 inch wide and slightly longer than 34 inches. The sabre knot is lightweight white buff leather ⅝ inch wide and 18 inches long over-all. Officers' grips are fishskin instead of leather. Drawn from specimens in the author's collection.

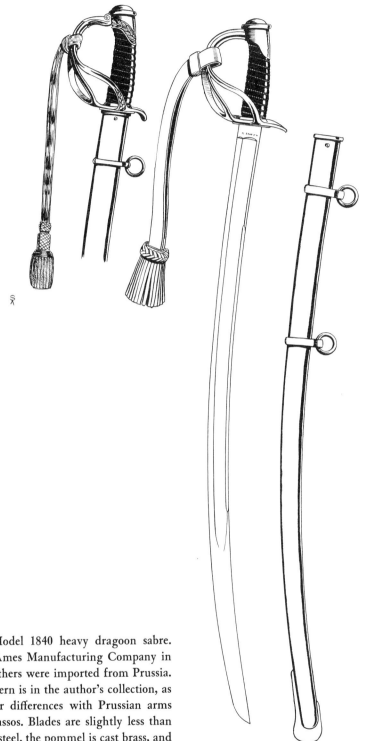

FIGURE 68. The U.S. Model 1840 heavy dragoon sabre. Many were made by the Ames Manufacturing Company in Massachusetts, but many others were imported from Prussia. An Ames sabre of this pattern is in the author's collection, as well as 2 with very minor differences with Prussian arms makers' stamps on the ricassos. Blades are slightly less than 36 inches long, of polished steel, the pommel is cast brass, and the grips are wood covered with leather and wound with twisted brass wire. The blades are about 1¼ inches wide at the hilt. This sabre is commonly known as "old wristbreaker" in the mounted service, and was patterned after the French light cavalry model of 1822. The enlisted man's sabre knot is heavyweight white buff leather 1 inch wide and 18 inches long. At left is the officer's model of the 1840 sabre. The blade is ornately etched on both sides with scrolls, figures, trophies, and the letters "U.S." The grips are like those of the service sabre, but the hilt is made of gilded brass. The Model 1851 knot is gilt lace and is the only one prescribed for officers in the regulations, although contemporary photographs show officers in the field with the wide leather service knots. Scabbards for officers and enlisted men are polished iron. Drawn from specimens in the author's collection.

August 28, 1840, for 2,000 of the French-type sabres. The cost to the Army was 3 *thalers* and 25 silver *groschens* each. ("Prussian Sabers for First Dragoons," by R. T. Huntington, in Vol. I, No. 4 of *The Guidon*, Journal of The Cavalry Collectors Association.)

At least one other Prussian firm was awarded a contract for this model sabre, for I have one in my collection marked "W. Clauberg, Solingen."

Just when Ames made the first delivery to the Ordnance Department is not known to me, but by 1842 it would seem, from the absence of further criticism from Colonel Groghan, that all mounted units were armed with the new heavy "old wristbreakers," as the dragoons called them.

Figure 68 shows both the officer's model, left, and the issue pattern for enlisted men. The sabre knot on the officer's sabre is the 1851 pattern. But the standard knot prescribed for officers from 1840 until the uniform change in 1851 was the one made of gold cord with the acorn end, as shown on the illustrations of earlier dragoon officers armed with the 1833 sabre.

The white buff sabre knot shown on the enlisted man's sabre at the right is the type used with "old wristbreaker" until about 1855, although some black harness-leather sabre knots may have been issued before then, since the leather accoutrements for officers and men were changed from white to black in the 1851 regulations. From the beginnings of the U.S. Army, it has been the standard policy to use old uniforms and equipment until the supply was exhausted, and such probably was the case with the old white buff sabre knots. Contemporary photographs and drawings certainly confirm this point.

According to theory, at any rate, sabres were the primary weapons for dragoons, and pistols were next in importance in mounted action, at least. Figure 69 shows the pistols with which the dragoons were armed during their early years. The flintlock system of ignition was not replaced by the percussion lock until about 1845 on dragoon pistols, in spite of the fact that the dragoons were armed the first year with the very first percussion firearm to be adopted by the U.S. Army—the Hall breech-loading carbine.

Single-shot pistols were used by dragoons until late in the Mexican War, when a few *may* have gotten their hands on Colt revolvers. It is a fact, though, that at least *part* of the Regiment of Mounted Riflemen received Colt Walker revolvers late in 1847.

An interesting fact concerning dragoon pistols is found in Hicks's *Notes on United States Ordnance*. From early correspondence Major Hicks uncovered the following information concerning pistol contracts by Ordnance with Robert Johnson and Asa Waters, both makers of the 1836 pistols with which the dragoons were armed:

Robert Johnson	June 27, 1836	contract for	3,000 @	$9.00
Asa Waters	Sept. 22, 1836	"	" 4,000 @	9.00
Asa Waters	Feb. 7, 1840	"	" 15,000 @	7.50
Robert Johnson	March 14, 1840	"	" 15,000 @	7.50

Of course, the quantities shown were for arming the officers and enlisted men of all corps authorized to be armed with pistols, not just dragoons and mounted riflemen.

Apparently several other types of pistols had been issued to dragoon companies, for Colonel Groghan's report on Fort Leavenworth dated July, 1840, stated, ". . . pistols are of three different patterns—only one with ram rod on swivel is worth anything." Undoubtedly he was referring to either of the two patterns shown in Figure 69, for both the Model 1819 and the Model 1836 pistols were fitted with such ramrods.

Figure 70 shows the first percussion pistol to be issued in any quantity to regular mounted troops in the U.S. Army. Although designated by the Ordnance Department as the Model 1842 percussion pistol, actual manufacture was not started until 1845, when a contract was awarded to Henry Aston on February 25 for 30,000 pistols at a cost of $6.50 each. This pistol was identical to the Model 1836 flintlock pistol except that the side plate had less swell and all the furniture was brass instead of iron.

The story of Sam Walker and his negotiations with Sam Colt that resulted in delivery of the first 1,000 revolving firearms to the Army, then involved in the war with Mexico, can be found in many places, and I will not repeat it here. Let it suffice to relate that at least some companies of the Regiment of Mounted Riflemen, including Sam Walker, received a number of Whitneyville-Walker revolving pistols late in 1847. The story goes that Walker himself was killed in the first fight he participated in after receiving his presentation pistols from Colt.

Be that as it may, the Whitneyville-Walker Colt was designated as the U.S. Repeating Pistol and was manufactured by the Eli Whitney Company at Whitneyville by assignment from Samuel Colt.

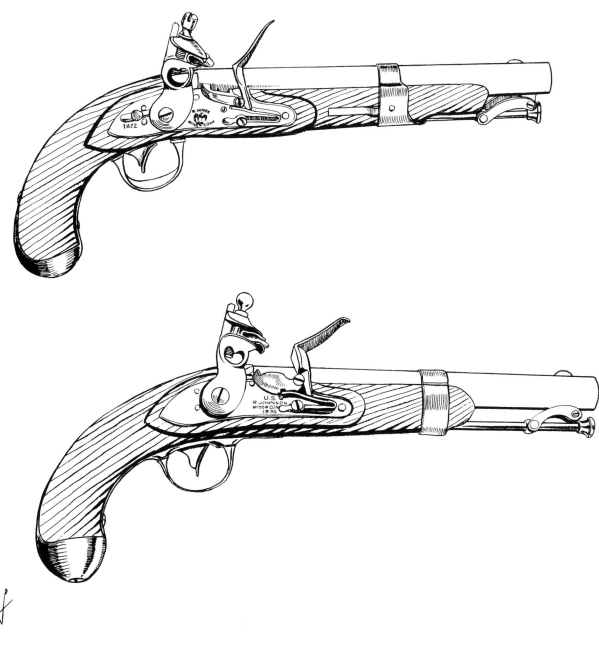

FIGURE 69. Flintlock pistols issued to the Regiment of Dragoons, 1833–45, and carried in saddle holsters. Top: S. North Model 1819 army flintlock pistol, caliber .54, with a 10-inch round, smoothbore, browned barrel with brass sight on muzzle end. Mounts are iron, and the pan is brass. The swivel ramrod prevents the dragoon from dropping the ramrod when reloading on horseback. Bottom: The Johnson Model 1836 army flintlock pistol, caliber .54, with an 8.5-inch round, smoothbore, bright barrel; brass front sight and pan; and polished iron mountings. The ramrod has a swivel mount, usual for dragoons. Drawn from specimens in the West Point Museum collection.

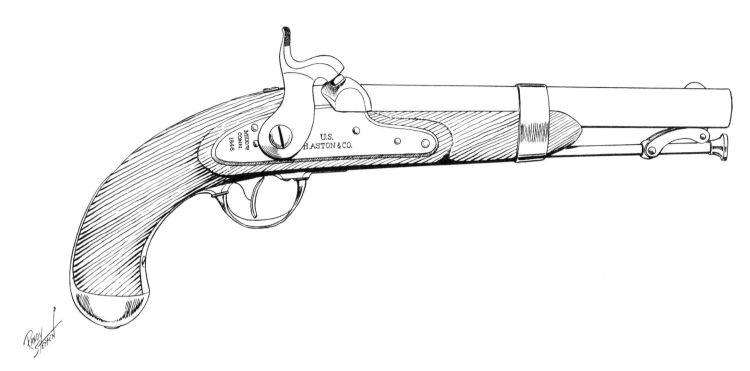

FIGURE 70. The U.S. Model 1842 smoothbore single-shot percussion pistol, caliber .54, issued to some dragoon companies. The barrel, ramrod, and brass mountings were finished bright. Manufacture of these pistols by Henry Aston of Middletown, Connecticut, was not started until 1845, and issue was made to some dragoon companies the same year, and to several companies of the Regiment of Mounted Riflemen after they were recruited the next year. Drawn from a specimen in the West Point Museum collection.

In February, 1849, the War Department finally got around to issuing a general order directing that all infantry arms with flintlocks (thousands had been used by regular foot troops in the war with Mexico) be converted to the percussion system. Until 1845 all dragoons had been equipped with flintlock pistols, but the cavalry tactics manual had never been revised to instruct the recruit in handling and loading the new percussion pistols with which they were now mainly armed. As noted before, many were armed with the new Colt's revolving pistol by this time, but apparently these were in the minority.

In November a circular was issued by the Adjutant General's Office with a standard procedure for loading percussion pistols—the Model 1842 single shot, and this circular is reproduced here as a matter of interest:

War Department
Adjutant General's Office
Washington, Nov. 17, 1849.

The following substitute for the present method of loading the pistol is adopted and published for the information and guidance of the army.

Cavalry Tactics—paragraph 389—the instructor commands: Load in 6 times.

    1. *Load*
        1 *time.*

At this command, place the pistol in the left hand, which seizes it below the band, the lock to the front, the barrel slightly inclined to the right; carry the right hand to the cartridge box, and open it.

    2. *Handle—Cartridge.*
        1 *time 2 motions.*

1. At the command of execution, take a cartridge between the thumb and two first fingers, then place the end of it between the teeth.
2. Bite off the end of the cartridge, and insert it in the muzzle of the pistol;—forcing the ball with the thumb;—seize the butt of the ramrod.

    3. *Draw—Ramrod.*
        1 *time.*

At the command of execution, draw the ramrod, turning the swivel—place the small end of it upon the ball.

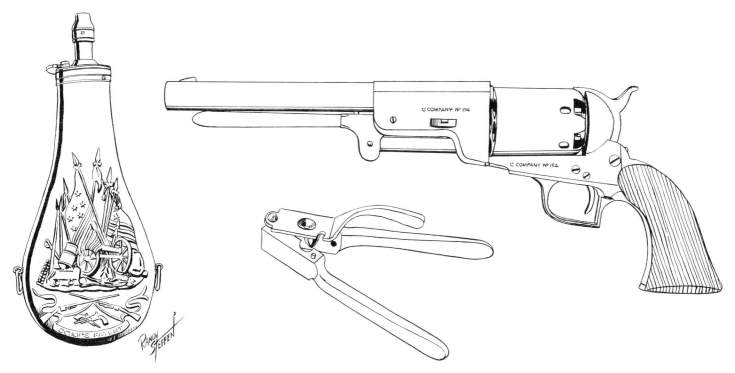

FIGURE 71. The Whitneyville-Walker Colt revolver that armed at least part of the Regiment of Mounted Riflemen in late 1847. The largest of any Colt revolver produced, the "Walker" weighs over 4½ pounds and has a 9-inch barrel that shoots a .44-caliber conical or round bullet. The Walker shown here is accompanied by the issue powder flask and bullet mold (slightly larger than scale). At first one flask was issued with each pair of revolvers, and one bullet mold with each 10 revolvers (one gang mold with each 50 pistols). But with the second 1,000 delivered to the Army, the orders specified one flask to each pistol. This weapon replaced the Model 1836 single-shot flintlock pistol where it was issued, but a number of years were to pass before all dragoons and mounted riflemen were armed with Colt's revolvers instead of the older "horse pistols." Drawn from specimens in the West Point Museum collection. Data on issue from Serven and Belden & Haven.

4. *Ram—Cartridge.*
    1 *time, 2 motions.*
1. At the command of execution, force the cartridge to the bottom and ram twice.
2. Draw out the ramrod, turn the swivel, return the ramrod, leaving the hand on the butt of it.
    5. *Prime.*
    1 *time, 2 motions.*
1. At the command, lower the muzzle of the pistol, directing over the horse's head on the left; half cock with the thumb, the fingers under the small stock, remove the exploded cap, and carry the hand to the cap box.
2. Place a cap upon the nipple, press it down with the thumb, and seize the pistol at the small stock.
    6. *Raise—Pistol.*
    1 *time.*
At the command of execution, raise the pistol with the right hand to a vertical position, the guard to the front, and wrist at the height of, and six inches in front of the right shoulder.

By Order:
R. Jones, Adjt. Genl.

The big Walker Colt revolver shown in Figure 71 was the first of four large-frame revolvers issued to various mounted units. Figure 72 shows the other three that were manufactured and issued as late as 1860 to some companies of dragoons and mounted riflemen, as well as the two new cavalry regiments authorized in 1855.

While the Third Model Hartford Dragoon revolver at the bottom of this illustration was not issued during the period covered by this chapter, I show it here so a comparison of details can be made with the other two Hartford-made pistols.

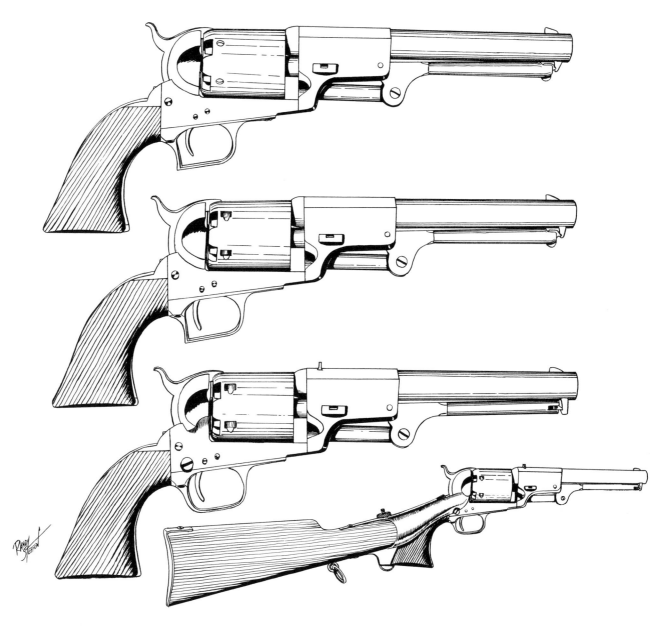

FIGURE 72. Colt's Hartford Dragoon Pistols issued to United States mounted troops, 1848–60. Top: First Model Hartford Dragoon Pistol, manufactured from 1848 to 1850. This weapon is a refinement of the previous big Walker model. Like all the Hartford Dragoon models, it is .44-caliber and has a 7½-inch barrel. This model weighs 7 ounces less than the Walker. It is distinguished from subsequent Colt Dragoon models by its oval cylinder stops. Drawn from a specimen in the West Point Museum collection.

Center: Second Model Hartford Dragoon Pistol, manufactured from 1850 to 1851. Its distinguishing external features are the new rectangular cylinder stops resulting from the mechanical improvements of the locking bolt and frame orifice, which has been changed to a rectangular shape. Other internal improvements of this model make it more reliable in the field. The Second Dragoon model still retains the square-back trigger guard. Drawn from a specimen in the author's collection.

Bottom: Third Model Hartford Dragoon Pistol, manufactured from 1851 to 1860, when production of the 1860 new-model Army belt revolver made all dragoon revolvers obsolete. Its most obvious feature that makes it stand apart from the other two Dragoon models is, of course, the round-back trigger guard. After 1855 some of this third model were made with provisions for attaching a shoulder stock (as shown here with rear sight), and a few were equipped with folding adjustable rear sights. In 1857 or 1858, Colt's pistol-carbines with detachable stocks were issued to 5 companies of the Second Dragoons on requisition of Brevet Colonel May (Report of Chief of Ordnance, July 17, 1858). Drawn from a specimen in the West Point Museum collection.

The Model 1833 Hall carbine was designed specifically for arming the Regiment of U.S. Dragoons. The recognized secondary sources of information regarding this arm are Major Hicks's *Notes on United States Ordnance* and Colonel Arcadi Gluckman's *United States Muskets, Rifles and Carbines* (Buffalo, Otto Ulbrich Co., 1948). Both have much contradictory information concerning calibers of the various models with which the mounted arm was armed from 1833 to the adoption of the U.S. Model 1847 cavalry musketoon, and this writer makes no bones about being uncertain of actual calibers.

A third writer, and a most conscientious researcher, is Lieutenant Colonel R. T. Huntington, who has written a book on the Hall carbines, *Hall's Breechloaders*; George Shumway, publisher; York, Pa. 1972. Colonel Huntington has been of immeasurable help in supplying completely documented information on very early dragoon equipments, his specialty, and I have quoted him a number of times in the earlier parts of this chapter. The following is an excerpt from his article, "Dragoon Accouterments and Equipments, 1834–1849: An Identification Guide, from the November, 1967, *Plains Anthropologist*:

HALL BREECHLOADING RIFLES AND CARBINES, AND THEIR ACCESSORIES

Although the Hall carbine was developed specifically for arming the two dragoon regiments, there is some mention of the use of Hall rifles as well. For this reason it appears appropriate to include the rifles in a brief discussion of Hall arms.

Characteristic of all Hall breechloaders is the movable receiver, which is pivoted at its rear and is elevated for loading. The receiver is in effect a short-barreled muzzle-loading pistol (Fig. 7b). It is charged by inserting the powder from either a flask or a paper cartridge, and placing a round ball above the powder, pushing it into place with the thumb. The receiver is then pushed down, and locked into alinement with the barrel. After priming, the piece is ready to fire.

The Model 1819 rifle, made both by John H. Hall at Harpers Ferry and by Simeon North at Middletown, Connecticut, was made with flintlock, although many specimens were later altered to percussion. The .52 caliber barrel, rifled with 16 lands, is 32.75 inches long. A very similar percussion model was made at Harpers Ferry in 1841–1842.

The first Hall carbine, and the first United States percussion arm, is the Model 1833 carbine made by Simeon North. It can be recognized by its 26-inch barrel and its rod-bayonet. The first thousand-odd carbines were made in caliber .579, but from 1836 through 1839 this model was made in caliber .52 smoothbore.

In 1836 Hall, at Harpers Ferry, brought out a somewhat heavier carbine that was made up with rifle components. Also a percussion arm, it had the rifle's offset sights that have misled many into considering the arm a conversion from an originally flintlock carbine. Barrel length is 23 inches, with a rod-bayonet.

Beginning in 1840, Simeon North delivered Model 1840 carbines which are characterized by an improved opening device (either an elbow lever or fishtail lever), and a 21-inch barrel with a conventional rod, which was used for cleaning the bore. In 1843 North brought out the most common of the Hall models, the Model 1843 side-lever carbine, still with the 21-inch barrel and rod.

To complete the tally, there is a Model 1842 carbine made at Harpers Ferry which can be recognized by its brass fittings: butt plate, trigger guard, and barrel bands. It had a fishtail opening lever similar to North's Model 1840 fishtail-lever arm.

All carbines were delivered to the government as smoothbore arms; later, during the Civil War, many carbines of all models were rifled.

One change that was introduced in early 1842 production may be helpful in dating finds. This was the provision of a bar and sliding ring on the left side of the receiver, for use with the wide post-1840 carbine sling, instead of the ring on the underside of the butt or (for the Model 1836) the ring-bolt through the small of the stock.

All government-issue Hall breechloaders carry the name of the manufacturer and the date on the receiver. Unfortunately, receivers can be interchanged between arms of all models but the Model 1842 and 1843, so that care must be taken to see that the other features are consistent with the date and maker on the receiver. Rifle receivers have at times been placed in carbines to make a "flintlock" carbine; but usually the deception is not difficult to detect.

A wiper and combination tool were issued with each Hall carbine, in fact, the Model 1833 and 1836 carbines had a recessed implement box in the butt of the piece to accept them. Both carbines used a five-inch wiper, but the combination nipple wrench—screw-driver—pricker differed in design. Some bullet-moulds and spring-vises were also issued with both rifles and carbines. We have no clear idea of the appearance of the Hall mainspring vise; it may have been a simple C-clamp.

The Hall rifle mould, of conventional scissors-type, casting one round ball, is usually stamped HALL'S RIFLE; the Hall carbine mould cast one round ball and three buckshot (to make a buck and ball cartridge) and such moulds should be readily recognizable. The writer knows of just one mould of this type.

The illustrations of the Hall carbines in this chapter have rather comprehensive captions which contain information concerning the calibers of the various models as best I have been able to interpret them from the information available to me. The reader who wants more certainty regarding this detail should avail himself of the pertinent Ordnance Department correspondence, which probably can be found in the masses of such records in the National Archives.

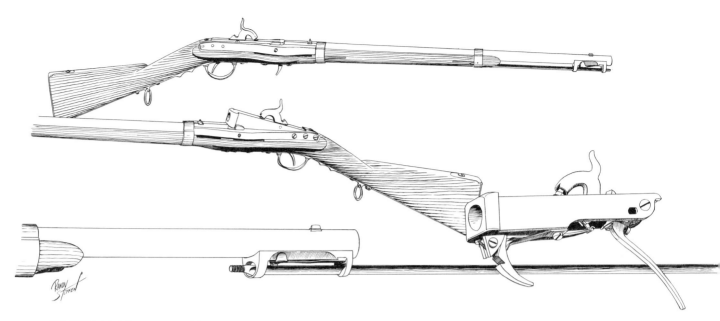

FIGURE 73. The U.S. Model 1833 Hall carbine made by S. North in Middletown, Connecticut. This is the first breech-loader to be used in the United States mounted service, and it is bored smooth for the .58-caliber ball. The barrel is 26⅛ inches in length, and all metal parts are browned with a lacquer finish for protection. Made specifically to arm the Regiment of Dragoons authorized in 1833, it was fitted with a sliding bayonet. As with all subsequent models of the Hall carbine, the lock could be removed from the piece by unscrewing a single screw that acted as a pivot—so the dragoon could carry it concealed on his person and use it as an effective handgun if it became necessary to protect himself in the wild frontier cantinas off the post. This practice was strictly against regulations, but it was done, as told by Sam Chamberlain in his "My Life." Drawn from a specimen in the West Point Museum collection.

The Model 1833 Hall carbine, shown with details of its construction and design in Figure 73, was the first percussion firearm in the United States service, and was the first arm to be made with a ramrod bayonet. Major Hicks's work tells that the first 1,026 made in 1834 were caliber-.69 smoothbores; Colonel Huntington claims the first order for the dragoon service were made in caliber .579, but from 1836 through 1839 they were made in .52-caliber smoothbore. Both men are recognized experts on U.S. ordnance, and yet their published findings reveal two distinctly different claims.

The Ordnance Regulations published May 1, 1834, describe the musket caliber as taking a ball weighing 1/18 of a pound, and the caliber for Hall's carbine to accommodate a ball weighing 1/32 of a pound. The former is .69-caliber, and the latter .54-caliber.

Personally, I believe the 1833 model was delivered in .58-caliber, and that the Model 1836 was made in the larger .69-caliber for arming at least some companies of the Second Dragoons for their use in Florida against the Seminoles. A letter from Colonel George Bomford, Ordnance, to Captain Bradford at the New York Ordnance Depot on August 11, 1836, confirms this statement:

. . . It having been decided to arm the 2nd Reg't of Dragoons with carbines carrying a ball weighing 1/18th of a pound (.69 cal.) you will cause the tin tubes of 1000 of the 2500 carbine cartridge boxes to be made large enough to receive a musket cartridge, the remaining 1500 being made agreeably to the present pattern.

The sling swivel on the Model 1833 Hall carbine was an iron ring held by a boss at the forward end of the hinged cover of the recessed implement box in the butt stock. It is surmised, as mentioned earlier in this chapter, that the carbine slings before 1839 were narrow, like the rifle slings, only 1¼ inches wide, and fitted with some sort of simple swivel for attaching the sling to the carbine. No identified specimens of this early sling exist to prove or disprove this theory.

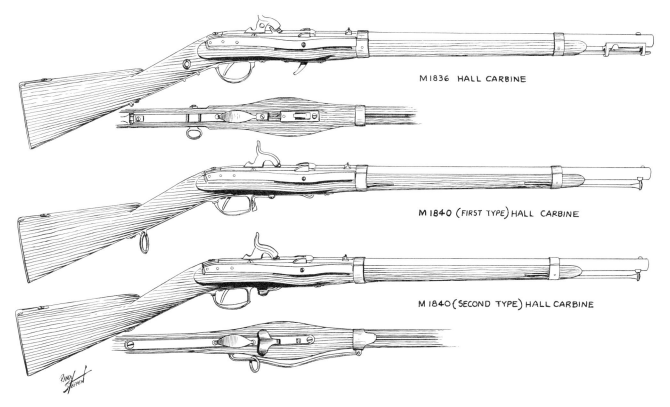

M 1836 HALL CARBINE

M 1840 (FIRST TYPE) HALL CARBINE

M 1840 (SECOND TYPE) HALL CARBINE

FIGURE 74. Top: The Model 1836 Hall carbine, a variation of the 1833 Hall carbine, with a shorter 21-inch barrel bored smooth for the .64-caliber ball. It was ordered by the Ordnance Department for arming the newly authorized Second Regiment of Dragoons. The bottom view shows the sling swivel ring used on this model. Drawn from a specimen in the O. C. Peterson collection, Fort Pierce, Florida.

Center: The U.S. Model 1840 Hall carbine, the first of which were made with a new L-shaped operating lever because the older spur-type lever seemed to present a hazard to the dragoon's person. Made with a 21-inch barrel in .54-caliber smoothbore and with a ramrod in place of the sliding bayonet, only 500 were delivered before the L-shaped lever was declared

unsatisfactory. Drawn from a specimen in the West Point Museum collection.

Bottom: The U.S. Model 1840 Hall carbine, second type, with the fishtail operating lever that superseded the first type (center). Six thousand were delivered before another change in 1843 made this arm obsolescent. The second-type Model 1840 was made in .54-caliber, but was rifled to use the elongated bullet. Drawn from a specimen in the West Point Museum collection.

There was also a Model 1842—the Model 1840, second type, with all brass mountings. These were manufactured at Harpers Ferry during 1842 and 1843. See bottom view.

Figure 74 shows three subsequent models of the Hall carbine issued to dragoons. The larger-bore Model 1836 carbine, made in .69-caliber for issue to the Second Regiment of Dragoons, at the top of the illustration, has a forged eyebolt through the small of the stock for attaching the sling swivel and sling. This was the last model made with the ramrod bayonet. Like the 1833 carbine, the Model 1836 has a recessed implement box in the butt stock. Both the 1833 and 1836 carbines had breeches that opened by pushing

forward a projecting steel triggerlike lever forward of the trigger guard. This projection caused a number of injuries to dragoons and was replaced on the revised 1840 carbine by an entirely different mechanism.

The third production Hall carbine was designated the Model of 1840, of which there are two distinct types. The first, shown as the second carbine from the top of Figure 74, incorporated an L-shaped lever to open the breech. But after 500 were made this system of breech operation was declared unsatisfactory and

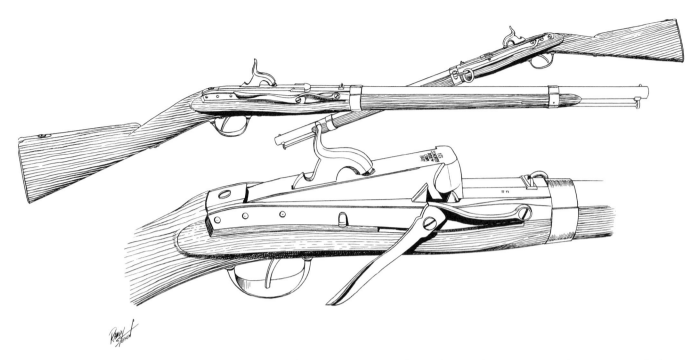

FIGURE 75. The U.S. Model 1843 Hall breech-loading carbine. This was the last production model of this dragoon arm, and it featured an improved side-lever method of breech operation patented by Savage and North. The lock itself has major changes over previous models; otherwise, this carbine is similar in operation and general appearance to previous Models 1838 and 1840. Pulling down on the side-lever release on the right side of the receiver frame raises front of the hinged receiver for loading with a paper cartridge. It was made in .54-caliber smoothbore, with a 21-inch browned barrel. The furniture is browned, and the breech block, hammer, release plate, release lever, and trigger are case-hardened in mottled blue-gray colors, as are these same parts on all previous Hall carbines. The trigger pull is adjustable on this model by a screw through the sear. Drawn from a specimen in the West Point Museum collection.

the familiar fishtail lever immediately forward of the trigger guard replaced it. This carbine was known as the second type of the Model 1840 Hall carbine. This model was made to shoot the elongated ball and was rifled, according to most sources.

A brass-mounted model, commonly called the Model 1842 Hall carbine, was made at the Harpers Ferry Arsenal during 1842 and 1843. This was the first of this arm to be made with a rod and sliding ring on the left side of the stock for attaching the sling swivel. One thousand of this model were delivered to the Ordnance Department for issue to the dragoon regiments.

The last Hall carbine to be manufactured was the Model 1843 with the so-called North's Improvement incorporated in its design (see caption for Figure 75). These were manufactured and issued until about 1850 (Gluckman).

Primer boxes, probably of brass, were issued with most Hall carbines. As stated before, my conjecture is they were of the round-shaped type, commonly known as cap-feeders, that would fit conveniently into the small pockets on the front of the dragoon jackets.

Colonel Stephen Watts Kearny, commanding officer of the First Regiment of U.S. Dragoons, expressed his concern over the lack of a definitive method of handling the carbine in his recently organized dragoon regiment by compiling a manual for the carbine, a photocopy of which is in the author's collection (from the original in the Library of Congress). In it he set forth detailed rules for exercise with the carbine on foot and on horseback, as well as maneuvers when fighting dismounted. Date of publication was January 4, 1837.

One section of this manual describes dismounting and mounting with the carbine, and since this same procedure was followed almost as long as the carbine sling and swivel were a part of the mounted man's accoutrements, I shall quote it here:

To dismount with carbine slung

92. At the command "prepare to dismount," the carbine will be passed behind the back to the near (left) side, hanging by the swivel, muzzle downwards.

To mount with carbine

93. At the command "prepare to mount," the carbine will be unswiveled and seized with the right hand at the lower band, and carried to the off side of the saddle; after mounting, the carbine will be placed in the left hand, swiveled, and then brought to the "advance."

Other carbines than Hall's were tried out for dragoon use. Ganoe (*History of the United States Army*) tells on page 185 of an Ordnance Department trial of the Jenks rifle. Even though they considered the Jenks rifle unsuitable for use by infantry, it was thought that a similar carbine might be practicable for dragoons. The board that rendered a negative decision felt convinced, as did most military men in that time, that breech loading produced no advantage and was slower, especially because of the fouling of the piece. They thought that since the muzzle-loader had to be rammed each time before firing, the bore would be kept cleaner than in the case of a breechloader.

But Samuel Colt took the bull by the horns and went to Florida himself. In some manner he arranged for a board of officers to be convened for the express purpose of examining his *revolving* carbine. In *Journey into Wilderness*, by Jacob Rhett Motte (Gainesville, University of Florida Press, 1953), the journal of a surgeon serving at times with the Second Dragoons in 1838, Dr. Motte tells of Colt's visit to Fort Jupiter in March, 1838. The special board reported

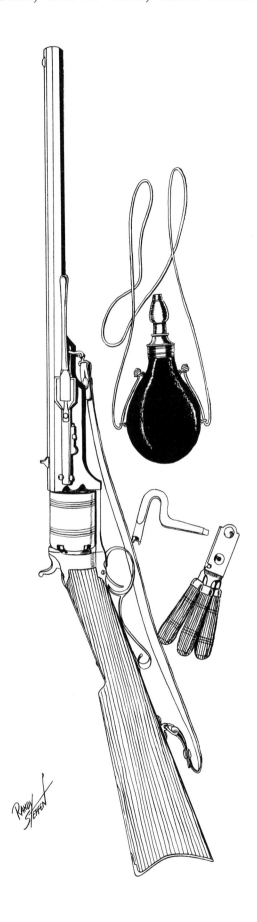

FIGURE 76. A Paterson Colt revolving carbine of the type used by 100 of Lieutenant Colonel Harney's troopers of the Second Regiment of Dragoons in Florida, 1838 and 1839, during the Seminole War. These arms were issued when Harney submitted a request for a test to a board of officers in 1838. Shown here with the carbine are the accessories issued with it—powder flask, combination tool, and bullet mold. This carbine shoots a caliber-.525 bullet from its smoothbore 24-inch barrel, and its cylinder holds six shots.

favorably on the revolving carbine, and 50 of the arms were purchased immediately and issued to 50 picked dragoons, who turned in their Hall's carbines for the new arm.

The board of officers appointed to test the Colt carbine consisted of Colonel Twiggs; Lieutenant Colonel Gates; Major Lomax; Captains Washington, Fulton, and Beall; and Lieutenant Tomkins.

Special Order No. 71, March 3, 1838, in the order book of General Thomas S. Jesup for 1838 (manuscript in the P. K. Yonge Library of Florida History, University of Florida), reads:

> Among other points the Board will examine particularly the structure of the arm, and whether its cylinder, in revolving, is invariably adjusted with perfect accuracy to the barrel by the process of cocking; and whether it is not liable to be frequently out of firing order by the loss of screws, wedges, and other essential parts of its works. The process of loading will be examined to ascertain whether the mode of the invention insures invariably the proper charge. The arm will be fired at various distances from 50 to 300 yards, to ascertain the accuracy as well as the force of its fire.

Theodore F. Rodenbough, in his history of the Second Dragoons, *Everglade to Canõn with the Second Dragoons* (New York, D. Van Nostrand, 1875), tells of having seen dragoons on two different occasions armed with "Colt's patent rifles." This very early Colt revolving firearm is shown in Figure 76, along with the combination screwdriver-nipple wrench, bullet mold, and powder flask that most likely are the types issued to the dragoons selected to be armed with the new weapon. Whether any further quantity ever reached the dragoons is not a matter of record.

In 1847 the Ordnance Board recommended the adoption of the Springfield cavalry musketoon for the mounted service, and this arm was officially designated the U.S. Model 1847 cavalry musketoon. It probably was not issued in more than very limited quantities before late 1851. Two versions of the 1847 musketoon are shown in Figure 77.

So far we have seen what arms were provided for the regiments of U.S. Dragoons. Now, to cover the subject of weapons in the hands of mounted troops included in the time period covered by this chapter, we must examine the arms issued to the Regiment of Mounted Riflemen, organized at the beginning of the war with Mexico.

McBarron, in text describing his Plate No. 18 in the *Military Uniforms in America* series published by The

Company of Military Collectors and Historians in 1950, quotes from documented sources that the regiment was equipped with muzzle-loading percussion rifles designated as U.S. Rifle, Model of 1841, commonly known as the *Mississippi Rifle*. This shorter-than-usual rifle, well known to all collectors, was slung across the mounted rifleman's back.

In addition, he carried a flintlock muzzle-loading pistol, most likely the Model 1836 (see Figure 69), and a sabre, which by this time was the Model 1840 heavy dragoon sabre—"old wristbreaker," shown in Figure 68. Figure 78 shows a mounted rifleman, mounted, with complete arms and equipments for service in the field.

ACCOUTREMENTS

According to current dictionaries, the word "accoutrement" has no plural, and relates to all the equipage of a soldier, not including arms and clothing. The modern spelling is *accout-er-ment*, but, as with many terms used in this book, I have used the spelling that was current with the period being described.

Army regulations of the nineteenth century, and correspondence of the various bureaus of the War Department, indicate the regular usage of the plural, correct or not, and I shall use it the same way throughout the eras covered by various chapters until the usage changes.

Normally, officers wore only the sabre belt, whether in dress uniform on parade or in field uniform on campaign. Figures 44 and 47 show the black patent-leather sabre belt called for in the regulations. The belt plate has already been described and illustrated in detail in the text accompanying the first illustration in this chapter. The belt is 1½ inches wide. Slings, according to early remaining specimens, were ¾ inch wide and were attached to belt and sabre scabbard rings as shown on the illustrations.

The same patent-leather belt was worn by officers in the field, although it is probable that some officers bought more serviceable belts for hard wear on campaign.

The accoutrements of the enlisted dragoon consisted of the sabre belt, carbine-cartridge box, pistol-cartridge box, and the carbine sling with sling swivel attached.

The sabre belt, of white buff leather, as described in the section concerning uniforms, was issued *without*

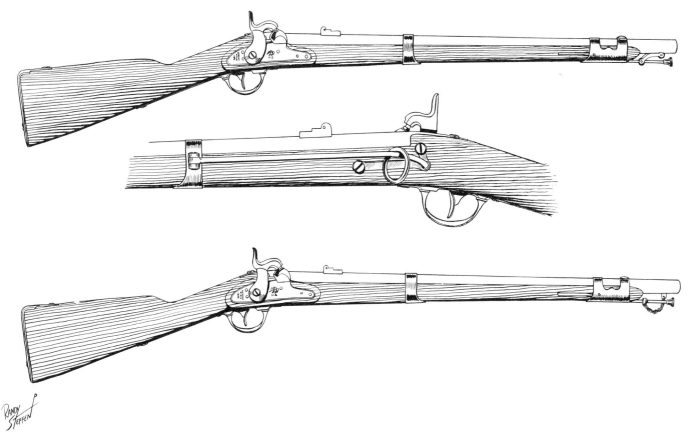

FIGURE 77. The U.S. Model 1847 smoothbore cavalry musketoon as adopted for the mounted service upon recommendation of the Ordnance Board of 1847 (Fuller; Hicks). Top: The original model, as adopted in 1847, with the ramrod swivel. This arm is .69-caliber and is brass mounted throughout. Center: The sling ring bar on the left side of the musketoon. Bottom: The U.S. Model 1847 cavalry smoothbore musketoon with the new chain attachment for the ramrod, as altered on recommendation of the Ordnance Board at its meeting December 29, 1851 (Fuller; Hicks). When the elongated bullet was introduced, many of these musketoons were rifled and reissued.

the supporting shoulder strap from 1833 until about 1837 or 1838, when the strap was added to help support the heavy load carried by the sabre belt, for it held sabre and both cartridge boxes when the dragoon was in the field. (See Figures 51 and 59.)

The pistol-cartridge box, carrying 12 rounds, was a leather box containing a wooden block drilled to hold the paper cartridges in individual holes of the proper size. The flap that closed the cartridges had an eagle with a scroll above, and borders of leaves, as shown on the drawings.

The carbine-cartridge box was of the same pattern, only larger, and contained a drilled block holding 30 rounds. Both boxes were made of black leather and had loops on the back through which the sabre belt passed. The carbine-cartridge box had a small flat pocket sewed to the front, under the flap, for holding the carbine tools, no doubt.

The earliest carbine slings, as we have seen before, were made of white buff leather, and were only 1½ inches wide, with a simple swivel, perhaps of brass, that snapped to the sling ring on the carbine stock.

Upon the organization of the Second Regiment of U.S. Dragoons in 1836, Colonel George Bomford, head of the Ordnance Department, wrote to Captain J. A. J. Bradford in the New York Ordnance depot on August 11 and directed that 1,000 of the sabre belts then on order were to be made of buff leather and

FIGURE 78. Corporal, Regiment of Mounted Riflemen (ca. 1846), with full field pack on the new Grimsley dragoon saddle with which the regiment was equipped. He is armed with the single-shot muzzle-loading U.S. Model 1841 rifle (the Mississippi rifle), a U.S. Model 1836 single-shot muzzle-loading flintlock pistol, and the dragoon sabre.

"afterwards dyed black." There seems to be no logical explanation for this seeming deviation from a uniform color in belts, unless the black belts were meant for use in the field, and the white ones were to be reserved for dress. Returns for the next several years showed quantities of both black and white belts on hand.

The year 1837 marked a number of changes in new manufactures of dragoon accoutrements. The report of the Board of Ordnance for that year included this statement:

... and for like reason [improvement and freedom from ornament] the Board recommends that the Cavalry or Carbine

Cartridge Box [the new pattern] be adopted and that the boxes instead of having the leather stamped or embossed as heretofore, be marked with the U.S. mark in brass. . . . The Board recommends that Major Baker, commanding Allegheny Arsenal, where accoutrements are made, be instructed to institute a rigid experiment into the expediency of rejecting the wooden box, and substituting therefor the tin case and method of delivering cartridges to the soldier in packages, as is understood to be the mode adopted in the armies of other countries. . . . the dragoon sabre belt with shoulder straps is considered by the Board as a decided improvement; but inasmuch as no member of the Board had at any time belonged to a Dragoon Corps, they respectfully recommend that the opinion of experienced officers of Dragoons be obtained before its final adoption. . . .

So we see that it was in 1837 that the embossed cartridge boxes, pistol as well as carbine, I am sure, were replaced with those having the small oval brass "U.S." instead of the embossed eagle design. It is also apparent that not too many months passed before the tin liner for these boxes was also made standard to replace the old wooden blocks. Just how much longer it took to approve the packaged cartridges I have not been able to document, but I suspect it was soon.

And it was this year that the Ordnance Department initiated tests on the shoulder belt for dragoons, so we can be safe in estimating the adoption during 1838, and issue by 1839, since the belt *without* the shoulder straps was listed in the 1839 Ordnance Regulations as "old pattern."

As late as 1839, sabre belts in both black and white leather were worn by the Second Dragoons. An extract from General Wood's inspection report dated October 30, 1839, notes, "Three companies were equipped with the old black belts and cartridge boxes, and three with white belts and new cartridge boxes; the latter appeared to be well made."

The new carbine sling and swivel, identical in design to the familiar so-called wide *Civil War* pattern, was issued by 1839, for both old and new slings are listed in Ordnance Regulations for that year. It was made of buff leather, white, with a brass double-tongue buckle and brass tip. The swivel was iron, probably polished, and had a link between the D roller and the snap hook itself, as shown in my drawings. The white buff-leather sling is 2½ inches wide and 56 inches long.

A new edition of the Ordnance Manual was published in 1841 that, among many other things, incorporated all the recent changes in its descriptions of

arms, accoutrements, and horse equipments. The following are the descriptions covering cavalry accoutrements, which include the carbine bucket, holsters, and holster covers that I have chosen to cover with the horse equipments, since they are only used when the trooper is mounted.

CHAPTER SEVENTH.

ACCOUTREMENTS.
NOMENCLATURE, DIMENSIONS.
Cavalry Accoutrements.

SABRE BELT, buff leather—*Waist belt*, 2 inches wide; 36 in. to 40 in. long—1 *square loop* and 2 *D rings* (brass,) for attaching the slings and shoulder strap—1 *belt plate*, brass, oval, 3.6 in. long, 2.2 in. wide, lettered *U. S.*—1 *shoulder strap*, 1⅓ in. wide, 41 in. long, with 2 *hooks*, brass—2 *sabre* slings 1⅓ in. wide; front sling 17 in. long, rear sling 34 in.—4 *studs* for do., brass—1 *sabre hook*, brass wire.

SWORD KNOT, buff leather—*Strap* 1 in. wide, 36 in. long; one end of the strap is fastened to a *tassel* 3 in. long; the other end is passed through the tassel after going round the guard of the sabre, and is fastened by one of the tags of the tassel—1 *sliding loop.*

CARBINE CARTRIDGE BOX, light bridle leather, black—Exterior length 7 in., width 1.3 in., height in front 5 in.—*inner cover* 4 in. wide—*flap* 7.5 in. deep, 8.5 in. wide at bottom, 8 in. at top where it is connected with the box—*pocket* for implements—*strap* 1 in. wide—*button*, brass, on the bottom of the box—*lining*, tin, edges turned over; 2 *lower divisions*, each 2.6 in. deep and 3.4 in. wide, to contain a bundle of 10 cartridges, (musket calibre;) 5 *upper divisions*, each 1.35 in. square, to contain 4 cartridges—*plate*, brass, oval, 2.8 in. long, 1.6 in. wide, lettered *U. S.*

PISTOL CARTRIDGE BOX, similar to the carbine box: Length 6.2 in, width 1.3 in., height in front 3.5 in.—*inner cover*, 3.5 in. wide—*flap*, 6.6 in. wide at top, 6.8 in. wide at bottom, 6 in. deep—*tin*: 2 *lower divisions*, each 2 in. deep and 2.9 in. wide, to contain a bundle of 10 cartridges; 5 *upper divisions*, each 1.2 in. square, to contain 4 cartridges, (rifle calibre)—*plate*, same as for carbine box.

CARBINE SLING, buff leather. Length 56 in., width 2.5 in.—1 *buckle* and 1 *tip*, brass—*swivel* and D with *roller*, iron, bright, 2.62 in. wide—*link* and *hook*, iron—*guard-spring*, steel.

Notice the unusual dimensions given for the widths of the sabre belt shoulder straps and slings—1 1/3 inches.

Another item considered accoutrement not mentioned before in this chapter is the trooper's canteen. From 1833 to 1837 I am quite satisfied in my own mind that the wooden canteen, the same type carried during the War of 1812, was a standard item of issue for the dragoon regiment.

In the annual report of the commissary general of purchases for 1837 there is a listing for both wood and tin types, along with their prices:

canteen, wood, complete _____ .40
canteen, tin, complete _____ .49

Therefore we can assume that both the wood and tin canteens were packed on the saddle during and after 1837, and that gradually, probably no longer than 3 years, the tin canteen completely replaced its wooden counterpart.

The percussion *cap pouch* was developed sometime around 1845, and its description appears in the *1850 Ordnance Manual*. That part of the manual covering the cavalry accoutrements is reproduced here. Both the carbine- and pistol-cartridge boxes underwent changes in size and compartmentation to accommodate the new ammunition; and the shoulder strap and slings of the sabre belt were narrowed from the 1 1/3-inch dimension specified in the *1841 Ordnance Manual* to 1 1/8 inches. Saddle holsters were changed slightly in some dimensions as well, but these shall be discussed in the next section under the category of "horse equipments."

ACCOUTREMENTS [1850]
Cavalry Accoutrements.

CARTRIDGE BOX, for carbine or musketoon; like the rifle cartridge box [see "Rifle Accoutrements" below].

PISTOL CARTRIDGE BOX. It is like the carbine cartridge box, except in its dimensions; length 6.2 in., width 1.3 in., height in front 3.5 in.—*inner cover*, 3.5 in. wide—*flap*, 6.6 in. wide at top, 6.8 in. at bottom, 6 in. deep—*Tins*, 2 lower divisions, 2 in. deep, 2.9 in. long, 1.2 wide; 5 upper divisions, 1.2 wide by 1.15 in. long and 1.5 in. deep.

CARTRIDGE BOX PLATE, for carbine or pistol cartridge box; the same as for the rifle.

CAP POUCH,
CONE PICK, } the same as for the infantry.

SABRE BELT (buff leather)—*Waist belt*, 2 inches wide, 36 in. to 40 in. long—1 *square loop* and 2 *D rings* (brass,) for attaching the slings and shoulder strap—1 *shoulder strap*, 1.125 in. wide, 41 in. long, with 2 *hooks*, brass—2 *sabre* slings 1.125 in. wide; front sling 17 in. long, rear sling 34 in.—4 *studs* for do., brass—1 *sabre hook*, brass wire.

SABRE BELT PLATE—Like the rifle waist belt plate.

SWORD KNOT (buff leather)—*Strap* 1 in. wide, 36 in. long; one end of the strap is fastened to a *tassel* 3 in. long; the other end is passed through the tassel after going round the guard of the sabre, and is fastened by one of the tags of the tassel—1 *sliding loop*.

CARBINE SLING, (buff leather.) Length 56 in., width 2.5 in. —1 *buckle* and 1 *tip*, brass—*swivel* and *D* with *roller*, bright iron, 2.62 in. wide—*link* and *hook*, iron—*guard-spring*, steel.

HOLSTERS. *Pipe* (sole leather, black); diameter of cylindrical part 2 in.; length of do. 7.5 in.; width of the mouth, 4.8 in.; depth, 2.2 in.; whole length, 14.5 in.—*pocket*, (light upper leather,) 3.2 in. long, 2.5 in. deep, lined with *tin* and covered with a *flap*—5 *cylindrical divisions*, diameter 0.6 in., each for one cartridge—1 *centre piece* forming the backs and connecting the two holsters, (bridle leather, black,) length 22 in., width 5.75 in.—2 *straps* 14 in. long, 0.75 wide, with 2 buckles, to attach the holsters to the saddle—2 *surcingle loops*, (light bridle leather, black,) 1.5 in. wide, 3.5 in. long, doubled.

Two holster covers, (black leather;) 10 in. long, 9.5 in. wide over the cartridge-pocket—*straps*, 4 in. long, 1 in. wide, to button on 2 *brass studs* on the holster pipes....

Rifle Accoutrements.

CARTRIDGE BOX. The leather parts are like those of the infantry cartridge box [see "Infantry Accoutrements" below]; length 7.2 in., depth in front 5 inches, width 1.6 in. *Two loops* are placed upright on the back of the box, to receive a 2 in. waist belt. The *tin lining* has 2 lower divisions, each 3.3 in. long by 2.8 in. deep, and 5 upper divisions, 1.35 in. square by 2.1 in. deep.

Infantry Accoutrements.

CARTRIDGE BOX, (black bridle leather.) Length 7.2 inch; width 1.6 inch; depth in front, 5.8 inch—*inner cover*, (light upper leather,) 4 inches wide, with end pieces sewed to it, so as to cover the ends of the box—*flap*, 8.5 inches wide at bottom, 8 inches at top, with a button hole *strap* sewed near the bottom —*brass button*, riveted to the bottom of the box—*implement pocket* (light upper leather) sewed to the front of the box; 6 inches long, 3.5 inches deep, with a *flap, strap,* and *loop*— 2 *loops*, on the back of the box, near the top, for the shoulder belt to pass through.

CARE OF ACCOUTREMENTS

During the first few years of service the dragoons were guided in the care and cleaning of their accoutrements by Article 29 of the *General Regulations of the Army* as revised by Major General Scott in 1825.

Three different methods for cleaning buff or white leather were given, and they are quoted directly from General Order No. 7, February 24, 1835 (Cost of Clothing for the Army), as follows:

Article 29: Accoutrements—Buff or white leather will be cleaned as follows:

First method—Take several handfuls of bran, and boil it in water, which afterwards draw off clear; make a paste of pipe clay with this water, and when cold apply it to the buff.

Second method—Take pipe clay and steep it a quarter of an hour in pure water; change the water, and dissolve a sufficient quantity of soap in it. This mixture is recommended for the cleaning of buff or white leather.

Third method—Clean off the buff with a brush dipped in clear water; leave it to dry in the shade; take white lead, steeped at least twenty-four hours in pure water, (several times changed to deprive the lead of its corrosive qualities) and by means of a brush, put on as many coats of this whiting as may be necessary, taking care to let each coat dry in the shade before another is added. The whiting should be tempered with water so as not to be too liquid or too thick.

Note: Pipe clay—a natural clay, one of the names given to impure kaolin or china clay.

In 1847 *General Regulations for the Army* included different instructions for cleaning white leather and a note on polishing black leather accoutrements:

Article 149 . . . white lead will not be used in cleaning belts and gloves, as it is prejudicial to health; pipe-clay or whiting will be used in stead.

Article 150. Cartridge boxes and bayonet scabbards will be polished with blacking; varnish is injurious to the leather and will not be used.

But in 1862 the *Ordnance Manual* contains formulas and instructions for preparing varnish for "holsters, scabbards, etc. . . ." quite typical of the philosophies which guided the Army under different men in different eras.

In the 1862 *Military Dictionary*, a privately printed book popular with military men, another formula and directions for making "whiting" for cleaning white buff accoutrements, which by this time had long since disappeared from dragoon equipage, was given. Apparently this was a method that had been used during the last part of the period that saw white sabre belts and carbine slings in use, and I quote it here for what it is worth:

WHITING. To make whiting for accoutrements, it is necessary to boil many handfuls of bran enveloped in linen. Dissolve afterwards pipe-clay in this water. Whiten with it when cold. When the buff leather is greasy and does not receive the whiting, scrape it, and apply to it a solution of pipe-clay and Spanish whiting.

Another receipt, calculated for one hundred men, is the following: Pipe-clay, 3½ lbs.; Spanish whiting, 8 ounces; white lead, 4 ounces; glue, 1½ ounces; starch, 6 oz.; white soap, 5 oz. Put the pipe-clay and Spanish whiting in about five gallons of water; wash them and leave them to soak for six hours; 2d, throw out the first water, and replace it by 5½

gallons of pure water; add the white lead, glue, and white soap. Cook them together, taking care to stir constantly the composition. At the moment that the foam shows itself on the surface, withdraw the vessel from the fire without suffering the composition to boil; put then the starch in the whiting, and mix all well together.

Before getting into the subject of horse equipments of the mounted corps in this first period, there are a few details of interest to the serious student of cavalry that must be incorporated into this work. I include them here in order that they be discussed somewhere near their correct chronological position.

The 1847 *General Regulations for the Army* contains a detailed description of standards and guidons for dragoons and cavalry which follows just as it appears in the regulations:

Article 853. Each regiment will have a silken standard, and each company a silken guidon. The standard to bear the arms of the United States, embroidered in silk, on a blue background, with the number and name of the regiment, in a scroll underneath the eagle. The flag of the standard to be two feet five inches wide, and two feet three inches on the lance, and to be edged with yellow silk fringe.

Article 854. The flag of the guidon to be made swallow-tailed, three feet five inches from the lance to the end of the slit of the swallow-tail, and two feet three inches on the lance. To be half red and half white, dividing at the fork, the red above. On the red, the letters U.S. in white, and on the white, the letter of the company in red. The lance of the standards and guidons to be nine feet long, including spear and ferrule.

This, then, marks the change from the original guidon pattern, on which the word "dragoons" appeared.

According to a specimen in the West Point Museum collection, and the description on the accession card, the standard for the Regiment of Mounted Riflemen in 1846 was:

of yellow silk now turned brown . . . 26 × 29 inches, trimmed with yellow fringe; 13 gold stars; shield solid bright blue chief with 13 white and red stripes; 6 arrows; painted red scroll held in beak of eagle with motto in yellow; name of regiment in yellow on red scroll. . . .

Although the above description of the standard with its yellow field is contrary to the regulations published the following year, it can be assumed that the mounted riflemen had at least one year of service under this distinguishing banner. As seen in the 1847 regulations, a blue field was prescribed for dragoons

FIGURE 79. The 1849 Ames knife issued to the Regiment of Mounted Riflemen.

and cavalry, which I feel sure must have been meant to include the Regiment of Mounted Rifles.

Another article of accoutrement, since it cannot, in my opinion, be classified as an article of uniform or a weapon in the true sense of the word, was the *rifleman's knife* made by Ames Manufacturing Company in 1848 and 1849 for issue to the Regiment of Mounted Riflemen. Specific ordnance specifications governed the pattern of the knife, and Figure 79 shows the knife and its scabbard as it was issued. The contract was for 1,000 knives with scabbards at a cost to the government of $4 each. This was the first knife ever made for the Army.

The blade is 11¾ inches long and 1⅝ inches wide, with a spear point and a short false edge; the guard was brass and the handle, walnut, with a brass-lined hole at the pommel for a thong or lanyard. The blade was stamped "Ames Mfg. Co./Cabotville/1849.

The scabbard is black leather with brass tip and throat fitted with a stud for attachment to a belt frog. No doubt this knife saw much good use on the regiment's march to Oregon at the close of the war with Mexico. This was to be the last knife made specifically for the Army until the Model 1880 U.S. Army Hunting Knife was made for issue to both cavalry and infantry.

HORSE EQUIPMENTS

Horse equipment of the Regiment of U.S. Dragoons, upon their organization in 1833, has been a long-time mystery to military historians. Stanley J. Olsen, in his article, "The Development of the U.S. Army Saddle," that appeared in the Spring, 1955, issue of *Military Collector & Historian* was correct in identifying the first dragoon saddle as the one illustrated and described in the 1834 War Department publication, *A System of Tactics*. But since there seemed to be nothing that backed up this assumption besides the above little known publication, few serious historians and military illustrators were convinced enough to use this information as fact.

During one extensive trip in 1962 to gather material for this book, I stopped for several days at Fort Riley, and spent a few hours in the small post museum there. An old saddle, obviously an early military one, was in a glass display case in one section of the museum, but there was no identification except the donor's name, which I failed to note at the time.

Being certain the saddle had a military history from the presence of staples and rings that were beyond question for the attachment of military pommel and cantle packs, I photographed it from every angle and made copious notes concerning its construction. These photos and notes were destroyed 5 months later when my California studio burned and the original manuscript, illustrations, and research material for this book were destroyed. Later, at my request, Mark C. Endsley, the Fort Riley Public Information Officer, was kind enough to supply me with a set of prints from negatives the post photographer had made at my request.

In 1964 I found a copy of the 1834 publication, *A System of Tactics*, and thought I recognized the saddle illustrated therein as the Fort Riley saddle. The little manual was in the West Point library, and I could hardly wait to get back to my studio, then in California, to compare the photographs I had with the photocopies I had made of the 1834 manual. My elation was great when a comparison revealed the saddle at Fort Riley and the one in the 1834 manual were identical! This removed the uncertainty about the first dragoon saddle and proved Dr. Olsen's assumption was correct.

This same *A System of Tactics* contained excellent descriptions of the other horse equipment issued with the saddle, and my illustrations are based on the Fort Riley saddle and the descriptions from this book.

I have little doubt that other military historians have had the opportunity to study this manual. But I am equally certain that most of them were thrown off balance, as far as associating its illustrations with the 1833 horse equipments was concerned, by the statement in the beginning of the manual telling of its submission to the Secretary of War in 1826. This threw me for some time, too. But after a great deal of study I concluded that the section on horse equipment had been more recent than the date on the fly page indicated, and I am convinced this is the case.

The information in the text on training the horse, on the School of the Trooper, and on the School of the Squadron undoubtedly had been written in 1826 or earlier, but since all the drills and maneuvers described in this part still held good for the later date of publication, no changes were made. But the saddle and other horse equipment illustrated on the plates did not correspond with the terminology used to describe the saddle in the text, reference being made to more than one girth, for example. The hussar saddle, also shown on the plate with the English-type saddle, was explained in a footnote by the statement that the men *preferred* the older-type saddle, but the description

was for "the saddle, bridle, and other equipments, commonly in use in the United States, as here described."

The hussar saddle, used extensively during the War of 1812 and later, until the abolishment of the mounted arm in 1821, did have two girths, as did a second type of dragoon saddle described in Chapter II. I feel certain the text alluded to these saddles, and *not* to the *Fort Riley* saddle illustrated along with the earlier hussar saddle.

Figure 80 shows the Fort Riley saddle with its related equipments drawn according to the descriptions printed below just as they appear in the 1834 manual:

ARTICLE FIFTH.

41.   *Of the Equipments of the Horse.*

*The Saddle.** (PLATE 2.) Its several parts, as seen in its covered state, are:

1. The head, or pommel.	5. Two flaps.
2. Seat.	6. Loop for halter strap.
3. Cantle.	7. Two loops for strap of
4. Two skirts.	holster pipe.

*The saddle, bridle, and other equipments, commonly in use in the United States, are here described.

The *Hussar Saddle* is, however, preferable, and is accordingly recommended; it is covered with a skin called a *Schabraque*, through which the cantle peak passes, protecting the valise as well as the holsters; the surcingle is buckled over it.— See *Plate 2, 2d Fig. 1 and 2.*

The saddle has the following appendages:

8. Two stirrup straps.
9. Two stirrups, (each consisting of an eye, 10; and bottom iron, 11.)
12. Girth.
13. Housing.

The breast plate. (PLATE 2. 2d No. 7.)

Crupper. (PLATE 5.)

Holsters. (The upper part called the body, the lower the pipe. The right holster ought to contain a horse shoe, nails, currycomb, and brush, &c., and ought to be six inches wide. PLATE 3.)

The Bridle, (snaffle and curb; the front uniting the two head stalls,) consisting of the following parts: (PLATE 4.)

1. Head piece.	6. Snaffle reins.
2. Cheek piece.	7. Curb reins.
3. Front.	8. Snaffle bit.
4. Nose band.	9. Curb bit.
5. Throat strap.	

The Halter, (PLATE 5,) consisting of—

1. Head stall.
2. Two linking rings.
3. Halter strap, (10 feet long, and tapering 2 feet from the end.)

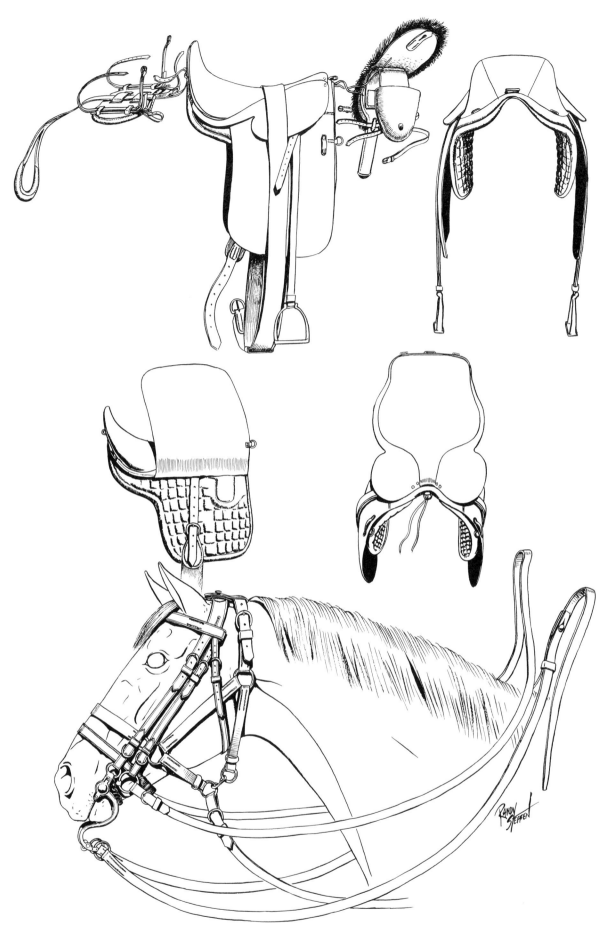

FIGURE 80. 1833 dragoon horse equipments from "A System of Tactics, 1834." Saddle drawn from a specimen in the Fort Riley Museum.

FIGURE 81. Lieutenant, Regimental Staff, the Regiment of Dragoons (ca. 1834), in full-dress uniform and with housing over regulation 1833 dragoon saddle. He is armed with a pair of U.S. Model 1819 S. North single-shot muzzle-loading flint-lock pistols, and the 1833 officer's dragoon sabre.

The officer in Figure 81 is in full dress, and rides the 1833 dragoon saddle with the *schabraque* over the saddle, as was prescribed for mounted parades. Slits in the *schabraque* accommodate straps at pommel and cantle that secure holsters and valise to the saddle. The bridle in this case is worn on the horse *without* the halter for parade.

The captain in Figure 82 is dressed for field duty, and his saddle is girthed on top of the regulation folded horse blanket *without* the *schabraque*. His great coat is strapped to the pommel *under* the holsters.

Breast straps are shown with both dress and field equipments, as was proper.

Figure 83 shows a corporal of dragoons with the proper horse equipments for parade. No halter is worn under the bridle, and the short half-housing illustrated in the 1834 *A System of Tactics* is shown as it was worn over the saddle blanket, or horse blanket, as it was called then, and under the skirts. This half-housing attached to the girth billets by small buckled loop straps on each side.

The combination holster-pouch can be seen clearly on this drawing, as can the carbine bucket in which the muzzle of the carbine rested when it was not carried in the hand or *hooked up* (to the carbine sling). The carbine bucket is buckled to the **D** ring fastened to the leading edge of the off-side skirt. The carbine strap, which secures the carbine to the saddle (shown in Figure 84), hangs loose over the dragoon's right leg in this drawing.

Figures 84 and 85 show dragoons in field dress and with full field equipment on their 1833 saddles. The off-side details are shown in Figure 84, while the method of carrying the canteen and forage net is shown on the near side in Figure 85. The canteen strap is looped over the off side of the valise and blanket roll atop it. The canteen is the same wooden type as was used in the War of 1812.

Both Figures 84 and 85 show the leather loop and stud on the crown piece of the headstall that was used to keep the halter in place.

The dragoon in Figure 85 has a canvas haversack slung over his right shoulder, and his tin drinking cup is secured by its handle to the buckled strap that closes the flap on the haversack.

While no mention that I can find has been made of the color of leather used in the 1833 dragoon saddle, black was used for all leather equipment and accou-

trements except the sabre belt and carbine sling. So I believe it can be safely surmised that this saddle was made of black leather. The saddle in the Fort Riley Museum, although in remarkably fine condition, has been worn by much riding, and the color is hard to determine because of its age.

Bridle and halter were made of black leather, as were the crupper and carbine sling. As noted in Colonel Kearny's letter at the beginning of this chapter, girths and surcingles were to be made of blue webbing, and breast straps were to be yellow leather, "the same color as the facings of the uniform."

Stirrups on the 1833 saddle were brass, according to a photocopy (in the author's files) of the *Return of Articles* purchased for the Regiment of U.S. Dragoons by Major Aeneas Mackay, assistant quartermaster at Philadelphia in the years 1833, 1834, and 1835.

The valise is carried on the mail pillion, or pad, in order to prevent the cantle pack from making contact with the horse's back.

The 1834 *A System of Tactics* gives explicit instructions for folding the cloak (great coat):

50. The cloak will be folded wrong side outwards; the sides laid inwards, equally and smoothly, so that the cloak may be two feet in length, when fixed; it will then be rolled neatly and tightly. When not in use it will be strapped in front of the holsters.

The next paragraph instructed the dragoon as to the contents and method of packing the valise:

51. The valise ought to be made of stout leather; and should be eighteen inches long, eight inches wide, and six inches deep, and should be limited to the following articles: two shirts, one pair of stockings, one handkerchief, one stable jacket, one pair of gloves, one pair of overalls (trousers), a forage cap, and shaving case; all to be neatly folded and packed, and the articles most in use to be placed uppermost. In the flap, one pair of shoes, a fatigue apron (stable frock), clothes brush, spoon, blacking, whiting, and a knife.

The uniform regulations for 1833, 1836, 1839, 1841, and 1847 give the descriptions of officers' *schabraques*, or housings, as well as of bridles and the metal parts of the horse furniture (equipments). You will notice that all parts, including bits, are of yellow metal (brass for enlisted men; gilt for officers).

No colors were specified for the colors of the enlisted man's half-housing illustrated in *A System of Tactics*, but I am certain the field was blue with yellow

FIGURE 82. Captain, the Regiment of Dragoons (ca. 1834), in fatigue dress and with the regulation 1833 horse equipments packed for service in the field. He is armed with a pair of U.S. Model 1819 single-shot muzzle-loading flintlock pistols and the officer's model of the 1833 dragoon sabre.

FIGURE 83. Corporal, the Regiment of Dragoons (ca. 1834) in full-dress uniform and with the half-housing used with the 1833 horse equipments for parade.

cloth trim and with the "U.S." embroidered in yellow thread.

Contents of the pouch half of the holsters are noted in a copy of the description of horse equipments from the 1834 *A System of Tactics*. They consisted of a spare horse shoe, nails, curry-comb and brush, and so forth.

That saddlebags were an item of dragoon issue there can be no doubt, for the statement of the cost of clothing and equipage for 1837 lists saddlebags as having cost $4.75. And in Colonel Groghan's report on equipment and arms at Fort Leavenworth in August, 1838 (*Army Life on the Western Frontier*) he complains about the size and shape of the saddlebags:

> The saddle bags are by no means suited to the nature of our Dragoon service; they are not only much too large, but are besides so badly shaped that when packed they cannot be carried on the saddle without greatly inconveniencing both the rider and his horse.

I have shown no saddlebags on the dragoon illustrations for the simple reason that I have not been able to find a description or a specimen from which to draw them. But saddlebags there were! I would guess that they must have been simple pouches of leather, with straps sewed between the pockets so they could be carried behind the cantle, similar to those shown on the drawings of the Continental Dragoons in Chapter I. But of this I am not certain, so I have refrained from showing any at all. Certainly they must have been used by *some* dragoon companies on the frontier in place of the usual valise.

Chain halters are also listed as items of dragoon equipment in the 1838 list on the cost of clothing and camp equipage. No known specimen or description of this type of halter exists, although it must have been a simple leather collar that buckled around the horse's neck, with a length of chain, probably with a toggle attached to the free end, that was used as a stable halter, and a means to lead horses to water so the field halter would not get wet and brittle.

Sometime prior to the publication of the *1841 Ordnance Manual*, probably in 1839 when changes in other dragoon accoutrements and equipments were made, a board of officers must have been convened to consider the subject of improvement of dragoon items, as well as for the other corps of the Army.

The *1841 Ordnance Manual* contains detailed descriptions of all equipments for the mounted service,

as well as accoutrements for dragoons, infantry, and artillery. All the recent changes have been included, and it is an accurate source for this work—in spite of the fact that there are no illustrations. I have used these descriptions to supplement a lifelong association with horse gear, and many years of study of military horse equipment in particular, to "reconstruct" the 1841 horse equipments shown in Figure 86, since I have not been able to find a surviving specimen of the 1841 saddle.

The descriptions from the *1841 Ordnance Manual* that follow can be compared with details of the drawings in Figure 86:

Horse Equipments for Dragoons—Pattern of 1841.

The leather parts are made of strong black leather, unless otherwise specified.

The *buckles* and *rings* are made of wrought iron tinned, and all the buckles have *rollers*.

NOTE. For an explanation of some technical terms, see *Page* 84.

Halter.

The *nose band*—2 *chin straps*; 1 *loop* for ditto—the *throat strap*—2 *cheek straps*, forming also the throat lash; 1 *buckle* and 2 *loops* for ditto—1 *loop* with a button hole, which serves to fasten the halter to the crown piece of the bridle—all these pieces are 1 in. wide; they are connected together by 2 *square cheek loops*, (iron,) the lower sides of which are covered with leather, and by 2 *throat strap rings*—the *shank*, (or *hitching strap*,) 1 in. wide, with 1 *buckle* and 1 *loop*—1 *billet* sewed to the shank, to connect it with the lower throat strap ring.

Snaffle Bridle.

HEAD STALL: The *long cheek* on the off side, the *short cheek* on the near side, ¾ in. wide—1 *buckle* and 1 *loop* for ditto—the *brow band* made with two loops through which the cheek straps pass.

SNAFFLE BIT, (wrought iron, burnished,) 2 *mouth pieces* connected by eyes; the outer ends pierced with holes for 2 *rings*.

REIN, ¾ in. wide—1 *buckle* and 2 *loops*.

Curb Bridle.

Crown piece 2 in. wide, split at each end into two equal parts, to fit 2 *billets* on the near side and 1 *billet* and 1 *throat lash* on the off side—1 *buckle* and 2 *loops* for the throat lash—3 *loops* for the *spare curb chain*; the loop on the top of the crown has a *button* for attaching the button-hole strap on the halter—the *brow band*, 1¼ in. wide, with 2 *loops* at each end for the billets of the crown piece—2 *brass plates*, for marking and numbering the bridle—2 *cheek straps*, each with 1 *buckle* and 1 *loop* at the upper end, and 1 *buckle* and 2 *loops* at the lower end—2 *bit billets*, sewed to the under side of the cheek straps—the *nose band*, 1 in. wide in rear, passing through openings between the cheek straps and bit billets; 1 *buckle* and 1 *loop* for ditto.

FIGURE 84. Sergeant, the Regiment of Dragoons (ca. 1837), in fatigue dress and with the 1833 horse equipments packed for service in the field. He is armed with the 1833 Hall single-shot breech-loading percussion carbine, the U.S. Model 1819 S. North single-shot muzzle-loading flintlock pistol, and the Model 1833 dragoon sabre. Off side.

BIT, wrought iron, burnished: 2 *cheeks*, the upper part straight, with an eye for the bit billet and another for the curb chain; the lower part an *S*, with an eye for the *bridle ring*—the *mouth piece* dovetailed and riveted to the cheeks; the *port mouth*—the *bar*, riveted to the lower ends of the cheeks—the *curb chain*, (tinned iron,) fastened by a *hook* to the off cheek and by an *S* to the near cheek—2 *scutcheons* (brass,) riveted to the cheeks.

The bits are made of three sizes and of three varieties in the form of the portmouth and the degree of severity. In a large number, one-sixth are *mild*, one-sixth *severe*, the rest *medium*. One fifth of each kind are 4.625 in. wide between the cheeks, three-fifths are 4.875 in. wide, and one-fifth are 5.125 in. wide.

REINS, 1 in. wide, made of one piece of leather split in two —2 *bit billets* with 2 *buckles* and 2 *loops*; 1 *sliding loop* and 1 *button*—the *whip*, of braided leather.

Saddle.

WOODEN PARTS, (beech or maple.) The *pommel*—the *cantle*—2 *side bars*. The pommel and cantle are dovetailed into the side bars, fastened by wooden *pins* and glued. The trees are

FIGURE 85. Private, the Regiment of Dragoons (ca. 1837), in fatigue uniform, and with the 1833 horse equipments packed for service in the field. Near side.

of two sizes, 12 in. and 13 in. wide between the lower ends of the pommel.

IRON PARTS. The *pommel plate*, fastened to the front of the pommel by 6 *screws* and 2 *rivets*—2 *pommel squares*, each fastened to the side bar by 3 *rivets*—*the cantle plate*, fastened to the rear of the cantle by 6 *screws* and 2 *rivets*—2 *cantle squares*, each fastened to the side bar and to the rear of the cantle by 6 *rivets*—2 *stirrup-bar plates*, each fastened to the side bar and to the pommel by 4 *screws*—2 *valise staples*, riveted over 2 *burrs* on the front of the cantle—*cantle moulding* (sheet brass,) fastened to the cantle with small *nails*.

LEATHER PARTS. The thongs used for connecting the parts together are made of strong raw hide or alum dressed skin.

The seat (or *straining*,) raw hide, alum dressed, *nailed* to the pommel and cantle and laced to the side bars with *thongs*.

The pad, covered with russet sheep skin, lined with strong canvass, stuffed with curled hair, and quilted; it is attached to the tree by 4 *strings* and 4 *loops* passing over the pommel, the cantle, the girth and the girth billet.

The girth 2¾ in. wide, attached with a *thong* to the off side bar of the tree—1 *buckle* and 2 *loops* for do. the *girth billet*, made double by means of a *layer* 2 in. wide, and attached, in the same manner as the girth, to the near side bar.

2 *Chapes*, with 2 *buckles* and 2 *loops* for the crupper straps, fastened to the points of the side bars with *thongs*.

STIRRUPS, of wrought iron, japanned black; the *bar*, double and roughed on the upper side; the *sides*; the *eye* for the stirrup leather—2 *stirrup leathers* 1¼ in. wide, stitched double for a length of 10 in. from the buckle, the stirrup resting on the double part—2 *buckles* and 4 *loops* for do. The

151

stirrup leather passes over the stirrup bar through a mortice in the side bar.

CRUPPER. The *dock* stuffed with wool or paper—the *body* 2 inches wide, split into 2 *straps* 1 inch wide, to which the dock is sewed, and into 2 *billets* 1 inch wide, by which the crupper is attached to the saddle.

BREAST PLATE, 1 inch wide, with a *buckle* at the lower end to form a loop for the girth; at the upper end a *heart* covered with a *brass plate*—2 *stays* ⅞ in. wide, sewed to the upper end of the breast plate; 2 *buckles* and 4 *loops* for do.—1 *breast plate strap* ⅞ in. wide; it passes through 2 mortices in the connecting strap and under the band on the pipe of the holster and the loop on the holster bag, and is buckled to the stays.

HOLSTER: black leather, jacked and varnished; the mouth is stiffened with iron wire covered with leather—a *band* round the pipe, passing through a *loop* in a *strap* attached to the connecting strap.

HOLSTER BAG, for combs, brushes, &c.; *mouth strap* passing through 2 *loops* sewed on the bag—1 *buckle* and 1 *loop* for do.—1 *loop* for the bag strap.

CONNECTING STRAP, to which the holster and bag are fastened by *thongs*; it is doubled and stitched, with an opening in the centre through which the head of the pommel passes. The strap is fastened to the pommel with 2 *thongs*; the holster being on the near side and the bag on the off side.

STRAPS, ⅞ in. wide. 1 *Holster strap* and 1 *bag strap*, passing round the lower ends of the holster and the bag, through the loops made for that purpose; used to strap up the cloak, &c.; each strap has 1 *buckle* and 2 *loops*—1 *middle cloak strap*, passing through a loop made with a thong in the head of the pommel—1 *buckle* and 2 *loops* for do.—2 *double cloak straps*, each with 2 *buckles* and 2 *loops*: these straps pass round the holster and bag, under the thongs which attach the connecting strap to the saddle tree; each strap has but one *billet* which is buckled first over the cloak and then over the schabraque, one of the buckle straps being passed through a slit made in the schabraque for that purpose.

1 *Middle valise strap*; 1 *buckle* and 2 *loops* for do.—2 *double valise straps*, each with 2 *buckles* and 3 *loops*: these straps pass through the valise staples and through slits in the schabraque; they are buckled first over the valise and then over any light package that may be carried on the valise.

Two SHOE POCKETS, attached to the rear of the side bars of the tree with the same thongs that hold the chapes for the crupper buckles.

CARBINE BUCKET, sole leather, jacked like the holster; it is made of two pieces, with a *band* sewed round the mouth and a mortice in the lower part—the *bucket strap* 1 inch wide, with 1 *buckle* and 2 *loops*: it passes through the mortice and through 2 loops in the band of the bucket, and is attached to the saddle by passing under a *thong* tied to the connecting strap and to the lacing of the seat.

CARBINE STRAP, ⅞ in. wide; 1 *buckle* and 2 *loops* for do: it passes through a loop in the thong that holds the connecting strap of the holster and bag, on the off side.

BLANKET, wool, dyed brown, 54 inches square, weighing not less than 3¼ lbs.

SCHABRAQUE, dark blue cloth, trimmed with the color of the facings of the corps, lined with strong canvass; the *seat*, white sheepskin dressed with the wool on; the skirts are faced with leather in the middle and lined with leather at the flanks—The schabraque is pierced with several *slits* for the passage of the straps of the saddle; it is secured to the saddle in front by the two double cloak straps, in rear by the two double valise straps, and in the centre by the surcingle.

SURCINGLE, leather 2¾ in. wide; it has at one end a *chape*, with a buckle and 3 loops; at the other end, a *billet* 1⅜ in. wide.

VALISE, dark blue cloth, trimmed like the schabraque; diameter inside 6 in., length 21 in.; the ends stiffened with plates of leather—it is *lined* with strong canvass and closed, under the flap, with *lacings* of strong twine—3 *straps*, with *buckles* and *loops*, and 3 *billets* are sewed to the outside of the valise.

SPURS, wrought iron, japanned black: the *plate* attached to the heel of the boot by a *point* behind and 2 *screws* at the sides—the *shank*—the *rowel*, (steel.)

CARBINE BUCKET, sole leather, black: Diameter 1.5 in., length of front part 6 in., back part 7.5 in.—*strap*, heavy bridle leather, black, 1 in. wide, 22.5 in. long, clear of the bucket; the strap passes round the sides and bottom of the bucket.

HOLSTERS. *Pipe*, sole leather, black: diameter of cylindrical part 2 in., length of do. 7.5 in.; width of the mouth, 4.7 in.; depth, 2.5 in.; whole length, 14.5 in.—*pocket*, light upper leather, 3.2 in. long, 2.5 in. deep, lined with *tin*—5 cylindrical *divisions*, diameter 0.6 in., each for one cartridge—1 *centre piece* to connect the two holsters, light bridle leather, black; mean length about 8 in., width 5.25 in.—2 *straps* 14 in. long, 0.6 wide, with 2 buckles, to attach the holsters to the saddle—2 *surcingle loops*, light bridle leather, black, 1.5 in. wide, 3.5 in. long, doubled.

HOLSTER COVERS, black leather; 23 in. long, 9.5 in. wide over the cartridge pocket, 7.5 in. in the middle—*straps*, 6 in. long, 1 in. wide, to button on the holster.

If you will refer back to the descriptions of the 1833 dragoon horse equipments as reproduced from the 1834 edition of *A System of Tactics*, you will see again the reference made to the preference for the *hussar* saddle over the English type which characterized the 1833 dragoon saddle. It is not surprising, therefore, to find the Model 1841 saddle a somewhat modified hussar type, complete with laced suspension seat, wooden pommel, cantle, and sidebars, and even the woolskin seat on the dress *schabraque*—as you refer to Figure 86 and check it against the foregoing description.

The 1965 edition of *Horses and Saddlery*, by Major G. Tylden, published by the J. A. Allen Company in London, contains excellent photographs and descriptions of the British hussar saddle of 1805, and strangely enough its construction is amazingly similar to the

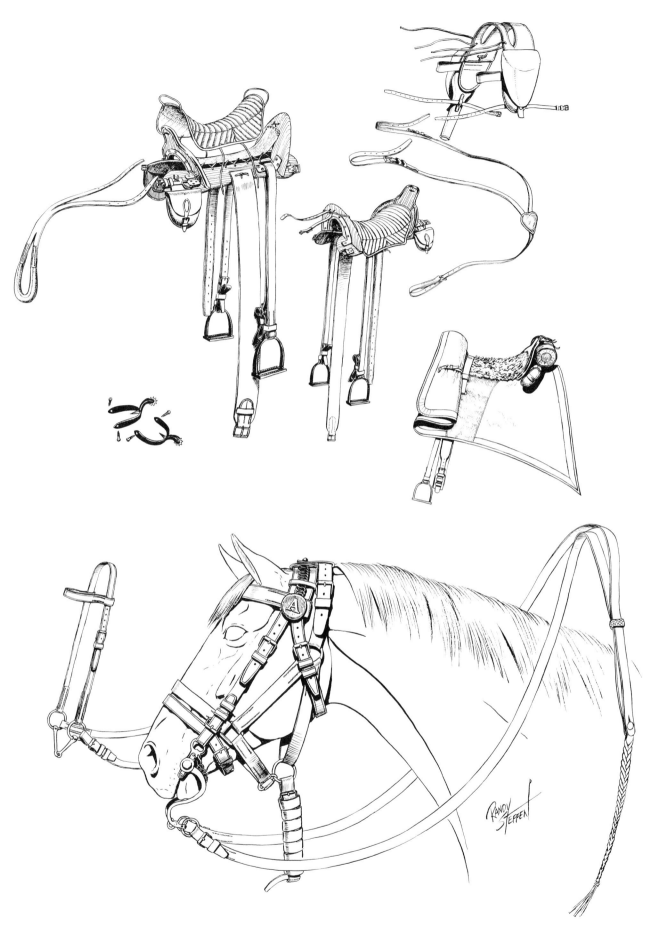

FIGURE 86. The 1841 dragoon horse equipments.

description of the U.S. Model of 1841. It is evident that this British saddle played an important part in the design of the American saddle, even to the shape of the pommel and spoon cantle and the use of a loose padded seat. While the British model does have side flaps, or skirts, which were eliminated on the Model 1841, the important features of the two are unmistakably similar.

In contrast to the webbing girths of the 1833 saddle, both girth and surcingle of the 1841 model are leather. The seat, a rawhide strip, is laced to the sidebars in typical hussar fashion, and just as on the British counterpart is fastened to pommel and cantle with nails.

The bridle shows much European influence in design, and especially in the method of carrying an extra curb chain on the crown piece. The halter is a slight modification of its predecessor, and the watering bridle, with its separate headstall, can be used as a bridoon for handling the horse with double reins if future orders made this mandatory.

Stirrups are wrought iron, japanned black, replacing the brass stirrups used on the 1833 saddle. Later, in 1844, brass stirrups will be used again when the Ringgold saddle is adopted, and in 1847 when the Grimsley becomes the standard-issue saddle for the mounted service.

Spurs, too, are to be made of wrought iron painted black, and are to be attached to the heel with two screws instead of spur straps, as had been used with the brass-plated iron spurs requested by Colonel Kearny in 1833.

The 1841 edition of *Cavalry Tactics* was the first really comprehensive manual published for the mounted corps, and contained detailed instructions for training the trooper in every phase of horsemanship, as well as instructing him in the complex evolutions of cavalry. One section was devoted to the standard method of packing the effects of the dragoon in valise and wallet, and another contained detailed directions for packing his effects on the horse. This section is particularly valuable in revealing the contents of the cavalry pack, and is reproduced in its entirety below:

page 24—Manner of packing up the effects

The Uniform pantaloons, folded the length of the valise should be well spread out on the bottom.
The shirts, unfolded, are laid on the white pantaloons.

The soldier's book on the shirts.
The cap cord on the book.
The shaving case, the pocket handkerchiefs, the gloves, and the socks, divided equally at the ends.
The second pair of boots under the flap of the valise.
The plume in its case, along with the boots.
The stable jacket in the valise wallet; and also the forage cap, which is placed in the middle.
The stable-frock rolled the length of the cloak, in the forage-sack.

page 28—Manner of packing the effects on the horse
Light Cavalry

The *schabraque* being on the saddle, the front part turned back on the seat, the packing straps run thro' their holes, fasten the cloak and the forage-sack containing the stable frock, drawing the middle-strap very tight, that the cloak may be in front of the pommel, falling down in front of the holsters. With the cloak straps, fasten the ends of the cloak and forage sack in such a manner that the ends shall not project beyond the schabraque. Place the pistol in the holster inside of the cloak, and fasten the strap in the ring in the butt. Place the *hatchet* in its case, turn down the front of the schabraque, and pass the gun-strap through its hole. Extend the right and left packing straps upon the croup; place the *wallet* flat against the cantle; lay the middle packing strap over the wallet, place the valise with buckles towards the saddle, fasten it tightly to the *peak* with this strap; fasten the wallet and the valise together with the side-straps; then attach the forage cord, rolled and twisted into a circle, on the left side, under the schabraque; in the same manner attach the watering bridle on the right side to the straps which are fixed to the saddle for that purpose; see that there is no fold in the valise.
Fasten the lock-cover to the cloak-strap on the right side, the buckles against the schabraque.
When blankets are used instead of schabraques, they will be folded twice, with the edges placed on the off side. To have the effects well packed, the three straps must be tightly buckled, and must come up straight 3 inches from each other; the three buckles on the same line in the middle of the valise; the valise and wallet square, so that both can be seen from behind.
The *valise* and *wallet* should not incline to either side.
The cloak and other articles in front should be so arranged as to raise the bridle-hand as little as possible.
Nothing should project beyond the schabraque.
If a bundle of forage is to be carried, it is placed on the valise, a little to the rear, and tied to the packing-straps. When the carbine is in the boot, it is placed that its end may be 4 or 5 inches from the horse's shoulder, without projecting beyond it; it is fastened to the saddle by a gunstrap, which makes two turns round the small of the stock.

No mention is made in the *1841 Ordnance Manual* of the *wallet* designated in the above excerpt from the 1841 *Cavalry Tactics*, nor have I been able to find a

FIGURE 87. Sergeant, Second Regiment of Dragoons (ca. 1842), in dress uniform, and with the pattern-of-1841 horse equipments properly arranged for a ceremonial exhibition with the schabraque reserved for formal occasions. He is armed with the Model 1833 Hall single-shot breech-loading percussion carbine, the Model 1836 single-shot muzzle-loading Johnson percussion pistol, and the Model 1833 dragoon sabre.

description of this item anywhere else. It is evident, from the above, that it was an enclosed container of the same length as the valise, and from the name, I assume it was somewhat flat in shape. I show the ends of my interpretation of this wallet in Figure 86, and under the valise on the drawings of the mounted dragoons riding the 1841 saddle in Figures 87 and 88.

The dragoon sergeant in Figure 87, in full dress and urging his horse into the gallop for an exhibition sabre charge, is riding the 1841 dragoon saddle covered by the *schabraque*, reserved, generally, for parade and ceremonial use. Like the *schabraques* of the current European armies, this one folds back in front to form a cover for the holsters and great coat. The straps and buckles visible hold the fold in place until an order is given to draw pistols, at which time the buckles are undone and the fold laid back to expose the holster and pistol.

Unlike the 1833 breastplate, the Model 1841 is black leather, as are all leather parts of the horse equipments, including girth and surcingle.

Figure 88 shows a private of the Second Regiment of U.S. Dragoons with the 1841 horse equipments dressed and equipped for field duty. Instead of the dress *schabraque*, he uses just the plain brown horse blanket. Holsters are strapped to the saddle over the greatcoat.

The lead strap, attached to the throat-latch ring of the halter, is wrapped in the manner that was customary through the 1860's, and in some mounted companies on into the 1870's.

Model 1841 horse equipments were made by private contractors for the Army. Contracts and correspondence in the National Archives show that saddles and other items of horse equipment were made and delivered by John Fairbairn & Co., Saddlers of Philadelphia, at a cost of $12 each for saddles, complete; $5 for bridles and halters as a set; $2.50 for valises; $0.75 for carbine buckets; and $3.50 per set of holsters.

Until 1841 horse equipments had been furnished by the commissary general of purchases, although at times the Quartermaster Department was called on to supply some items of horse gear when time was important. But General Order No. 24, published by the Adjutant General's Office April 24, 1841, directed that the duty of furnishing horse equipments was to be transferred to the Ordnance Department. A little more than a year later, October 22, 1842, General Order No. 67 revealed that the Secretary of War had

decided to make the Quartermaster Department responsible for the issue of horse equipments, thus relieving the colonel of ordnance of this duty.

THE RINGGOLD SADDLE
1844–47

Correspondence and records in the National Archives indicate rather conclusively that a saddle designed by Sam Ringgold, an officer of artillery in the Regular Army, was given field tests in 1841, 261 of his saddles having been made for the Quartermaster Department, according to a statement submitted to the quartermaster general by Major Crossman of the Philadelphia Clothing Department. This same statement shows the total number of Ringgold saddles and saddle trees made by private contractors between 1841 and 1845 as requested by Commander C. Ringgold, probably a brother of Sam, in a letter to the Secretary of War in 1857. Major Sam Ringgold had been killed in the Mexican War, and no doubt this was an effort on his brother's part to collect whatever royalties were due the major's estate from the manufacture of Ringgold saddles in the above span of years. This fairly well indicates that no more Ringgold saddles were made after 1845.

The statement cited above indicates a total of 1,147 Ringgold saddles were made by John Fairbairn, Isaac Young, and Magee Tabor & Co., all private saddlery contractors. Unless additional quantities were made for the Ordnance Department, which no longer was officially responsible for the purchase and issuing of horse equipments after 1842, it would seem to indicate that comparatively few Ringgold saddles were used by the mounted services, which, of course, included the light artillery.

A report dated August 16, 1844, and labeled Document 95 in Book 3 of Quartermaster Correspondence in the National Archives, is Major Ringgold's description of his saddle. This was submitted about the same time he applied for a patent on his saddle, which had already been used quite extensively in field tests by dragoon and artillery companies, and by individual officers through purchase from private contractors.

This appears to be the only description on record besides the one used in the patent issued to Ringgold in October of 1844. Major Ringgold's description follows:

FIGURE 88. Private, Second Regiment of Dragoons (ca. 1842), in fatigue dress and with the Model 1841 horse equipments packed for service in the field. He is armed with the Model 1833 Hall single-shot breech-loading percussion carbine, the 1836 Johnson single-shot muzzle-loading percussion pistol, and the 1833 dragoon sabre.

The saddle calculated for the use of Horse or foot artillery . . . light or heavy dragoons . . . or for the purpose of carrying packs.

Note: The arches of the pommel and cantle are strengthened by pieces of iron conforming to & screwed into the wood. The sheet iron is screwed into the side bars, then bent up and screwed into the pommel and cantle. The upper part of the pommel and cantle is also strengthened by pieces of iron forming an arch.

The saddle tree is made of the best seasoned ash—it consists of six pieces—
1.—The two side bars. 2.—The pommel in 2 pieces forming an arch over the withers. 3.—The cantle in two pieces forming an arch over the backbone. These pieces by an ingenious contrivance form a joint by crossing each other and overlapping, giving the arches great strength. The parts that form the pommel and cantle are joined to the side bars by iron pins, which passing through them are firmly clinched and rivetted on the sides. The pommel and cantle are mortised into the side bars rendering the whole firm and compact.

The side bars are open at the top, and just wide enough to admit of free action to the vertebrae and prevent pressure on the ridge of the back, the withers and loins. They are supplied with four rings behind—two to attach the crupper and horse shoe pouches—two for the nose bag and forage cord. They have three rings in front—two for the breast strap and one for the carbine socket.

The side bars in front of the pommel and behind the cantle are covered with sheet iron through which staples are passed in front of the cloak straps & rings. Staples are also passed through the cantle to support the valise against it and prevent its touching the horse's loins.

An iron plate is attached to each side bar to hold the girth strap. The stirrup leathers pass through a mortice in the wood which is strengthened by a plate secured to the pommel & affording a strong brace.

The tree has a brass moulding on the pommel and cantle to protect the wood of each, and a small staple passes through the side bars to secure the stirrup leather in its place.

The seat of the tree is covered with webbing strongly stretched and again with rawhide both firmly fixed to the tree with copper nails which prevents the covering from rust and from coming loose.

The flaps extending sufficiently low to prevent the rider's legs from being soiled cover two interior flaps which protect the horse's sides from the girth buckles. The flaps are secured firmly to the side bars with copper nails.

In constructing a military saddle and arranging the equipments there are certain indispensable conditions that must be fulfilled. Among the rest may be enumerated:
1. Protection to the horse from injury by a proper formation of the saddle.
2. Transportation of the effects of the soldier without embarrassment to man or horse in travelling, maneuvering and the use of weapons.
3. Durability, strength, and a view to proper economy.
4. Fitness for campaign & war.
5. As much as possible the ease and comfort consistent with a correct military seat.

It is confidently believed that the saddle I have the honor to offer for inspection fulfills these conditions.

The cantle is no higher than is necessary to sling a valise clear of the loins. The pommel is no higher than to raise the arch over the withers and carry the holster & cloak free of pressure.

THE BRIDLE

1. The bridle consists of a bitt, curb and headstall.
2. Of the Halter & watering bridle united together.

The use of the curb is necessary to enable the horseman to restrain and govern his horse with one hand whilst the other is free to defend himself & unemployed except with the use of his weapons.

A snaffle bit is necessary for purposes of instruction in riding, and for a watering bridle. It is ingeniously attached to the halter rendering a double headstall unnecessary.

The breaststrap and crupper are attached to the saddle by rings which maintain it in its place. Girths, a surcingle passing through the flap, a nosebag, forage cord, two horse shoe pouches, a carbine sling and bucket, a blanket, valise straps, & cloak and holster straps complete the equipment.

All which is respectfully submitted
(signed) S. Ringgold

Even though Ringgold was granted Patent No. 3,779 on October 7, 1844, records show that less than 500 Ringgold saddles were made for the Army after 1844. By that time the Grimsley saddle, a greatly improved dragoon saddle that was not so prone to make the horses' backs sore, had become popular with dragoon and artillery officers, and the government refrained from buying new saddles until the demands of the Mexican War made it necessary. And then it was the Grimsley pattern that was purchased in 1846 to outfit the new Regiment of Mounted Rifles.

The Ringgold saddle and its related equipments are shown in Figure 89. Details of the iron-reinforced tree are from the patent drawing. The saddle itself was drawn from the excellent specimen in the West Point Museum that had been used by Colonel Duncan, an artillery officer in the Mexican War. While the West Point saddle no longer has girth, stirrup leathers, or stirrups, it is likely they were like the ones shown on this drawing. Records of returns for the Regiment of Mounted Riflemen show that the stirrups were brass, and girth and surcingle, which passed through slits in the skirts to pass *over* the seat and *under* the skirts to buckle on the near side over the girth, were of blue woollen [*sic*] webbing.

The seat, padded with hair, was goatskin or light morocco leather, and was secured to the pommel and cantle by brass nails.

All leather in this saddle was black. Metal parts, except for brass moldings on pommel and cantle, and brass stirrups, were iron with japanned black finish.

Figure 89A shows a specimen of the Ringgold saddle recently added to the Fort Sill Museum collection after having been identified by the author as a Ringgold in the private collection of Norm Flayderman. It is my supposition that the Fort Sill specimen was manufactured at a later date than the Duncan saddle at West Point and that it is an improved version issued to dragoons and light artillery after the West Point specimen was purchased privately by Colonel Duncan.

Comparison with Figure 89 will show a number of apparent differences and modifications. The tree appears to be almost identical to the tree of the West Point saddle, except for the length of the horseshoe-shaped iron reinforcing pieces at the front of the pommel peak and at the rear of the cantle peak; those on the Fort Sill saddle are shorter and do not extend all the way to the heavy iron arches at both pommel and cantle. Rawhide, nailed to pommel and cantle and laced to the sidebars with leather thongs, similar to the seat in the 1841 saddle, replaces the heavy webbing used in the West Point specimen. A single ring at the forward ends of the sidebars differs from the two on the Duncan saddle.

The quilted seat on the Fort Sill saddle has a much simpler design than the one shown in Figure 89, with the pommel and cantle ends of the seat neatly held in place by the brass moldings. Brass shield-shaped escutcheons are nailed to the top sides of pommel and cantle peaks, protecting the edges of the coat and valise-strap mortices through the wood tree. Both cantle and pommel peaks are slightly curved with more rounded ends than the Duncan saddle (Figure 89), and the over-all workmanship and design of the Fort Sill specimen seems to be much improved over the earlier model.

Since stirrup leathers, stirrups, girth, and surcingle are missing, it must be assumed that they were either very similar or identical to the equipments shown on Figure 89. I believe it is safe to surmise that the improved Ringgold saddles were issued to dragoons with the heavy brass stirrup with perforated treads and to light artillery with the lighter brass stirrup with roughened solid tread.

A telephone conversation with Norman Flayderman during the fall of 1974 revealed that two other improved Ringgold saddles have been sold from his New Milford, Connecticut, military-goods store to private collectors, but the locations of these two saddles are unknown to me.

The headstall was not unusual, it being of the current military design. An extra curb chain was carried on the crown, which was fitted with a brass stud and leather loop used to hold the halter in place behind the horse's poll. The halter was of slightly different design from the Model 1841, for the ring on the lower part of the noseband was joined to the throatlatch by a doubled and stitched leather strap with a metal two-headed stud at the ring end to strengthen it.

The watering bridle, or snaffle-bit attachment, was unique, and was the first of a series of watering bits that attached to the halter squares by means of a chain and toggle. This was one of Ringgold's innovations that was to last as standard pattern until 1885.

At least one modern writer has criticized Ringgold's method of reinforcing the tree with iron plates, but this was not the factor that made it unsatisfactory for service—it was a very *strong* tree. The fact that the *shape* of the sidebars caused so many sore backs among dragoon and artillery horses was the characteristic that influenced the government to replace it with the Grimsley saddle in 1847.

Figures 90 and 91 show dragoons using the Ringgold horse equipments, with saddles packed for duty in the field. Pommel and cantle packs are held up clear of contact with the horse, and the snaffle-bit chain-and-toggle attachment to the halter is visible.

The carbine strap and bucket are not unlike those described in the 1841 descriptions of horse equipments.

Figure 92 shows a corporal of the Second Dragoons in a sabre duel with a first sergeant of the Mexican Seventh Regular Cavalry Regiment. The American dragoon is using the Ringgold equipments. The Mexican cavalryman is uniformed and equipped according to the regulations for his regiment during the Mexican War period. His saddle is the crude wood hussar type, copied from the common European hussar equipment.

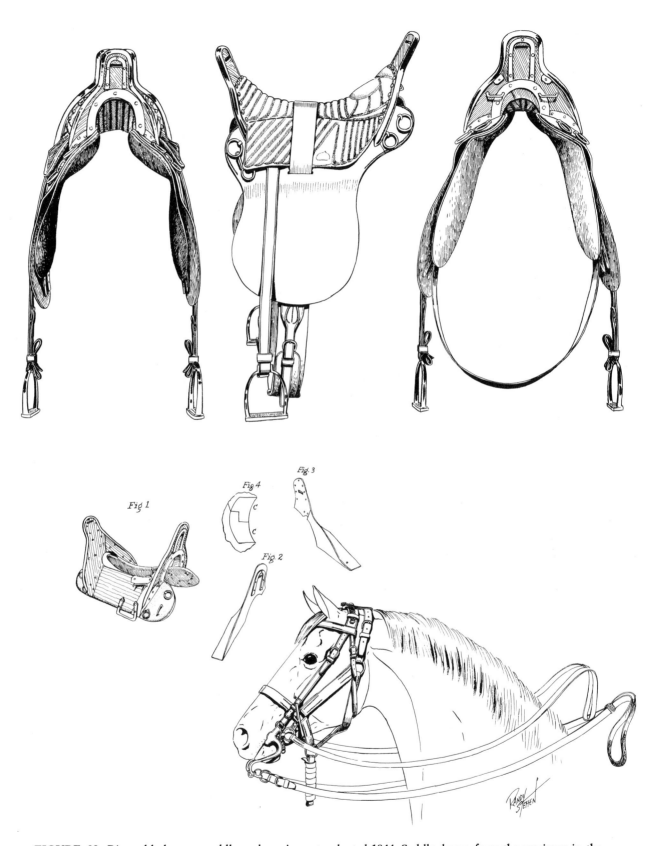

FIGURE 89. Ringgold dragoon saddle and equipments adopted 1844. Saddle drawn from the specimen in the West Point Museum collection.

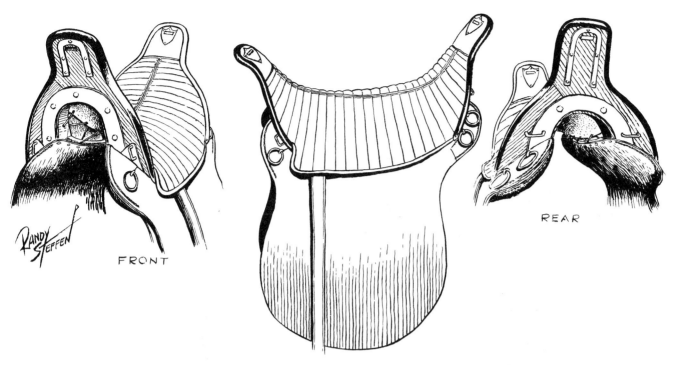

FRONT

REAR

FIGURE 89A. The improved Ringgold dragoon and light-artillery saddle issued before the adoption of the Grimsley saddle in 1847. There is little doubt that this saddle was issued to the Regiment of Mounted Riflemen when it was organized in 1846, before the special contract with Grimsley was completed to supply saddles to the new regiment. Drawn from the specimen in the Fort Sill Museum collection.

THE GRIMSLEY SADDLE

1847-59

When the Second Regiment of U.S. Dragoons was authorized in 1836, President Andrew Jackson appointed Thornton Grimsley of St. Louis a first lieutenant in the new regiment, but Grimsley declined to accept the appointment and remained in St. Louis (*Everglade to Cañon* by Rodenbough, 19, 20).

By 1844 Grimsley had a large saddlery company in St. Louis. It was in April of this year that he first wrote the quartermaster general soliciting contracts for the manufacture of horse equipments for the dragoon service. His letter mentioned the remounting of the Second Regiment of Dragoons and left no doubt he was interested in furnishing their horse equipments. His letter mentioned that he could save the government some money, and that all he needed to submit a bid was a set of patterns for the equipment required, for which he would quickly post the necessary security. He mentioned casually that letters from Lieutenant Colonel Kearny and Major Aeneas Mackay, deputy quartermaster general in charge of the St. Louis depot, would reach the general's office in the same mail.

Grimsley and Major Mackay must have had a very satisfactory relationship, for by September, 1846, Mackay had awarded Grimsley the contract for furnishing the horse equipments for the new Regiment of Mounted Riflemen without requiring competitive bids. His letter to the quartermaster general announces his action, and is of enough interest to reproduce here in full.

Deputy Quartermaster General's Office
1 September 1846

General

The Company of the 1st Dragoons which has been recruiting for some time back under the direction of Lt. Col. Kearny is I believe nearly complete in the compliment of men and horses, & Mr. Grimsley, with whom the Board of Officers arranged the pattern saddle, etc., has nearly finished the Horse Equipment for it. The extra blankets, spurs, etc., required

FIGURE 90. Private, Second Dragoons (ca. 1846), with the regulation Ringgold horse equipments and full pack for field service. He is armed with a U.S. Model 1842 single-shot muzzle-loading percussion pistol, the Model 1843 Hall single-shot breech-loading percussion carbine, and the Model 1840 dragoon sabre. Near side.

FIGURE 91. Private, Second Dragoons (ca. 1846), with the regulation Ringgold horse equipments. He is armed with a U.S. Model 1842 single-shot muzzle-loading percussion pistol, the Model 1843 Hall single-shot breech-loading percussion carbine, and the Model 1840 dragoon sabre. Off side.

FIGURE 92. Sabre duel during Mexican War.

by them, can be furnished at any moment they are called for, so that it will depend on the exertions of the officers in their organization & drill to enable them to take the field immediately.

With respect to the saddles and bridles of the Mounted Riflemen, I came to the conclusion that as they were to be made on the model of Mr. Grimsley and he had the most perfect knowledge of their construction, was the best workman and the most extensively engaged in the business in this place, and had in the opinion of all that I consulted on the subject, fixed the price as low as he could reasonably afford to furnish them, it was decidedly preferable to engage him to make them, than to risk their imperfect construction by any who might endeavor to under bid him in getting the job. He has engaged to do the work and to put such force upon it as shall insure their being completed as fast as the Reg. shall want them. He is to receive the same compensation as was fixed upon with the Board which made the report upon the Saddle & Equipments and arranged the price of each article.

Colonel Kearny took out with him as an experiment a number of these Saddles, and has never made any objection to them & the popularity of them has become so great that I

have been obliged to prohibit the private sale of them to the Officers & others, to enable Mr. Grimsley to complete in time the number required by the Dragoons

I have the honor to be, &
with great respect
Your mo. Obd. Servant
(signed) Aeneas Mackay
Supt. & Ac. D.Q.M. Gen.

Major General Tho. S. Jesup
Qr. Master General
Washington, D.C.

We see from the above that by this time Grimsley had already worked with the Board of Officers convened to select the best saddle for the mounted services, and that his saddle and equipment designs had been selected for adoption, although the official adoption did not come until December 2, 1847, 15 months later.

The usual procedure of the Quartermaster's Department was to have horse equipment contracts put out for bid to any saddler whose facilities were adequate to produce the quality and quantity required. In 1844 Ringgold sought to collect royalties from the manufacture of his saddle pattern by patenting his saddle. After his death his brother made some effort to determine the number of saddles and saddle trees that had been made after the date of patent, evidently with the intent to collect royalties for the estate on saddles of the Ringgold design made after the date of patent.

Grimsley followed the same procedure by applying for a patent in the fall of 1847, figuring, I am sure, on being awarded all contracts for manufacture of the Grimsley equipments, knowing the government was reluctant to pay royalties when not absolutely necessary.

In late September, 1847, Grimsley wrote Lieutenant Alfred Pleasanton, Second Dragoons, who was stationed at the Cavalry School, Carlisle, Pennsylvania, in reply to a letter of praise for his saddle, in which a set of equipments to be used as a sample at the school was ordered. Grimsley said:

... The complete success which has attended every exertion to bring in to use a saddle superior to any in service, and the many testimonials of the highest respectability in its favor has caused me to yield to the solicitations of friends and have it patented.

I have all my drawings completed and in a few weeks will be in Washington with my samples, descriptions, etc., etc. when I shall hope to see our brave and chivalrous Colonel May, Genl. Jessup, and yourself.

I shall bring with me two or three sets, and hope to be able to convince the Q.M. Genl. of the utter falicy [sic] of the practice of purchasing the important articles of Horse Equipments of men east of the mountains who never rode on horse back probably five hundred miles in their lives. Be so kind as to say to Col. May that I should be happy to "furnish" a set of equipments for the School of Practice at Carlisle, and will get them up in a stile [sic] superior to any he has ever seen, and forward them to him in a shorter time than he can procure them anywhere in the U. States. I have about 130, and can make him 100 sets in 20 days from the time I receive the order.

I manufacture my Bridle bits, and stirrups, and put all the company and regimental letters on the bridles, breast plates and valises.

If the Q.M. should feel disposed I will make a set of equipments and forward them to Carlisle where they may be inspected, and if they are not superior to anything in service I will receive them, and pay all charges of transportation, etc.

The price will be the same as heretofore. Col. McKay [sic], QM at this place purchased of me for Capt. [sic]

Kearny's command for the Mounted Rifle Regt., and for several other companies of the 1st and 2nd Dragoons.

Grimsley was a salesman, there can be little doubt of that! And there's little doubt that his saddle and equipments were highly thought of, from the letters written by dragoon officers praising the Grimsley pattern.

The Colonel May mentioned in Grimsley's letter to young Pleasanton was the Mexican War hero now in command of the Cavalry School at Carlisle. His letter, which follows, to the quartermaster general shows his own and others high regard for the Grimsley saddle. He puts subtle pressure on Jesup to limit the manufacture of the Grimsley saddle to the facilities of the patentee, and suggests that final steps be taken to adopt it for the Army.

> Carlisle Barracks, Pa.
> October 7, 1847
>
> General,
>
> I have the honor herewith to enclose a letter of Mr. Grimsley, Saddler of St. Louis, in reply to one I directed Lieut. Pleasanton to write to him ordering a saddle of his pattern to be sent to me.
>
> You will see by his letter that he has patented his saddle, and objects to furnishing it as a pattern.
>
> I have used his saddle in service, and consider it much superior to any we have ever used in our service, and for that reason specified his saddle in my requisition for Saddles for this Post—I am satisfied that when you see Mr. Grimsley's saddle you will be pleased with it—
>
> All the Officers of my Regiment, and of the 1st. Dragoons, who have used the saddle & with whom I have conversed, speak in the highest terms of it, and as I consider the Saddle of the greatest importance in the instruction of recruits, I hope the Department will comply with my wishes in furnishing me this saddle.
>
> Mr. Campbell whom I am informed has the contract to make the Saddles for this post, cannot, I am satisfied, make them as I wish, without he is furnished with a pattern.
>
> Would it not be as well on the arrival of Mr. Grimsley in Washington to convene a Board to examine & report on his saddle—
>
> I shall require about 40 saddles by the end of next month—
>
> I am, General,
> very respectfully
> Your Most Obdt. Servant
> C. A. May
> (signed) Brvt Lt Col 2nd Drags.
> Com. Of.
> General T. S. Jesup
> Q Master General, U.S. Army
> Washington City,
> D.C.

A letter from Grimsley to the quartermaster general October 11, 1847, confirms the fact that a number of Grimsley saddles were in extensive use by officers of the First Dragoons on their ride to California and Oregon in 1846, and by Donophan's army. This letter voices his eagerness to corral all contracts for Grimsley pattern saddles, and his reluctance to see them made by anyone else:

St. Louis, 11th Oct. 1847

Genl. Jesup

Col. Mackay of this City has ordered two complete sets of me, one he informs me is to be sent to you in Washington and the other to Col Stanton, U.S.Q.M. in Phila. They are in preperation [sic], and will be forwarded as soon as completed. The saddle tree on which I construct my military saddle is different from any I have ever seen in several essential points all of which I hope to be able to explain to you personally when I come to Washington, and I address you these few lines to ask you to suspend any contracts you may have to make for dragoon equipments until I arrive as I feel confident I can give you ample testimony of the superiority of my saddle over every other now in use. Should you think proper to contract with other persons than myself for equipments I will furnish the treese [sic] on a contract with you for a less price than you can procure them anywhere east of the mountains. I have furnished them to officers of every arm of the service though more of course to the dragoons and I assure you I have yet to find the first one to find fault with them.

They have been rode from St. Louis to California and Oregon, and have been tested in the service from the first braking [sic] out of the war, and have been resold after a years service under Col. Donophan at Saltillo Mexico for double my contract price.

I also manufacture a Splendid article of dragoon bridle bit and stirrups which I will also submit for your inspection. I hope you will give me the 100 sets for the School of Practice at Carlisle Pa. to make the proposition for which I have forwarded to Lieut. Pleasanton and asked him to submitt [sic] it to you.

I remain with greate [sic] respect
Your ob servant,
(signed) Thornton Grimsley

On the same date the above letter was written, Colonel Mackay wrote General Jesup a highly complimentary letter concerning the Grimsley equipments, saying:

. . . There can be no doubt I think, from the universal expression of that opinion, that the Dragoon Saddle furnished by him, of which we have procured so many for the service, is vastly superior to any other we have ever made use of. . . . Mr. Grimsley is able and willing to furnish them to any extent; but should it be the intention of the Department to procure Saddles from other makers, he will furnish *them* on reasonable terms with his Patent Saddle Tree on which the superiority of his Saddle greatly depends.

Grimsley left St. Louis on October 24 for his trip to Washington. With him he took a pattern saddle, patent drawings and description, and a letter of introduction from Mackay to the quartermaster general. In it he was most flowery concerning Grimsley's reputation, and said of his facilities, "He has in this city (St. Louis) one of the most extensive and perfect *Factories* of this kind in the United States."

On December 11, Grimsley wrote General Jesup to inform him that he had obtained a patent on his saddle, and since he had 1,000 of his new trees on hand he would be glad to receive an order for them.

Less than a month before, the Adjutant General's Office had published General Order No. 35, dated November 20, 1847, in which a board of officers was ordered convened in Washington on November 24 to determine the best pattern for saddles and other equipments for cavalry corps. The board consisted of Brigadier General S. W. Kearny; Major Thomas Swords, Quartermaster Department; Major P. St.G. Cooke, Second Dragoons; Captain and Brevet Lieutenant Colonel C. A. May, Second Dragoons; and Captain H. S. Turner, First Dragoons.

The board made its report on December 2, 1847. Following is the complete text of this document:

Washington
December 2d: 1847.

The Board met pursuant to the above orders—present, all the members—and having at several sittings freely discussed the subject of Cavalry Equipments, and examined the models presented for their inspection by Mr. Thornton Grimsley of St. Louis, respectfully submit the following report; and recommend the patterns hereinafter described, as being most suitable for Cavalry purposes, viz:

Bridle.

Bit—Of the form and pattern of that submitted to the Board by Lt. Col. May; being an S bit, with a strengthening crossbar, connecting the lower extremities of the branches. Mouthpiece of three patterns, made after those prescribed in the tactics, and to be supplied to companies in the proportion therein recommended: 1/6 mild, 4/6 medium, 1/6 severe. Branches all medium. Material of bit, steel thickly plated with brass. See Fig. 5 & 6.

Curb—Leather strap, 5/8 of an inch wide, with brass buckles. Fig. 3

Head-stall—Single cheek pieces, one inch wide, with brass wire buckle on each end; buckled to bit and upper part of headstall. Fig. 3

Throat-Strap—5/8 of an inch wide, with brass buckles on each side.

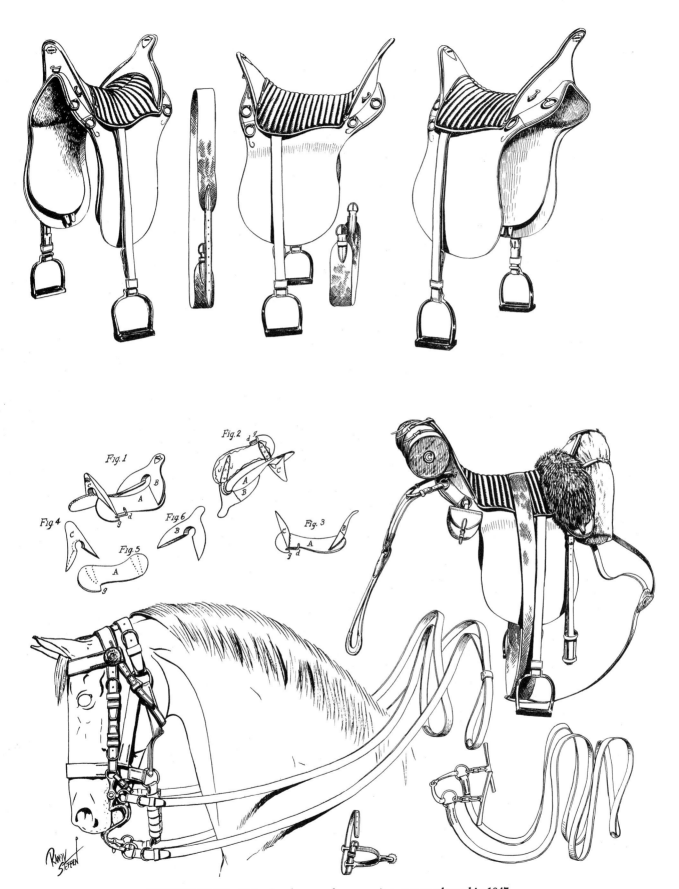

FIGURE 93. The Grimsley dragoon horse equipments as adopted in 1847.

Fig. 3

Front-piece—Single plain strap, one and a quarter inch wide; a brass circular plate, one and a half inch diameter on each extremity; with beaded edge and letter of company, one inch long, raised on it. Fig. 3

Reins—Leather curb-rein five feet six inches long. Snaffle-rein four feet six inches long. Both reins buckled to bit, and ⅞ inch wide. Curb-rein provided with a strong leather slide. Fig. 3

Buckles—Brass wire with oval top and strong tongue.

Halter

The same in pattern as that furnished the 1st Dragoons in 1839, and since. All the straps to be one and 4/8 of an inch wide; and made of strong harness leather. The cheek pieces to be connected with the neck and nose bands by iron rings: those for nose band to be *square*, one inch and a half inside; for neck band, *round*, one and ¾ inch in diameter. The strap, seven feet long, buckles into an iron ring, and should have the usual taper for ease in tying. Fig. 4

Watering Bridle

Plain ring snaffle, with single rein: to be attached to the lower side rings of the halter, by short chains & attachment bars. Fig. 4

Saddle. Figs. 1, 14, 15, 16, 17, & 18.

It is the unanimous opinion of the Board that, the best pattern of saddle for Cavalry service, is the one submitted by Colonel (now Brig. Genl.) S. W. Kearny to the Qr. Mr. Genl. in 1844, with the changes made in it by Mr. Grimsley since that time. A complete model of this saddle, as modified, was submitted to the Board by Mr. Grimsley, and they recommend its adoption, as it is, for Cavalry Corps. Combining strength, durability, peculiar fitness to the horse's back, and convenience for military fixtures, this pattern more than any other yet furnished for Dragoon service, gives an erect posture and easy seat to the rider, at the same time that little or no injury is done to the horse's back on the longest marches. Some of the members of the Board have had the fairest opportunity of testing the merits of this saddle, having used it on marches of more than 2000 miles in extent, and the result has been in every instance to confirm their belief in the superiority of this saddle over any other which has come under their observation. In outward appearance, the saddle resembles more the French Hussar saddle than any other with which the Board is familiar: it combines all the conveniences of the French saddle for attaching military and cavalry appurtenances, with the indispensable qualities requisite in a service tree. To prevent injury to the horse's back, the "side-bars" are so formed as to *fit* the back, bearing equally throughout their whole extent; and the forks of the high pommel and cantle are, in every case, and under all the circumstances of reduced flesh, raised above the withers and back-bone of the horse.

The details of finish to be precisely as in the model submitted by Mr. Grimsley. Stirrup leathers to pass through staples let into the lower edge of the side-bars. Girths to buckle to straps strongly nailed and rivetted to side-bars. Mortised holes in pommel and cantle for cloak and valise straps. Iron rings and staples on the cantle end of side-bars for attaching shoe-pouch and crupper. The tree to be protected and strengthened by a covering of raw-hide. Quilted seat sewed down and stitched as in the model presented. Leather skirts to protect the blanket (on which the trooper rides on service) and the pantaloons of the rider, from the sweat of the horse. Also small under skirts to protect the sides of the horse from the girth buckles.

Stirrup-leathers—Black: one and ⅜ of an inch wide, with oval brass buckles. Fig. 1

Stirrups—Brass, and of same pattern as those furnished the 1st Dragoons in 1834. Fig. 1

Holsters—Black leather: left side for pistol, right side made in the form of a pouch, for holding grooming articles; attached to saddle as in the model. Fig. 2

Holster-covers—Black bear-skin, extending two inches below the shoulder of holster-pipe on the left & to a corresponding distance on the right side; terminated by a leather strap one inch wide; strongly sewed to the cover—this strap buttons to a brass knob, firmly rivetted to holster and pouch. Fig. 2

Breast-strap—Same as that heretofore furnished the dragoons, and attached in the same manner. Fig. 2

Breast-plate—Plain brass heart, with letter of company one & a half inch long raised thereon. Fig. 2

Crupper—To buckle into rings on each side-bar, as in the model. Fig. 1

Carbine Strap & Boot—Same as that uniformly furnished for Dragoon Service, and attached to saddle by a ring & staple, rivetted to the pommel end of right side-bar. Fig. 9

Girths—Indigo blue, worsted webbing: three inches & a half wide; three feet nine inches long. Fig. 7

Surcingles—Indigo blue, worsted webbing; three inches & a half wide: five feet webbing, two feet strap. Fig. 8

Valise—Dark blue cloth; waterproof; five inches & a half diameter; eighteen inches long. Attached to saddle by three straps, the middle one of which passes through the mortise of the cantle, and suspends the valise effectually from the horse's back. A brass circular plate, one inch and a half diameter, with beaded edge, on each end of the valise, with the letter of the company one inch long raised thereon. Fig. 1

Saddle blanket—Plain dark blue, such as now furnished by the Q. Mrs. Department.

Spurs

Of brass, corresponding in fashion with the model presented by Mr. Grimsley; the leather strap to be ¾ of an inch wide. Fig. 11.

Pack-saddle. Fig. 12

Mr. Grimsley's pattern in every respect; except that, the girth must be four inches wide, and made of horse hair or Manilla grass.

Officers' equipments will not differ from those above described for enlisted men, except as follows, viz: Two holsters, instead of holster and pouch. Holster pipes to have plain brass tips, extending up two inches and a half. A raised star on Breast-plate, instead of letter of the company. A raised star on circular brass plates of the Bridle, instead of letter of the company.

Officer's Housing or Saddle cover. Fig. 13

Of dark blue cloth, with gold lace border for field officers & commissioned staff, one & a half inches wide, and yellow cloth border of the same width for company officers: this border to be set back, one quarter of an inch from the edge, which will be bound with patent leather. The saddle cover will be pointed in the flanks, & extend eleven inches behind the cantle, having thirty inches depth from back seam to the flank points. An embroidered silk star in each flank corner for company officers, with number of the regiment left on the cloth ground, in center of the star: the star to be of five points and two inches diameter.

Officers' valise to be bound with patent leather, with an embroidered star of five points and one inch & a half in diameter, on each end.

This star, both on housing and valise, to be of silk for company officers, and of gold lace for field officers and commissioned staff.

Carbine pommel strap 28 inches long; ¾ of an inch wide. Oval brass buckle.

The Board adjourned sine die.

(signed)   S. W. Kearny
Brig. Genl.

(signed)   Thos. Swords, Qr. Mr.

(signed)   P. St. G. Cooke
Maj. 2nd Dragoons

(signed)   C. A. May
Bvt. Lt. Col. 2nd Dragoons

(signed)   H. S. Turner
Capt. 1st Drags.

So it is seen that Colonel May's suggestion to the quartermaster general was carried out, and a special board convened for the sole purpose of adopting the Grimsley saddle and equipments.

An interesting side light on the origin of the Grimsley saddle pattern is the board's comment in the description of the saddle in their report about a saddle having been submitted by the then Colonel Kearny to a board in 1844. It is especially interesting in view of the text of a note written by Grimsley to someone in the Quartermasters Department shortly after the board's report had been published. The contents of the note are as follows:

The tree introduced by General Kearny was a complete compilation of the french, and Spanish and made by myself. The one now submitted is my improved tree, and the board specially refers to my improvements.

(signed) Grimsley

This note, as well as the above report of the board, and all other correspondence concerning the Grimsley saddle are from photocopies made of the originals in the National Archives collection of Quartermaster correspondence.

When this glowing report reached the quartermaster general, coming as it had from such distinguished warriors as those sitting on the cavalry equipment board, he was quick to get an approval from the Secretary of War, and the Grimsley saddle became the official pattern for the mounted service for the next 18 years. (Official approval published in G.O. No. 35, March 7, 1848.)

The patent protecting Grimsley on this saddle design was issued December 11, 1847 (Patent No. 5,396), giving him the right to collect license fees from any other manufacturer making saddles of his design for the government or for private sale to officers. It is doubtful that many were made outside the Grimsley factory at St. Louis.

Two features are outstanding in the design and construction of the Grimsley tree. The sidebars are contoured to fit the horse's back, with the lower surface rounded and curved so that in theory, at any rate, equal pressure is exerted on every surface contacted by the bars. In addition, the whole wooden tree is enveloped in rawhide, sewed on while wet in the fashion of the Mexican, or Spanish, tree, so that in effect it is one solid mass of great strength, where stresses are distributed over its entire surface.

The description accompanying the patent drawings contains much more of a detailed description of the tree and the other components than the abbreviated one in the Board's report. Since information on the Grimsley saddle has been more or less obscure in readily available publications up to now, I believe the inclusion of this description, as well as the illustrations that accompany it, will be of value to the student of cavalry history, so I include it here in its entirety.

UNITED STATES PATENT OFFICE.

THORNTON GRIMSLEY, OF ST. LOUIS, MISSOURI.

DRAGOON-SADDLETREE.

Specification of Letters Patent No. 5,396, dated December 11, 1847.

To all whom it may concern:

Be it known that I, THORNTON GRIMSLEY, of the city of St. Louis and State of Missouri, have invented a new and improved Saddletree Possessing Qualities That Particularly Adapt it to the Formation of Dragoon and other Military Saddles; and I do hereby declare the following to be a full, clear, and exact description thereof, reference being had to the accompanying drawings, making a part of this specification.

T. Grimsley,

Riding Saddle,

Nº 5396.

Patented Dec. 11, 1847.

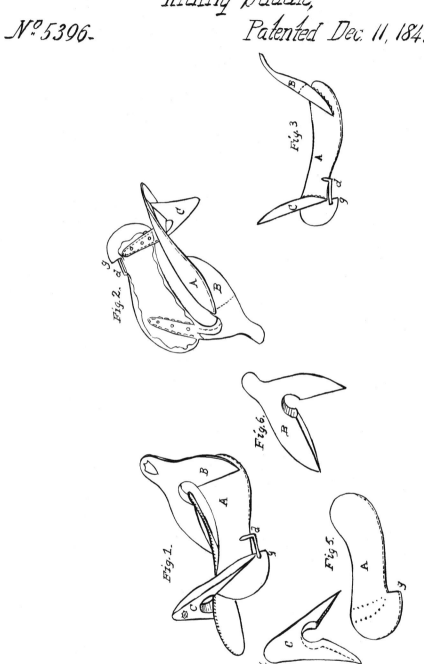

Figure 1, is a perspective view of my military saddle tree, standing in its natural position; Fig. 2, a perspective view of the same reversed; Fig. 3, a side elevation thereof, and Figs. 4, 5, and 6, represent the pommel, one of the side bars, and the cantle of the tree, detached.

Similar letters indicate like parts in all the figures.

A, A, are the side bars, B, is the cantle, and C, is the pommel of the tree.

The nature of my invention consists of an improvement upon the form of the pommel and cantle made use of in the construction of the French hussar (or old dragoon regulation) saddle tree, and in the combination—without metallic fastenings—of the French hussar or dragoon regulation style of pommel and cantle, or my improved form of pommel and cantle with winding side bars; of such a form, and arranged in such a manner, that they will bear so equally and uniformly in every part upon the back of a horse or mule, as to require no padding. The French hussar saddle tree has straight side bars, which do not fit the back of a horse with accuracy, and in consequence, it is necessary that they should be padded to prevent injury to the horse. The pommel and cantle of the French hussar saddle tree are combined and secured to the side bars by means of metallic fastenings.

I secure the pommel and cantle to the side bars of my military saddle tree by means of a rawhide covering, confined in the manner represented in the drawings; by which means my tree is much lighter and stronger than the French hussar tree. The side bars A, A, should be 19 to 20 inches in length, and the timber when rough, ought to be $3\frac{1}{2}$ inches thick. The two ends on their upper side, are brought to a plane surface where the pommel and cantle are joined to the same; the space between the pommel and cantle is shaved out to form a seat for the rider. The under sides of the side bars are worked off and so formed that they will rest on the back of a horse below the "great leaders"; and a sufficiently winding and oval surface is given to them (as represented in the drawings,) to insure their bearing with an equal and uniform pressure from front to rear. The side bars are from 5 to 7 inches wide, and vary from one fourth of an inch to an inch in thickness.

The pommel C, is twelve inches in height, from two to three in width at its upper end, and from 10 to 11 inches at its lower extremities. The pommel is plano-convex in its form; the front side being flat, and its rear surface convex. The top of the pommel is rounded off, and is slightly curved forward; an aperture is formed near the top of the pommel, faced on each side with ornamental metallic plates; which aperture is for the reception of a strap, with which to secure an overcoat or other luggage.

The height of the cantle (B,) is 14 inches; its width from two to three inches at its upper extremity, and from 11 to 12 inches at its lower extremities. The front or inner surface of the cantle, is worked out to a concave form, for the purpose of giving a safe and easy seat to the rider; (in this particular it varies from the cantle of the French hussar saddle tree, both the front and rear surfaces of which are of a convex form;) the rear side of the pommel (C,) is of an oval or convex form. One and half inches is the usual thickness given to the cantle

at its center. The narrow upper portion of the cantle curves gracefully to the rear, as represented in the drawings, and has an aperture near its extremity, faced on each side with ornamental metallic plates, for the reception of straps for suspending and securing the valise under the same. The forks in the pommel and cantle terminate in semicircular concavities, which are so far elevated as to be, in all cases of reduced flesh, above the withers and back of a horse. These four pieces—the pommel, side bars, and cantle—being formed as above described, are connected to each other by screws, nails, or pegs. Along the front and rear sides of the base of the pommel and cantle, a series of small apertures are formed in the side bars, as represented in Fig. 5; which apertures open into grooves f, f, formed in the under side of the side bars, as represented in Fig. 2.

The tree thus prepared, is covered with soft, wet raw hide of suitable strength in the following manner. The hide is stretched over the upper side of the side bars in one piece, covering both sides of the pommel and cantle, and is secured by thongs passing through the hide, and through the holes in the side bars; thus forming a seam on each side of the joints at the junction of the pommel and cantle, with the side bars; the grooves f, f, on the under side of the side bars, receive the thongs and prevent their making a prominence on the bearing surfaces of the same. The upper covering is then trimmed even with the edges of the tree, and the under covering of raw hide is fitted and sewed to the upper covering by thongs. In drying, the raw-hide covering shrinks upon the tree, binding and supporting equally every portion of the same; giving to the tree more than double the strength for its weight, that can be given to a tree in which the pommel, side bars, and cantle, are confined to each other by metallic fastenings. It will therefore be clearly perceived, that my military saddle tree is not only perfect in form, but is also much lighter and stronger than any military saddle tree ever before constructed.

Winding side bars have been used in the Spanish and Mexican saddle trees; the side bars of my improved military saddle tree have the following described improvement on the side bars made use of in those trees; viz,—a cut of some two inches in depth is made in the lower edge of each of the side bars, forming shoulders (g,) nearly in a line with the front side of each leg of the pommel; from the base of these shoulders, the lower edge of each side bar is curved off to the rear, as represented in the drawings. The object of forming this recess in the lower edge of the side bars, is to narrow the saddle in front, for the purpose of giving a firm and steady seat to the rider by giving free play to the muscles of the thigh. When a rider's thighs are so far spread by a saddle as to prevent this free play of the muscles, it necessarily gives him an unsteady and unsafe seat in the saddle. The stirrup bars d, d, are secured as represented in the drawings; their front ends are riveted to the shoulders g, g, and their rear ends to the lower edge of the narrowest part of the side bars.

As my military saddle resembles somewhat in its external appearance the French hussar saddle, I will here more particularly point out the difference between the trees on which they are constructed. The pommel of my military saddle tree curves slightly forward,—its front surface is flat, and its rear surface is convex; an aperture—faced with metallic plates,—is formed near its upper end for the reception of a strap or straps by which to suspend baggage. The pommel of the French hussar saddle tree is straight, and there is no aperture through the same for the reception of luggage straps: its form in other respects is like the pommel of my military saddle tree. The cantle of my military saddle tree has a concave inner surface and a convex outer surface, and has an aperture through the same near its upper end, faced with metallic plates for the reception of valise straps. The cantle of the French hussar saddle tree is convex on both sides and has no aperture faced with metallic plates through the same for the reception of valise straps; in all other particulars its shape is the same as that of the cantle of my military saddle tree. The side bars of my military saddle tree bear no resemblance to those of the French hussar saddle tree, as has already been particularly set forth. The pommel and cantle of the French hussar saddle tree are secured to the side bars by means of iron straps, angle plates, bolts, rivets, or screws. The pommel and cantle of my military saddle tree, are secured to the side bars by means of a strong raw hide covering in the manner herein set forth.

I am aware that saddle trees have been made in which the under side of the tree has been made to fit the form of the back of a horse, while the upper side of the tree was not shaped with reference to the comfort of the rider. But in my tree, the upper and under sides are quite different in form,—the under side fitting the horse's back, and the upper side shaped to suit the rider.

What I claim therefore as my invention and desire to secure by Letters Patent, is—

The form of my improved side bars,—the under side of which are adapted to the form of a horse, and the upper side and edges to the seat of the rider, as herein described and represented;—and the combining and securing the same to a high pommel and cantle by means of a raw hide covering substantially as herein set forth.

THORNTON GRIMSLEY.

Witnesses:
Z. C. ROBBINS,
CHAS. G. PAGE.

A little more than a month after the patent for the new dragoon saddle had been issued to Grimsley, a formal protest was made to the Secretary of State and the quartermaster general by Hezekiah L. Thistle, a former captain of Louisiana volunteers who had served in Florida during the Seminole Wars.

Thistle had invented a litter saddle that had been used in a limited way in Florida, and for several years before the Grimsley patent had been issued, the ex-volunteer captain had been flooding the Quartermaster General's Office with letters expressing his desire to make saddles and other equipments for the dragoon service.

In his letter to the Secretary of State, Thistle claimed, in 6 pages of vehement outrage, that Grimsley's patent had been examined and issued even though the application had been made only 30 days before, when an application for a similar dragoon saddle and pack saddle by Thistle had been laying on the commissioner of patent's desk at the time.

Thistle claimed that the Grimsley sidebars were a direct infringement of the patent issued to him in 1837 for a litter saddle to carry the sick and wounded, and that a letter from the Secretary of War to the patent commissioner had influenced his unusually quick action on the Grimsley application.

Apparently Thistle's claim was not valid enough for any action to be taken, for no further correspondence relating to it was found in the National Archives files.

On December 23, 1847, Thistle had requested that a board of officers be convened to examine his dragoon saddle, improvements to pack saddle, tents, and wagons. This was a month after a board had recommended the Grimsley saddle for adoption, and it is evident that Thistle must have exerted some annoying pressure, stressing "fair play," to get another board appointed and convened. Two weeks before, he had offered to make Grimsley-pattern saddles, complete with all equipments, for $8 (a real cut-throat proposition, since the Grimsley board had set a price of over $25 per set for Grimsley), and guaranteed to turn out 1,000 sets per month.

No contracts were awarded to him, but on January 7, 1848, a board of officers was appointed and ordered to convene on January 10 to examine Thistle's dragoon saddle, pack saddle, and tent. This must have gotten Thistle out of the quartermaster general's hair for a few days, for his letter to the Secretary of State was not delivered to that cabinet member until January 29, as related above.

Two days later, this eccentric gentleman again wrote the quartermaster general, offering this time to make Grimsley saddles and equipments for $25 per set and deliver at least 500 a month—acting as though nothing unpleasant had ever happened.

At least one other firm made the Grimsley-pattern equipments for the Army, for a letter from Major Ruff at Carlisle Barracks to Major Crosman in charge of the clothing depot at Philadelphia, dated November 15, 1852, referred to saddles of the Grimsley pattern being made by Magee Tabor & Co. for the dragoon companies in California.

This same letter contained a sharp criticism regarding the lack of quality of Grimsley saddles being made then in comparison with the quality found in earlier manufactures. This and other critical remarks concerning the equipments are worth quoting:

Grimsley's saddles are of several sizes and the difficulty is to get at *all* times the right size for each horse, the *result* of this difficulty is that in each Company a great number of the saddles "pinch" (or bear "unequally" upon) the horse's back. I know of no remedy for this; it is a common remark now (in our mounted service) that "Grimsley's saddles" are not made with the same care now as formerly.

The Arrangement of the Breast Strap is decidedly bad—it is not *fixed*, but connecting *with* the Holster Strap passes through loops on the Holster & slides (with a little wear) from one side to the other. They *should fasten* to the *saddle itself* & have no connection with the Holster. Nor is the Breast Strap *strong enough*, but is the very first part of the equipment which becomes unserviceable & thus the Holsters are also rendered unserviceable.

The present arrangement of the Holster is *decidedly bad*, and much complained of. There is no security for the Holster if the Trooper is galloping and the Breast Strap breaks (& nothing is more common) the Holster is certainly lost. So apparent was the insecurity that in Mexico the common method adopted by the men was to *drive a nail through the Holsters into the pommel of the saddle*. The saddles of the 1st Dragoons in '38 and up to the adoption of Grimsley's Pattern fastened the Holsters directly to the saddle by means of a small strap through the saddle skirt & around the "Holster *pipe*." I never heard of but one objection to that old arrangement & that same objection exists now in addition to the connection with the Breast Strap & is that after the great coat is unstrapped, there is no fastening for the Holster when it *passes over the pommel peak*. You will observe a small opening in the extremity of the pommel peak (to pass a strap through by which the Great Coat is fastened at that point). After then there is nothing to prevent the Band (connecting the Holster pipes and Brush pouch) from slipping over the pommel peak. The result of this is that when the horse is in rapid motion (the rider wearing his over coat) that the Holsters work over the pommel peak. This was the complaint with the old saddle & the occurrence is much more frequent now. . . . The *Shoe Pockets* I have never known used, & my experience with them is several years with the 1st Dragoons on their annual long marches, on the Western prairies, the whole of the Mexican War & finally in the very long march with the Mounted Riflemen from Jefferson Barracks to Oregon.

The Bridle Reins *are not too long*; our "tactical instructions" require the trooper to take the curb rein in his right hand, and carry it (preparatory to mounting) to the cantle peak. Any greater length than this would be superfluous.

The bits are *much too large*, & would be better if *narrower* in the *mouthpiece*. It is the common wish of nearly every cavalry officer to have restored the old "S Bit" used by the 1st Dragoons from about 1836 to 1840. I think any change that

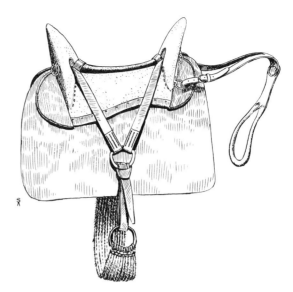

FIGURE 94. The Grimsley-pattern pack saddle approved for use by the mounted service.

would make the Bits *more severe* but of *much* less weight is greatly desired. Universally so, I believe.

Recently some of the Bits are made with a round opening for the cheek pieces of the head stall to fasten to. This is a *very great evil* & should be strictly prohibited; the rectangular opening ($\square$) for the cheek strap is the best & simplest plan to prevent vicious horses & a horse who should stumble in rapid motion from throwing the Bit up over his nose & of course thereby render both Bit & Reins useless to the rider.

The reins of the *Watering Bridle* might without detriment be made six (6) inches shorter.

In November, 1849, Grimsley requested permission to substitute molded leather covers for bearskin for holsters being made by him, saying that bearskin had become too difficult to procure on the market. But Jesup, the quartermaster general, refused at first, relenting several weeks later in a letter to Assistant Quartermaster General Swords, telling him that a recommendation for the change would be made to the Secretary of War. This approval was forthcoming a few days later.

Figure 94 shows the Grimsley-pattern pack saddle as adopted with the Grimsley dragoon equipments. This saddle, from its appearance, utilized pommel pieces at both pommel and cantle, modified to fit the sidebars, and the same type of sidebars as used in the dragoon saddle, with the lower contour modified to eliminate the step for the stirrup leather staple.

Leather sleeves over the ends of the sidebars are sewed to the large leather slabs that form the skirts of the pack saddle, and quarter straps over the sidebars and fitting in grooves under the tree form the rigging for this saddle. Rings attached to pommel and cantle by iron staples are for attaching the ropes used to secure the pack in place, and a crupper is provided to keep the saddle from slipping back on the animal's back.

Figure 95 is of an officer with field equipments on his Grimsley saddle purchased privately before this pattern was adopted as standard by the Army.

In Figure 96 the dragoon officer in dress uniform rides the Grimsley saddle with the dress housing described in the board of officers' report. All horse equipments on his mount are as prescribed.

MISCELLANEOUS

BANDS

Army regulations for 1832 did not provide for dragoon regimental bands, since the first dragoon regiment was not authorized until 1833. But the regulations did provide for a sergeant to act as master of the band (no chief musicians yet), and 10 men were allowed for the band. It is entirely likely that the same provision was made for dragoons.

In 1841 regulations provided for a portion of the post fund to be used to maintain the band and to purchase instruments for it, and a total of 12 bandsmen were allowed that year. The 1847 regulations increased the number of privates for the band to 16.

When various units of a regiment occupied several stations, the band was kept at the headquarters post of the regiment. (*History of Military Music in America*, by W. C. White, New York, Exposition Press, 1944.)

COOKS

There were no professional cooks in Army service during this entire period. Regulations provided that messes be prepared by "privates of squads, including private musicians, each taking his tour." Detailed instructions were set forth in solemn tones for the making of soup and the baking of bread, according to footnotes in Groghan's *Army Life on the Western Frontier* (note 5, pp. 201–205).

COMPANY HORSES

From the time the Regiment of U.S. Dragoons was constituted in 1833, it was customary to buy horses of the same color for each company, and each company had horses of a different color than the next. Besides instant identification in the field, there was another sound reason for this practice, as told by the late Colonel Harry C. Larter in an article that appeared in *Military Collector & Historian* (Vol. VI, No. 2, 1954, 67):

... a new horse of different color entering the corral [or] the troop column ... was due for a much longer probationary period of bites and kicks than that accorded a "recruit" of the same familiar hue as the veterans.

DRAGOON BAGGAGE WAGONS

Baggage wagons were used by the Regiment of U.S. Dragoons in the dragoon expedition of 1834. An account of this trip in *The Guidon* (Vol. I, No. 4) tells that "our waggons were all left at this camp." This was the march from Fort Gibson in Arkansas Territory to the Pawnee Pict and Comanche villages, June 15 to August 15, 1834.

Just what these wagons looked like is not known, although baggage-wagon design did not change much until the 1870's, when the old 6-mule jerk-line type gave way to the first of the 4-horse escort-wagon types.

According to bits and pieces of information uncovered during the years of researching government records for this book, the pattern for the early baggage wagons used by the Army must have been almost identical to the wagons used by the tens of thousands during the American Civil War. But, because there seems to be no documentary proof of this, I shall not attempt to describe or illustrate them. Drawings and descriptions of the Civil War baggage wagons will be found in the chapter covering that period.

Wagon harness used during the Mexican War, according to a description dated May, 1846, in the Quartermaster Correspondence section of the National Archives, was for *4-mule* teams, and was, for all practical purposes, the same as the harness used by the Army for 6-mule teams throughout the period when jerk-line teams were used instead of teams driven with lines to each animal.

The *wagon saddle* illustrated in the above-mentioned description was similar to the later saddle rid-

FIGURE 95. Lieutenant colonel, Second Dragoons (ca. 1846), in fatigue jacket and with a privately purchased Grimsley saddle. His bridle and halter are of the pattern of 1841. He is armed with a pair of U.S. Model 1842 single-shot percussion muzzle-loading pistols and the Model 1840 dragoon officer's sabre.

den by the teamster on the near-wheel mule, being built on a Spanish tree, but there was no girth, it being held in place by a "Spanish-type" surcingle that buckled over the saddle, with flat leather straps running behind the cantle and over the pommel, or fork. There were long side skirts on this saddle, nailed to the tree, and iron stirrups.

The 1847 *Regulations for the Army*, by the Act of March 3, 1847, specified

that to each regiment of dragoons, artillery, and mounted riflemen there shall be added one principal teamster with the rank and compensation of quartermaster-sergeant, and to each company of the same two teamsters, with the compensation of artificers....

FIGURE 96. Grimsley dragoon officer horse furniture (ca. 1847). Dragoon officer wears uniform that was regulation from 1833 to 1851.

While I have found no specific information regarding teamsters attached to dragoons for the earlier period, vague references seem to indicate that dragoon privates themselves drove the baggage wagons attached to the companies, with their mounts tied to the backs of the wagons.

CAVALRY TACTICS

The training of the dragoon was greatly helped by the publication of the first really extensive *Cavalry Tactics* in 1841. Issued by order of the War Department, this manual provided for a drill of 2 ranks. A regiment consisted of 5 squadrons and each squadron of 4 platoons; 2 platoons formed a division. A captain commanded a squadron with a junior captain second in command. Lieutenants commanded the platoons.

The text of the manual was from the French manual of the same period, and the illustrations were copied from the French ones, somewhat modified to show a *sort* of resemblance to the United States dragoon's uniform. But whoever did the art work had little idea of what the equipment looked like. These illustrations are completely useless for reference.

APPENDICES

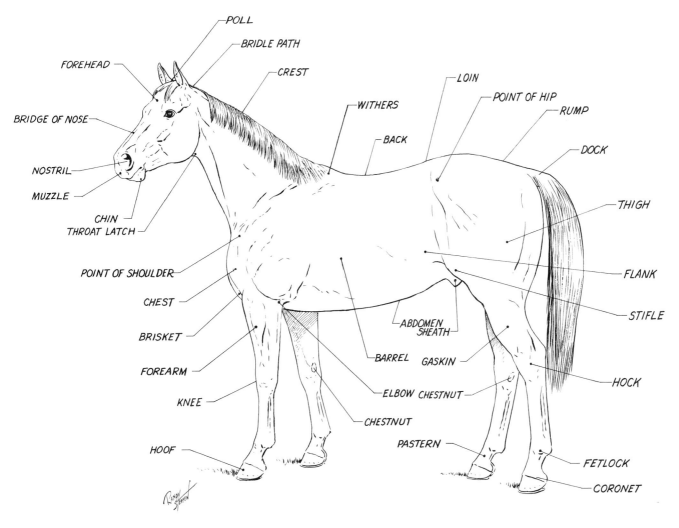

APPENDIX 1. Nomenclature (points) of the horse.

APPENDIX 2. Nomenclature of the horse equipments.
Above: Model 1847 Grimsley saddle and equipments. Below:
Model 1909 cavalry bridle; Model 1924 halter.

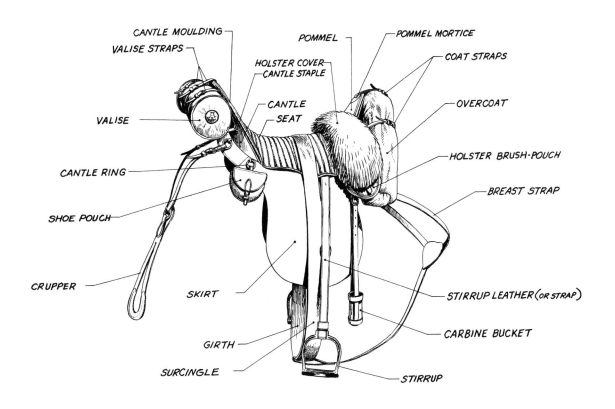

CANTLE MOULDING
VALISE STRAPS
POMMEL
POMMEL MORTICE
COAT STRAPS
HOLSTER COVER
CANTLE STAPLE
OVERCOAT
CANTLE
SEAT
VALISE
HOLSTER BRUSH-POUCH
CANTLE RING
BREAST STRAP
SHOE POUCH
CRUPPER
STIRRUP LEATHER (OR STRAP)
SKIRT
CARBINE BUCKET
GIRTH
SURCINGLE
STIRRUP

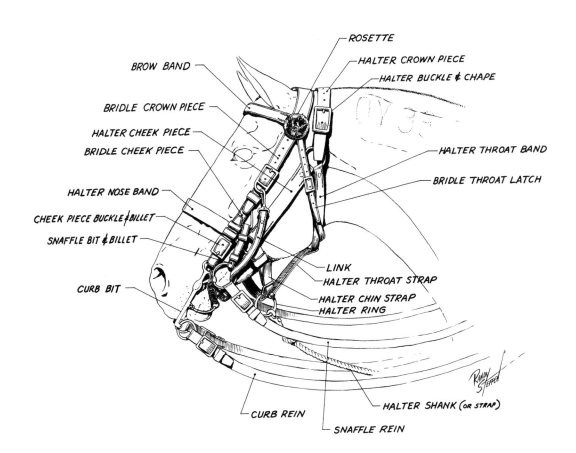

ROSETTE
HALTER CROWN PIECE
BROW BAND
HALTER BUCKLE & CHAPE
BRIDLE CROWN PIECE
HALTER CHEEK PIECE
BRIDLE CHEEK PIECE
HALTER THROAT BAND
BRIDLE THROAT LATCH
HALTER NOSE BAND
CHEEK PIECE BUCKLE & BILLET
SNAFFLE BIT & BILLET
LINK
HALTER THROAT STRAP
CURB BIT
HALTER CHIN STRAP
HALTER RING
CURB REIN
HALTER SHANK (OR STRAP)
SNAFFLE REIN

183

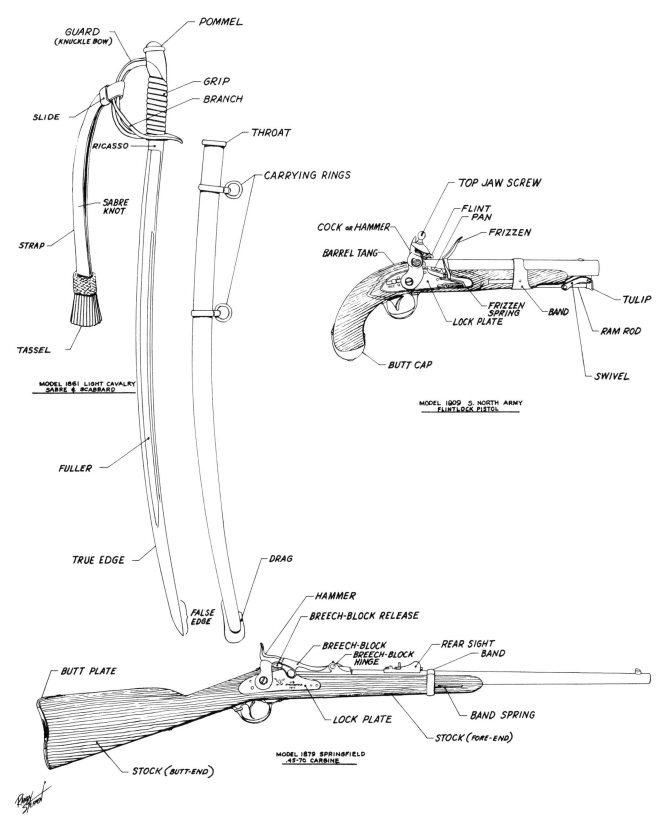

GUARD
(KNUCKLE BOW)

POMMEL

GRIP

BRANCH

SLIDE

THROAT

RICASSO

CARRYING RINGS

SABRE
KNOT

STRAP

TASSEL

MODEL 1861 LIGHT CAVALRY
SABRE & SCABBARD

TOP JAW SCREW

FLINT
PAN

COCK or HAMMER

FRIZZEN

BARREL TANG

TULIP

FRIZZEN
SPRING

BAND

RAM ROD

LOCK PLATE

SWIVEL

BUTT CAP

MODEL 1809 S. NORTH ARMY
FLINTLOCK PISTOL

FULLER

TRUE EDGE

DRAG

FALSE
EDGE

HAMMER

BREECH-BLOCK RELEASE

BREECH-BLOCK

REAR SIGHT

BREECH-BLOCK
HINGE

BAND

BUTT PLATE

LOCK PLATE

BAND SPRING

STOCK (FORE-END)

STOCK (BUTT-END)

MODEL 1879 SPRINGFIELD
.45-70 CARBINE

APPENDIX 3. Nomenclature of the arms. Above left: Model 1861 light cavalry sabre and scabbard. Above right: Model 1809 S. North army flintlock pistol. Below: Model 1879 Springfield .45-70 carbine.

APPENDIX 4

CAVALRY CALLS.

WARNING CALLS.

First call, guard mounting, full dress, overcoats, drill, stable, water, and *boots and saddles*; they precede the *assembly* by such interval as may be prescribed by the commanding officer.

In camp, where the men are near their horses, and known to be present, the *assembly* may be sounded immediately after *boots and saddles*, in which case the men immediately proceed to the horses and saddle.

Mess, church, and *fatigue,* classed as *service calls,* may also be used as warning calls.

First call is the first signal for formation on foot only; it does not precede, and is not used in connection with other warning calls, except *full dress* and *overcoats.*

Guard mounting is the first signal for guard mounting.

Boots and saddles is the signal for mounted formations; for mounted guard mounting or mounted drills, it immediately follows the signal *guard mounting* or *drill.*

The trumpeters assemble at *first call, guard mounting,* and *boots and saddles.*

When full dress or overcoats are to be worn, the *full dress* or *overcoats* call immediately follows *first call, guard mounting,* or *boots and saddles.*

Call to quarters; the signal for the men to repair to their quarters,

FORMATION CALLS.

Assembly; the signal for the troops or details to fall in,

Adjutant's call; the signal for the troops to form squadron; also for the guard details to form on the camp or garrison parade ground for guard mounting, it follows the *assembly* by such interval as may be prescribed by the commanding officer,

To the standard; the signal for the squadrons to form regiment; it is also sounded when the standard salutes,

ALARM CALLS.

Fire call; the signal for the men to fall in without arms to extinguish fire,

To arms; the signal for the men to fall in under arms, dismounted, on their troop parade grounds as quickly as possible.

To horse; the signal for the men to proceed under arms, to their horses, saddle, mount, and assemble at a designated place as quickly as possible; in extended order, this signal is used to remount the troops.

SERVICE CALLS.

Taps, mess, sick, church, recall, issue, officers', captain's, first sergeant's, fatigue, school and *the general.*

The general is the signal for striking tents and loading wagons preparatory to marching,

Reveille and *tattoo* precede the assembly for roll call; the *retreat* follows the *assembly,* the interval being only that required for formation and roll call, except when there is parade,

Taps is the signal for extinguishing lights: it is usually preceded by *call to quarters* by such interval as the commanding officer may direct,

Assembly, reveille, retreat, adjutant's call, to the standard, the *flourishes,* and the *marches* are sounded by all the trumpeters united; the other calls, as a rule, are sounded by the trumpeter of the guard or orderly trumpeter; he may also sound the *assembly* when the trumpeters are not united,

BUGLE CALLS.

The morning gun is fired at the first note of *reveille*; or, if marches are played before *reveille,* it is fired at the commencement of the first march,

The evening gun is fired at the last note of *retreat,*

DRILL SIGNALS.

The drill signals include both the preparatory commands and the commands of execution; the last note is the command of execution; the movement begins the instant the signal for execution terminates.

When a command is given by trumpet, the chiefs of subdivisions give the proper commands orally.

The memorizing of these signals will be facilitated by observing that all movements to the right are on the ascending chord, that the corresponding movements to the left are corresponding signals on the descending chord; and that changes of gait are all upon the same note.

It will be observed that *captain's* (or *troop commander's*) *call* is the first two bars of *officer's call* with the *attention* added,

Form rank and *posts* are the same,

The signals for the *turn and halt* are preceded by the signal *platoons*, *troops*, or *squadrons*, according to the unit or units that execute the movement,

The signal *right* (or *left*) *turn*, corresponds to the signal for the *turn and halt*, but with the signals *forward*, *march*, instead of the signal *march*, added, and except for simultaneous movements, the signal for the unit does not precede the preliminary signal.

In sounding the signals for simultaneous movements, the signal *platoons*, *troops*, or *squadrons* precedes the preliminary signal for the movement; *e.g.*, 1. *Troops*, 2. *Right front into line*, 3. MARCH, the signal *troops* would be sounded, and then followed by the signal *right front into line*, MARCH; 1. *Platoons right*, 2. MARCH.

Fours right and *by the right flank* are the same; in extended order at this signal, troopers deployed as skirmishers or foragers move individually by the right flank; and organizations or sub-divisions in close order move in column of fours to the right,

The same applies to the signal *fours left* and *by the left flank*.

To the rear corresponds to *faced to the rear*, but has the signal *forward*, *march*, instead of the signal *march*.

The signals are sounded in the same order as the commands are prescribed in the text.

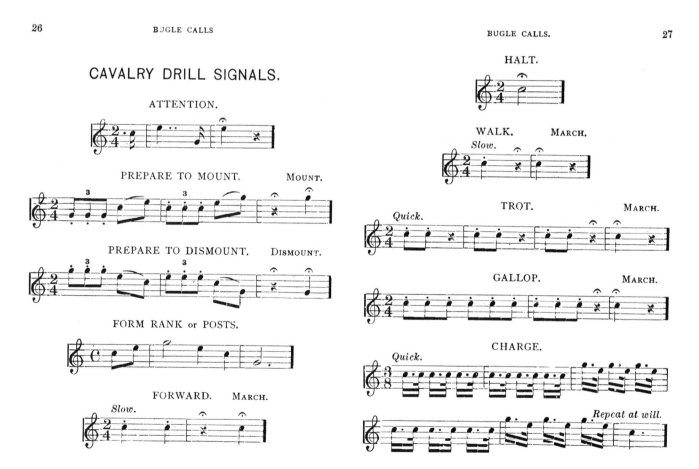

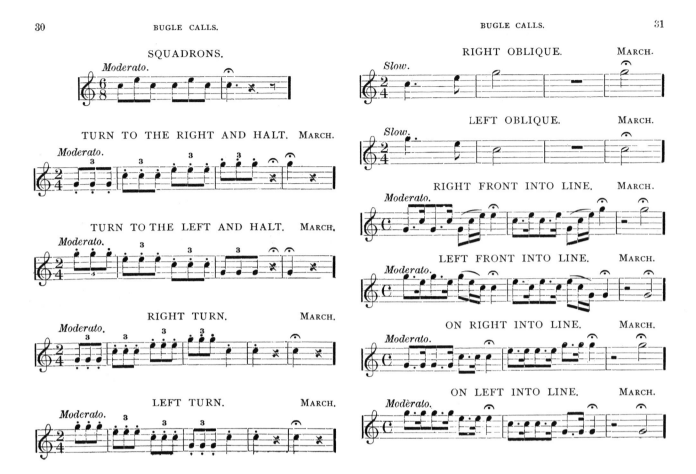

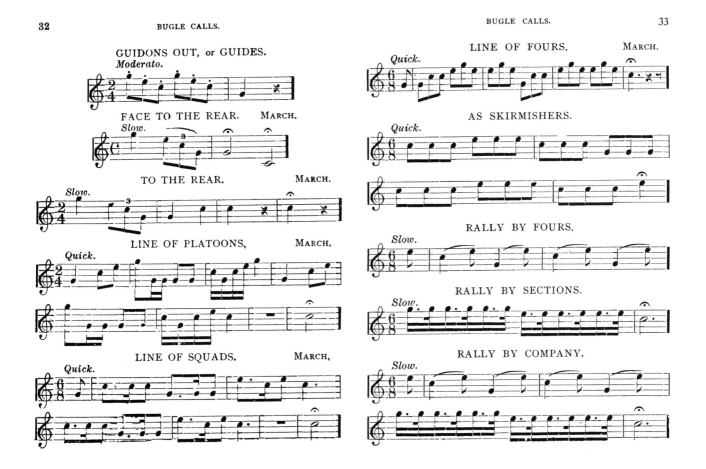

34 BUGLE CALLS.

TO FIGHT ON FOOT.

COMMENCE FIRING.

CEASE FIRING.

LIE DOWN.

RISE.

INDEX